THE GENDER GAP IN WHITE-COLLAR CRIME

A Multi-Country Study of Women Offenders in Economic Crime

THE GENDER GAP IN WHITE-COLLAR CRIME

A Multi-Country Study of Women Offenders in Economic Crime

by

Maryam Kamaei, PhD

Petter Gottschalk, DBA

Thomas E. Dearden, PhD

APPLE ACADEMIC PRESS

First edition published 2025

Apple Academic Press Inc.
1265 Goldenrod Circle, NE,
Palm Bay, FL 32905 USA

760 Laurentian Drive, Unit 19,
Burlington, ON L7N 0A4, CANADA

CRC Press
2385 NW Executive Center Drive,
Suite 320, Boca Raton FL 33431

4 Park Square, Milton Park,
Abingdon, Oxon, OX14 4RN UK

Library and Archives Canada Cataloguing in Publication

Library of Congress Cataloging-in-Publication Data

ISBN: 978-1-77491-826-5 (hbk)
ISBN: 978-1-77491-827-2 (pbk)
ISBN: 978-1-00356-832-2 (ebk)
DOI: 10.1201/9781003568322

About the Authors

Maryam Kamaei, PhD
Department of Criminal Law and Criminology, Ahvaz Branch, Islamic Azad University, Ahvaz, Iran

Maryam Kamaei, PhD, is the Director of the Law Department at Scientific and Applied University and a lecturer at the Ahvaz branch of Islamic Azad University. She holds a master's degree in criminal law and criminology and is currently a PhD candidate in criminal law and criminology at Islamic Azad University, Ahvaz branch. As of 2019, she is researching women and white-collar crime.

Petter Gottschalk, DBA
Professor, Department of Leadership and Organizational Behavior, BI Norwegian Business School, Oslo, Norway

Petter Gottschalk, DBA, is a Professor in the Department of Leadership and Organizational Behavior at BI Norwegian Business School in Oslo, Norway. He has published extensively on white-collar crime, convenience theory, and corporate investigations. Dr. Gottschalk held several chief executive officer positions in business before joining academia.

Thomas E. Dearden, PhD
Assistant Professor, Department of Sociology, Virginia Polytechnic Institute and State University (Virginia Tech), USA

Thomas E. Dearden, PhD, is an Assistant Professor of Sociology at Virginia Polytechnic Institute and State University (Virginia Tech), USA. His work focuses on the interaction of white-collar crime and cybercrime. He has more than a dozen academic publications and over 40 presentations to his credit. He has consulted for several organizations across the globe.

Contents

Contents

Preface

Historically, women were directly excluded from white-collar crime. This was done at the earliest stages, when Edwin Sutherland created a definition of white-collar crime that only included men. Even ignoring the definition, women have historically been left out of significant business sectors and economic markets generally. In recent years, this is beginning to change. However, research on white-collar crime is only beginning to catch up. Yet an interesting question remains: does this increase in economic participation by women lead to an increased proportion of women committing white-collar crime (sometimes termed pink-collar crime)? In this book, we wanted to examine women and white-collar crime both theoretically and empirically. In addition, we wanted to consider the international differences and how countries differ dramatically in economic and other participation by women.

This work is written for higher education professionals. This means that interested readers will likely be faculty, students, or others with a focus on white-collar crime. While we have written this book to be approachable by all, there is scientific nuance and a consistent focus on empirical and theoretical work. Certainly, anyone interested in advancing their understanding of white-collar crime, gender, criminological theory, and international differences in crime will find this book useful.

One note for readers: each chapter is meant to be largely a stand-alone chapter, meaning that individual pieces of this book may be assigned to students. It also means that some information is repeated in different chapters. Below is a guide to each chapter.

Chapter 1 largely introduces the topic of women and white-collar crime. It focuses broadly on the ideas that we further expound in this book. This is generally an introduction chapter.

Chapter 2 in this book considers the convenience theory motives of motive, opportunity, and willingness for female white-collar offenders. This chapter illustrates convenience themes that are gender-specific in favor of female offenders.

Chapters 3 and 4 introduce and apply the stage model for the gender gap in white-collar crime. While half of the population is female, the fraction of convicted women is much lower. The model explains this gap in terms of stages determined by relative needs, opportunity, motivation, justification, and detection. Different estimates for the determinants derive from the research literature, from surveys among business students in Norway, and from the Utah White-collar Crime Registry in the United States. These two chapters with student exercises are helpful in understanding gender and crime by the stepwise reduction in female fraction based on factors derived from previous gender research.

Chapter 5 continues to apply the Utah White Collar Crime Offender Registry to study female white-collar offenders' target selection. Using data from a required online registry, we consider the differences between the motives of female and male white-collar offenders.

Chapter 6 introduces the Norwegian database with several hundred white-collar offenders convicted to prison. The chapter evaluates the emancipation hypothesis by comparing gender fractions in Norway with the United States.

Chapter 7 presents a case study of corruption involving a woman, where the access to bribes for female offenders generally seems limited. Corruption requires more than one person, where women often feel excluded or prefer to avoid criminal groups and networks.

Scholars have emphasized the lack of case studies outside the United States for many years. Therefore, Chapter 8 presents a number of women offenders prosecuted and convicted in Norway.

Chapter 9 reviews women and white-collar crime through a comparative study of Iranian mafia and Norwegian offenders. Traditionally, women represent a small fraction of convicted white-collar offenders. The gender gap has been explained by low female participation in privileged positions due to gender inequality. The extent of gender inequality is measured by the global gender gap index. According to the 2022 index, Iran ranks 143 while Norway ranks 3 (out of 146 countries) in terms of gender equality. Iran and Norway thus represent two extremes on the index, making a comparative study relevant. A small sample of convicted offenders in Iran is compared in this chapter to a larger sample in Norway, indicating little support for the suggestion that the extent of gender equality can explain gender gap differences in white-collar crime rates. In addition to addressing the research question of how women and white-collar crime compare in Iran and Norway, this chapter emphasizes research literature and news reports from Iran, as little has been published so far about the phenomenon of white-collar crime in the Islamic Republic of Iran. Therefore, white-collar crime in Iran is exemplified by the meat mafia, the sugar mafia, the tea mafia, as well as the steel mafia.

Chapter 10 focuses on convenience themes in cybercrime by considering the importance of gender in the brief history of crime committed on the internet and the relationship between cybercrime and white-collar crime. This newer medium of crime has provided additional opportunities for offenders. However, current research suggests there are significant gender differences in cybercrime as well.

Chapter 11 revisits the question of convenience advantages for women offenders as introduced in Chapter 2. It discusses several convenience themes that depend on gender in favor of female offenders. Some themes are exclusively valid for women, while others are more pronounced for women compared to men.

Chapter 12 proposes potential paths for future gender research in the context of women in white-collar crime and convenience theory. The chapter emphasizes modeling and testing, the validity of main gender effects, and suggestions for advancing theory and practice.

Chapter 13 distinguishes between offenders and non-offenders, where the typical offender might be a man, while the typical non-offender might be a woman. However, this chapter presents no explicit gender research. That is why paths for future gender research were presented in the previous chapter. This chapter can only be implicitly understood from a gender perspective. The chapter presents an integrated theory of convenience, focusing on dimensions, themes, and structure. Convenience statements derive from the themes. The research suggests that potential offenders will find crime more convenient than potential non-offenders will. Seventy-one sociology and criminology students in the United States were either classified as potential offenders or non-offenders determined by their responses in survey research. Participants who believe it is understandable that top executives commit white-collar crime are classified as likely offenders, while participants who do not find it understandable are classified as non-offenders. The empirical tests show that participants labeled as offenders find more motive, opportunity, as well as behavioral convenience in crime compared to assumed non-offenders. Similar results were obtained from business students in Norway, who expressed a stronger understanding of top executive deviance.

Similar to Chapter 13, Chapter 14 does not explicitly discuss gender and crime. This chapter is more general in its attempt to identify convenience themes. Based on an empirical study of 268 convicted white-collar offenders in the state of Utah in the United States (the same database as in chapters 3 and 4), this research identified the frequency of various convenience themes within the opportunity dimension. The most surprising result was the large number of victims who had trusted funds in the hands of offenders with an expectation to receive substantial returns from their investments. We apply to this result the principal-agent perspective, which suggests narrow self-interest between both principals and agents. The interests of principals (victims) and agents (offenders) tend to diverge, they may have different risk aversion, there is knowledge asymmetry between the two parties, and the principal has imperfect information about the agent's contribution.

Chapter 15 returns to the topic of gender in terms of a case study from Denmark. For many years, a female employee in the social security service in Denmark was able to embezzle money at work. "Britta Nielsen is a committed employee, who takes on significant tasks in grant administration and is always willing when extra work is required." This is what Danish Britta Nielsen (64)'s employer wrote in a recommendation for the Queen's Merit Medal in 2016. Nielsen received the medal in silver. The occasion was 40 years of service as an employee at Socialstyrelsen (social security service in Denmark). It is from that point in time that Nielsen faces an accusation of having embezzled 117 million Danish kroner, about 20 million US dollars. In 2018, the police arrested her in South Africa, having been on the run for more than a month.

The final Chapter 16 draws conclusions. One of the key uncertainties regarding women in white-collar crime is the extent of gendered detection rate.

Introduction

Women and white-collar crime is an emerging area of research. In this book, we utilize a variety of theoretical perspectives to examine women and white-collar crime. There is a specific focus on convenience theory, an integrated theory originally created by Gottschalk to explain general white-collar crime. Both theoretical arguments and empirical work examine the validity of theory in explaining women and white-collar crime. Given the variety of different participation of women in economic systems around the world, we importantly consider international perspectives on white-collar crime. This work was written by authors geographically located around the world, adding an international focus to this book.

CHAPTER 1

Introduction

Historically, definitions of white-collar crime only included men. Today, we need to consider women who commit white-collar crime. A woman in white-collar crime is a female offender who abuses her professional status to commit and then conceal financial crimes that can benefit herself or the business (Daly, 1989a, b; Paxton, 2012). A woman in white-collar crime belongs to the elite in society, where she enjoys legitimate access to resources. She commits financial crimes in the course of her occupation. She is a person of respectability and high social status who commits crimes during the course of professional activities (Craig & Piquero, 2017; Friedrichs et al., 2018; Logan et al., 2019; Schnatterly et al., 2018; Sutherland, 1939).

This book applies the theory of convenience, which is an emerging new perspective on white-collar crime. Convenience was first introduced as a core concept by Gottschalk (2017). Recently, the theory has been reviewed (e.g., Chan & Gibbs, 2020; Hansen, 2020; Oka, 2021; Vasiu, 2021; Vasiu & Podgor, 2019) and applied by several scholars such as Asting and Gottschalk (2022), Braaten and Vaughn (2019), Dearden and Gottschalk (2021), Desmond et al. (2022), Gupta and Gottschalk (2022), Qu (2021), Stadler and Gottschalk (2022), and Sterri and Borge (2022). Reference to the theory of convenience is already made in numerous research publications (e.g., Almaqableh et al., 2022; Black et al., 2022; Clarkson & Darjee, 2022; Ghazi-Tehrani & Pontell, 2022; Hendricks, 2022; Morino, 2021; Othman & Ameer, 2022; Prabhakar & Chawla, 2022).

Historically, the notions of white-collar crime have been limited to men. The perception, and likely reality, was that few women committed white-collar crime. The reasons for this are multifaceted. It could be due to a lack

The Gender Gap in White-Collar Crime: A Multi-Country Study of Women Offenders in Economic Crime.
Maryam Kamaei, Petter Gottschalk, and Thomas E. Dearden (Authors)

of opportunity, motive, or willingness. Steffensmeier et al. (2013) studied how gendered focal concerns can inhibit criminal behaviors in females in the corporate context. One note, generally, the fraction of females who commit white-collar crime is increasing. It is worth examining why this is the case.

One limitation for women committing white-collar crime has been the opportunity structure. There are far fewer women in positions of trust. These positions of trust allow for the opportunity to commit white-collar crime. But is this the only reason? Are women only limited by their position from committing white-collar crime?

Women's experience in white-collar crime differs from men in several ways. One way is the roles they occupy in illicit networks and the financial compensation they receive from their crimes. These differences are illustrated in a series of cases prosecuted by the Corporate Fraud Task Force (CFTF). The United States established the CFTF after the Enron scandal. The CFTF prosecuted 83 large corporations for fraud between 2002 and 2009. Of the 436 defendants, only 37 (9%) were female (Steffensmeier et al., 2013). Furthermore, only 10 of the 37 were major figures or ringleaders in the respective cases. The remaining female offenders played either minor (51%) or in-between (22%) roles. In their analysis of corporate fraud, Steffensmeier and colleagues (2013) found that most frequently, women received directives and orders from others. They were largely included in the crime because their job duties made them pivotal in committing the crime. Differences between men and women were also observable in their respective takes or profits from crime. While over half of the women (56%) reportedly received either little or no profit, about 80% of men received over $100,000 in illicit earnings. Over three-quarters of females received less than their male conspirators regarding financial gain from their offenses.

Traditional gender research in the United States thus indicates that in ordinary street crime, women are generally less involved than men in most types of white-collar crime. Women appear to lack representation especially in cases which involve multiple offenders working cooperatively or in what can constitute criminal networks (Goncharov & Peter, 2019). When they are involved in criminal conspiracies, women more often play a minor or supporting role. They also benefit less from the crime, tending to receive substantially lower financial gains than men.

White-collar crime is a global problem. Fraud, manipulation, embezzlement, and corruption happen in every economy and society in the world. In the past decade, white-collar crime has been a threat to the economic and social health gains across the globe (König et al., 2020). Since the inception of white-collar crime as a sociological and criminological concept, special attention has been paid to how this form of crime can be unique from other forms of crime. Some of these differences include the socio-demographic backgrounds of individuals who commit white-collar crimes, generally associated with an "elite" class of men. These crimes are also often linked to legitimate occupational activities (Benson & Gottschalk, 2015).

The gendered structure of corporations often limits women's ability to achieve leadership roles (Holtfreter, 2015). Because women are limited in positions of power, they are also limited in the positions where they may commit white-collar crime (Dodge, 2009). However, these gendered positions are weakening. The emancipation hypothesis suggests that the percentage of white-collar crime committed by women will rise as more leadership positions are filled by women. Currently, empirical research does not support this hypothesis, as international comparisons have yielded little support (Benson & Gottschalk, 2015).

Certainly, the original definition of white-collar crime proposed by Sutherland recognized men as exclusive offenders of white-collar crime. Generally, research has supported this notion, albeit with more tempered conclusions. Cumming et al. (2015) found that women in male-dominated fields reduced the frequency and severity of fraud. Dollar et al. (2001) found that a greater fraction of women in parliament is associated with a lower extent of corruption. Dodge (2007) found that female board members talk most often about ethics.

This book discusses several gender differences related to financial crime by members of the privileged elite in society. This can include differences beyond opportunity. For example, Holtfreter (2015) found that strain may vary with gender. Not only are strains themselves different, but the responses to strain are different between men and women. Women may respond with more anxiety or depression (Brands & Mehra, 2019), whereas men may respond with anger or aggression. These differences may interact with the responses to opportunity within the workplace.

Gender can also influence the type of financial crime committed. Women comprise about half of the bank embezzlers but only 5% of the securities, bribery, tax, and antitrust offenders in the United States, while no convicted female offenders in Norway were involved in corruption (Benson & Gottschalk, 2015). The opportunity structure might explain that women have many positions in organizations where they handle money. Assuming that there is a gender difference in hurting others, the willingness to embezzle might be strong among women, as the offense does not directly harm or involve anybody else. Personal willingness for wrongdoing declines as the female offender can experience a stronger sense of retaliation desire in society. Rehg et al. (2009) suggest that wrongdoing by females can cause punishment to be a more desirable outcome for women compared to men.

A person with low risk aversion and high-risk willingness will likely perceive the detection risk as low, while a person with high risk aversion and low risk willingness will likely perceive the detection risk as not as low. Research suggests that there is a gender gap in terms of subjective detection probability (Dearden & Gottschalk, 2021). For example, women tend to have a stronger belief in not speeding when driving on the highway. Research has shown that men drive faster than women do on the highway because men believe speeding is less risky. Intuitively, this could be explained by the fact that females are generally more law-abiding than males. However, it is the gendered subjective probability of detection that prevents women from driving beyond the speed limit as often or as extensively as men do. While the objective detection likelihood is the same for male and female drivers in the same situation, the subjective detection likelihood varies.

Most published research on women and white-collar crime is from the United States. Comparative analyses are informative, as there is significant variation in women's participation in corporate organizations. This book is unique, as it focuses on data from three countries with vastly different structures. It uses data from Norway, Iran, and the United States. Each of these countries has diverse perspectives on gender equality, economic and state interactions, gross domestic product, government structure, and many other differences. These differences allow for a comparison to tease apart some of the potential differences in why women and men commit different types and quantities of white-collar crime.

Three general explanations for gender differences in white-collar crime are the emancipation hypothesis, opportunity hypothesis, and focal concern hypothesis. The emancipation hypothesis is concerned with gender equality, the opportunity hypothesis is concerned with equal access to resources to commit and conceal crime, while the focal concern hypothesis is concerned with gender differences in interests and priorities. We return to the various perspectives and explanations throughout the book.

A key element in understanding the business offender in the workplace is the opportunity to commit and conceal financial crime. Within convenience theory, the opportunity dimension focuses on the chance that the offender has to commit and conceal white-collar crime. Opportunity can be defined as a "potential course of action, made possible by a particular set of social conditions, which has been symbolically incorporated into an actor's repertoire of behavioral possibilities" (Coleman, 1987, p. 409). In philosophical terms, as suggested by Ramoglou and McMullen (2022), opportunity refers to confidence about what can happen. Opportunity can be realized, and if so, it will result in a different state of affairs. Opportunity does not actually exist as an undiscovered or created entity, but rather in what potential offenders imagine as possible. In the eyes of the potential offender, a favorable opportunity is some kind of non-physical social object. Opportunity is the confidence that a non-actual but desirable state of the situation can be achieved following a course of action when the conditions that make the imagined state of the situation non-imaginary are believed to be in place. Opportunity is the ability to do or achieve something. Aguilera and Vadera (2008, p. 434) described a criminal opportunity as "the presence of a favorable combination of circumstances that makes a possible course of action relevant."

Some of the material is repeated several times throughout the book, so that the reader does not need to read the text sequentially. Rather, each chapter is a complete text that can be read independently of other chapters.

CHAPTER 2

Theory of Convenience

Women's lack of financial motivation, organizational opportunity, and personal willingness to engage in deviant behavior have traditionally been the focus of research on gender and white-collar crime. This chapter approaches white-collar crime from the perspective of special female motivation, opportunity, and willingness, which is in contrast to conventional gender research. This chapter identifies gender-specific convenience themes that favor female offenders based on utilizing the theory of convenience. Within convenience theory, the motive dimension can be related to concern for others, and stress can lead to depression and anxiety (Brands & Mehra, 2019). In terms of the willingness dimension, female followers may be able to claim loyalty to their leaders to better justify their actions and alleviate any potential feelings of guilt than male criminal leaders.

The majority of studies on the proportion of women involved in white-collar crime have focused on women's reduced financial motivation, organizational opportunity, and personal willingness to deviate. Researchers like Cumming and colleagues (2015), Holtfreter (2015), Dodge (2007), Steffensmeier and colleagues (2013) highlighted a difference in women's motivation. Scholars such as Dodge (2009), Gottschalk and Smith (2015), Benson and Gottschalk (2015), Benson and Simpson (2018) emphasized the lack of opportunities for women. Still, some scholars such as Benson and Harbinson (2020), Galvin (2020), Goulette (2020), and Becker and McCorkel (2011) emphasize the reduced willingness of women to commit white-collar crime. However, the fact that some women engage in criminal activity indicates that females do not always lack opportunity, motivation, or willingness.

The Gender Gap in White-Collar Crime: A Multi-Country Study of Women Offenders in Economic Crime.
Maryam Kamaei, Petter Gottschalk, and Thomas E. Dearden (Authors)

This chapter seeks to address the following research questions: What are female motive characteristics? What aspects of female opportunity are there? This chapter considers the opposite of typical literature, by examining the unique special motive, opportunity, and willingness of women who commit white-collar crime. The theory of convenience can provide potential answers to gendered differences (Braaten & Vaughn, 2019; Dearden & Gottschalk, 2021; Gottschalk, 2022).

2.1 FEMALE WHITE-COLLAR OFFENDERS

A woman who commits and conceals financial crime in order to benefit herself or the business is known as a female white-collar offender. She has legitimate access to resources because she is part of society's elite. In the course of her employment, she engages in financial crime. She is a respectable individual with a high social status who engages in criminal activity while performing professional duties (Sutherland, 1939). Sutherland's definition is a notable and powerful depiction of unique differences in crimes committed by individuals in different social status (Friedrichs et al., 2018). According to Craig and Piquero's 2017 definition, "white-collar crime" is defined as "financial crime committed by privileged individuals in society who abuse their legitimate access to resources to violate the law" (Schnatterly et al., 2018). Financial crime committed by privileged individuals in a professional setting is known as white-collar crime because of the offenders' legitimate access to resources due to their positions and trust (Logan et al., 2019).

We should note that offender-based definitions are most often used in this book, though recent literature in white-collar crime utilizes a more offense-based definition (Goossen et al., 2016; Piquero, 2018; Piquero & Schoepfer, 2010). Yet, one of our arguments is that the heterogeneous nature of white-collar crime leads to unique differences in white-collar crime (Onna, 2020).

One common finding in criminology across all crimes is the high proportion of men as offenders (Benson & Gottschalk, 2015). Yet, the gender gap in criminal activity differs based on the type of offense. The proportion of men is highest in the commission of direct contact wrongdoing including homicide and burglary, while the percentage of women increases (though still not at an equal proportion) for minor vandalism such as shoplifting or robbery. For instance, in the United States, males are arrested for over

90% of robberies but only 65% of minor property crimes (Steffensmeier & Allan, 2000). This gender gap extends to white-collar offenses. It would appear that this gap still exists today. Only 7% of those involved in white-collar crime since Enron in the United States were women. In addition, the gender gap in white-collar crime varies across offense types, as it does with street crime (Benson & Simpson, 2018; Dodge, 2009). For instance, a study of people who were found guilty of antitrust, securities, tax, and bribery in the United States found that women made up less than 5% of those. Within those categories, nearly 50% of those women were found guilty of bank embezzlement. According to Holtfreter (2005), data from the Association of Certified Fraud Examiners shows there were differences in the kinds of fraud committed by men and women. Men were more likely to commit fraud that required more access to organizational resources. The orientation hole could diminish over time both by female culpable developing and by male culpable decreasing (Estrada et al., 2016; Steffensmeier et al., 2005).

In Norway, women comprise just 7% of middle-class detainees (Benson & Gottschalk, 2015). Estrada and colleagues (2019, p. 145) suggest that, "the fact that men commit a much larger number of offenses than women is one of the central findings in criminological research," there is still a gender gap in registered crime. In a similar vein, Messerschmidt (1997) suggests that gender is a factor in predicting criminal activity because men are much more likely to commit crime. Holtfreter (2015, p. 422) stated, "The gender gap in crime – the overrepresentation of males in virtually all official arrest statistics – has narrowed in recent decades and is substantially smaller for white-collar crime." Subsequently, one could guess that as orientation equity expands, women's contribution in middle-class wrongdoing will turn out to be more similar to men's, particularly assuming that orientation fairness is reflected in superior financial standing and business opportunities for men.

2.2 MOTIVE-OPPORTUNITY-WILLINGNESS

- Financial motivation, organizational opportunity, and individual willingness to engage in deviant behavior all play a role in white-collar crime. This examination applies the hypothesis of convenience, which is an emerging new perspective on middle-class wrongdoing, where the research literature is rapidly evolving. A three-dimensional synthesis of perspectives produces the integrated theory of convenience:

- **Convenience in Motive:** It is convenient to use fraudulent financial gain to explore possibilities and mitigate risks (Naylor, 2003), satisfy a need for recognition (Chatterjee & Pollock, 2017), achieve the American dream of financial success (Schoepfer & Piquero, 2006), fulfill the hierarchy of needs (Maslow, 1943), and restore feelings of fairness (Clark et al., 2010). Moreover, goal setting is common in organizations. However, these high-performance goals have been found to encourage unethical behavior (Welsh, Bush, Thiel, & Bonner, 2019). A perpetrator can exploit opportunities and potential threats by leveraging the additional illicit income from financial crimes. Since financial crimes and illicit income often bypass external and internal control mechanisms, including compliance functions, there may be added benefits from illegal profits (Kawasaki, 2020). Consequently, documented funds may not deter illegitimate financial gain from exploring opportunities and mitigating risks.

- **Convenience in Opportunity:** There are helpful opportunities when engaging in financial crimes. These include legitimate access to systems, facilities, and other closed systems (Benson & Simpson, 2018), special but normalized access for routine activities (Cohen & Felson, 1979), diffusing blame through erroneous attribution to other people or business entities (Eberly et al., 2011), and the decline of the institution (Rodriguez et al., 2005). The opportunity dimension of convenience theory incorporates a number of different points of view (see 2005). In contrast to many street criminals, a typical white-collar offender does not go into hiding. Instead, the offender conceals financial crime by omitting certain activities from financial or organizational books or by combining legal transactions with illegal ones to make illegal ones appear legitimate. A common white-collar criminal has easy and legal specialized access to commit a crime and can focus on hiding their crimes from the organization or external entities (Huisman & Erp, 2013; South & McClanahan, 2020).

- **Convenience in Behavior:** Criminals can conveniently justify their actions and avoid feeling guilty (Dearden, 2016, 2017, 2019), neutralize their behavior (Sykes & Matza, 1957), cascade into further illegal behavior (Welsh et al., 2014), lack self-control (Gottfredson & Hirschi, 1990), and engage in narcissistic attachment to an organization (Galvin et al., 2015). Some additional perspectives include professional deviant identity (Obodaru, 2017) and learning from others by differential association (Sutherland, 1983). The perpetrator may assert that the wrongdoing was morally justifiable (Schnatterly et al., 2018), and that a negative event in one's life has taken place (Engdahl, 2015). A white-collar criminal employs neutralization strategies when he or she denies guilt. It is convenient based on identity when a white-collar offender chooses crime (Galvin et al., 2015), reason (Pratt & Cullen, 2005), knowledge from other people (Sutherland, 1983), and an individual's self-concept as a member of an organization is their social identity (Piening et al., 2020).

- According to Mai and Olsen (2016), convenience is being able to carry on with something without putting too much effort or strain on the body. A helpful individual isn't genuinely terrible or sluggish. Conversely, when choosing a convenient option, the individual frequently exhibits both intelligence and reason (Blickle et al., 2006; Radon & Sundström, 2015). The crime-as-choice perspective is consistent with convenience theory as a relative construct.

The model of convenience theory is shown in Figure 2.1. It divides motivation into possibilities and threats, with the possibility being to commit and cover up a crime and the willingness being a choice and an assertion of innocence.

2.3 WOMEN CONVENIENCE THEMES

The motive, possibilities, and individual perspective are the first convenience dimensions in Figure 2.1. As a matter of social concern, one motive is to satisfy a desire or perceived need to assist others. Beyond simple self-interest, Agnew (2014) suggested that individuals could offend due to social concerns or a desire to help others. However, as Paternoster et al. argue (2018), charity can be a self-serving, rational, and socially conscious act. Despite the rise of materialism within feminism, feminine morality places more emphasis on social rather than material aspects (Sullivan, 2012).

Klenowski and colleagues (2011) conducted interviews with 20 female convicted white-collar offenders and found that "the most common way that females framed their actions was to show that their ultimate goals were to provide support and aid to those for whom they cared," such as:

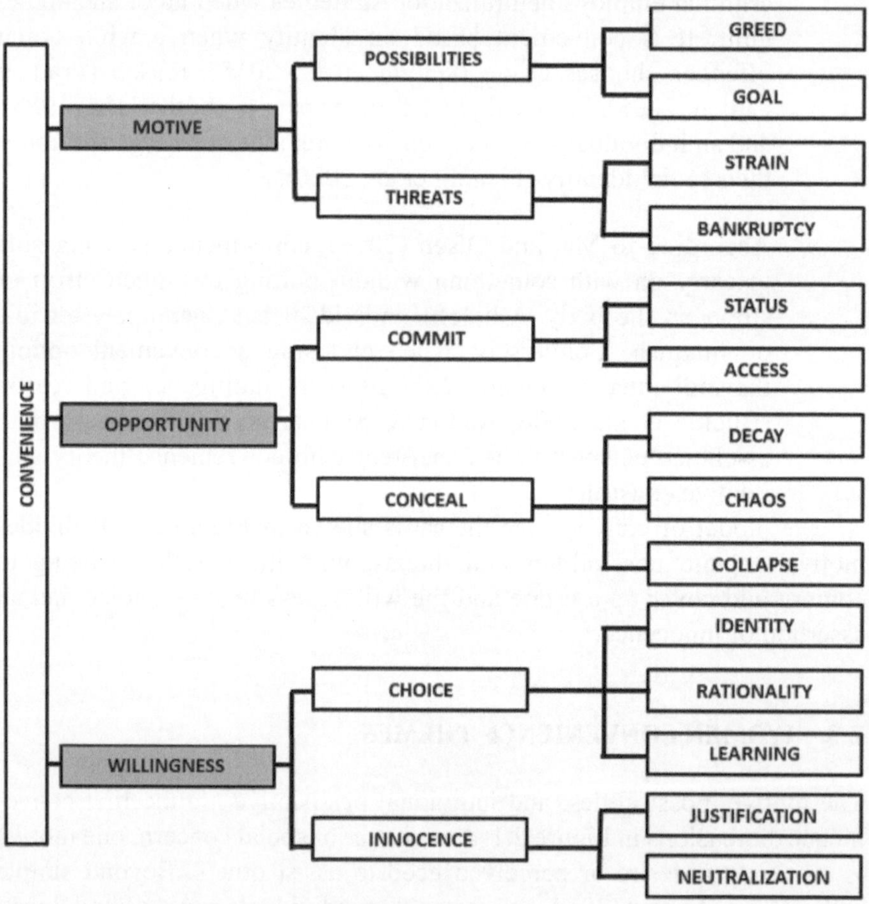

FIGURE 2.1 A model of convenience theory.

"Actually, my two daughters were sexually abused by their father when they were three and 5 years old in 1990 and 1991. I partnered with someone who could pay my legal fees to fight for custody and justice in that regard, so I guess I'm here because of what I did and should be here, but I don't think I should be here because of my motive. I had the impression that I was only doing what I had to do as a mother."

Under the assumption that women have different focal concerns, women are generally socialized to accept nurturing role responsibilities and communalistic orientations toward other people. Women develop identities as caregivers as a result of integrating these responsibilities (Steffensmeier et al., 2013).

One of the most prominent theoretical explanations for crime is the strain perspective (Agnew, 2005, 2012; Cleff et al., 2013; Froggio & Agnew, 2007; Hoffmann, 2002; Langton & Piquero, 2007; Ngo & Paternoster, 2016). The strain perspective emphasizes the dissatisfaction that comes from failing to complete a task, such as avoiding personal or corporate bankruptcy. Strains typically cause people to feel bad, which makes them feel pressured to take corrective action to close the gap between what they want and what actually happens. One possible response is to commit a crime. Individual and corporate threats depicted in Figure 2.1 may, as a result, elicit particular motivations from female offenders due to the gender differences in strains.

For opportunity, it is likely that women offenders focus more on the conceal dimension than opportunity structure. The gender difference in suspicion might be demonstrated by a straightforward experiment. Over the years, we have experimented by asking the following question to audiences in Norway: Who do you want to bribe? You want to construct a summer mansion on a state-regulated recreation property. Within the 100-meter belt, the property is on the shoreline at the oceanfront. The general public has priority access to it because it is on Norway's southern coast. You have the option of bribing a male or female municipal official who has authority to issue permits. They both have the same powers to approve your application. Considering all the audiences, a large majority exclusively vote for bribing the male official. Overall, less than 5% would involve the woman official in corruption. Generally, this stereotype is supported, as women have been empirically shown to be less involved in corruption (Bowman & Gilligan, 2008). Further, Steffensmeier et al.'s (2013) investigation of corporate fraud schemes found that women were only included in the criminal conspiracy because their jobs made them important to the execution of the crime and that most of the time, they received instructions from others. According to a study conducted in the United States, female white-collar crime rises when women are invited to participate by men (Becker & McCorkel, 2011).

In the willingness dimension of convenience theory, female criminals have gender-specific themes because they are more often followers than leaders. For instance, claiming loyalty could be used to neutralize women who are followers. According to Fehr et al. (2015), followers have a belief in the morality of the leader's pressure, which can cause them to feel shame and guilt if they fail to support the leader. Emotional regulation in relationships between leaders and followers was studied by Glas and Einarsen (2008). They found that adherents regularly stifle gloomy feelings like frustration, vulnerability, and irritation, while they normally express or feign good feelings like excitement, interest, and smoothness. It is possible for a leader to use language that followers may not necessarily comprehend. The messages of leaders are still trusted by followers (Ferraro et al., 2005), and language influences what people notice and ignore (Holt & Cornelissen, 2014; 2017 by Srivastava and Goldberg; Weick, 1995). Language used by leaders can lead followers to obey (Mawritz et al., 2017).

Within organizations, there can be a culture of "ends justifying means" in these goal-oriented businesses, where employees will do whatever, it takes to achieve objectives. Both the individual and the organizational level can have goals. The likelihood of committing crimes rises in such organizations when deviant means, such as crime, are justified in achieving objectives, goals, and ends. From our gendered perspective, the question of whether such organizations are more appealing to men or women arises. Jonnergrd and colleagues (2010) found that women are less likely to join businesses with a strong culture of management by objectives. They find that women prefer other metrics of success. This avoidance may lead to reduced opportunity to commit and conceal financial crimes.

In conclusion, this chapter considered the unique convenience dimensions faced by women in white-collar crime. In general, there may be specific differences across all dimensions that may lead to overall less frequent commission of crimes. Combined with lower detection rates, women appear to commit substantially less white-collar crime than men. We conclude this chapter with a case study highlighting convenience dimensions for one female offender.

2.3.1 THE CASE OF HARRIETTE WALTERS

The District of Columbia's tax assessments manager was Harriette Walters. She was found guilty of being a key player in the largest fraud scheme ever carried out by a District government official. Walters entered a guilty plea to charges of stealing over $48 million in district funds in September 2008. Forensic accountants from PricewaterhouseCoopers and lawyers from Wilmer Cutler Pickering Hale and Dorr were hired to look into how Walters was able to steal $48 million from the District of Columbia (WilmerHale & PwC, 2008).

Walters orchestrated a scheme lasting nearly two decades in which she processed bogus refunds for real estate taxes and arranged for the funds to be deposited in bank accounts owned by either herself or her friends and family. She cashed, for instance, refund checks that were returned after the death of the taxpayer recipient. Additionally, she created several checks for tax refunds. It gave the idea that Walters had sorted out that she triumphed ultimately the keep going eyes on the duty discount check and worked with little observing (Stewart & Nakamura, 2007).

Four managers were held accountable for failing to spot the fraud due to a lack of monitoring. The four supervisors who quit were: Stewart and Nakamura, 2007. They included the deputy chief financial officer Sherryl Hobbs Newman, the deputy director Matthew Braman, real property tax administrator Martin A. Skolnik, and chief assessor Thomas Branham.

The goal of the WilmerHale and PwC (2008) investigation was to figure out how Walters was able to steal for nearly 20 years and suggest changes to controls, oversight structures, and the work environment generally that could help stop similar frauds in the future. The money that was stolen should not be traced or how it was distributed or spent in the investigation. Nor did the command look to decide the culpability or honesty of any members in Walters' plan. Those issues had been addressed by federal authorities.

WilmerHale and PwC (2008) concluded, following the investigation, that Walters' lengthy fraud scheme was the result of a lack of control, a dysfunctional work environment, and oversight. The Office of Tax and Revenue (OTR) did not have policies or procedures that formally documented the process for processing real property tax refunds, making it impossible to guarantee the process's reliability. Managers and employees did not always adhere to existing policies or procedures. Administrators in the OTR did not test the discount cycle or find fundamental ways to analyze genuine local charge discounts. In fact, Walters' managers in the Real Property Tax Administration (RPTA) approved these refund vouchers at the beginning of her scheme without verifying the legitimacy of the attached documentation (WilmerHale & PwC, 2008, p. 3):

> Worse, Walters's direct supervisor in 2003 apparently made it clear in words or deeds that she no longer wanted to sign off on real property tax refund vouchers at all. This apparent abdication of managerial responsibility allowed Walters to process all real property tax refunds, regardless

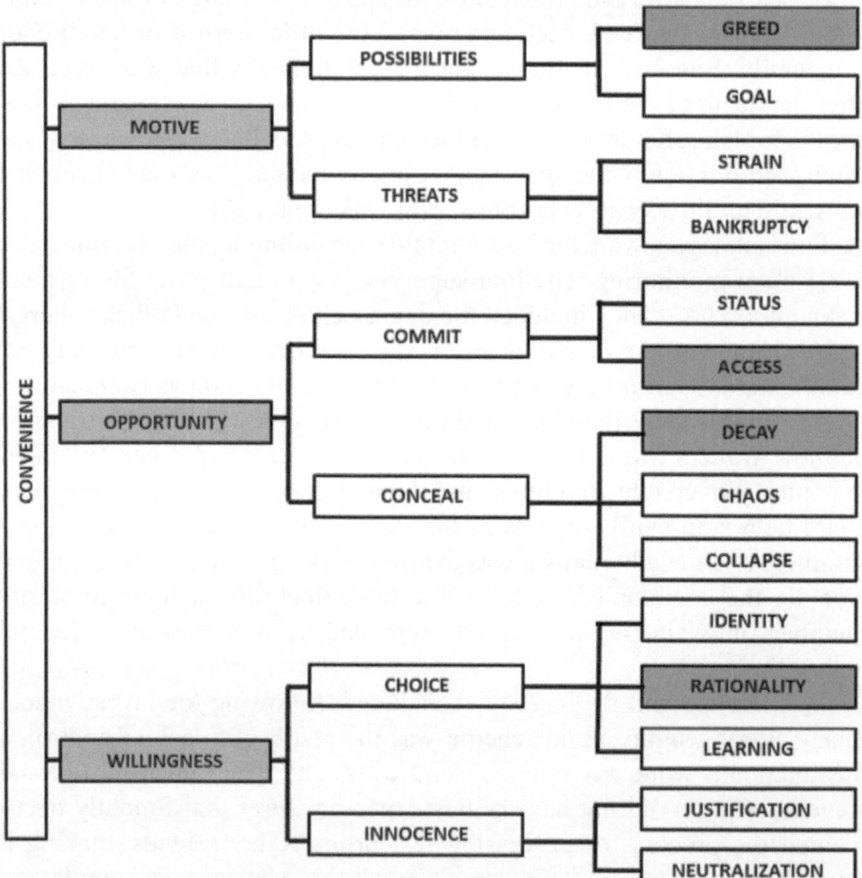

FIGURE 2.2 Harriette Walters convenience themes.

of amount, without needing the review and approval of a higher-level authority.

Walters processed all real property tax refunds without obtaining approval from upper management due to managers' failure to take responsibility. Additionally, there were no automated controls.

Walters admitted to the charges when he was finally caught. Ten additional individuals pleaded guilty in connection with his scheme, in addition to Walters. No one worked for the District. They were friends, relatives, and bank managers. Figure 2.2 depicts Walters' fraud scheme's convenience themes.

CHAPTER 3

Gender Stage Model Norway

We are aware that females make up half of Norway's population but only 6% of white-collar criminals in prison. To explain this discrepancy, we use a stage model to show gender differences. In this chapter, we present data from a group of business school students. While estimates from executive students indicated that 3% of women were in prison, estimates from bachelor students indicated that 10% of women were in prison. The most obvious difference between our two survey groups and the research literature is in their respective convictions. We suggest in this chapter, based on the literature, that female defendants can receive more severe convictions because they may feel more guilt for the crime, such as regret and shame. As a result, it's possible that women confess more readily. In this chapter, 62% and 69% of students disagree that women receive more severe convictions. Their suggestion that female white-collar criminals receive less severe sentences may be because family situations and other factors could be taken into consideration before a woman is convicted. Another significant error connects with identification risk. Women may have a lower detection risk than we estimated (30%), but the literature suggests this is not the case. 75% and 65% of executive and bachelor students, respectively, believe that there is no difference in detection between men and women.

Sutherland (1939), who coined the term middle-class wrongdoing, characterized it as wrongdoing carried out by an individual of decency and high economic well-being in their occupation. This offender-based definition, as opposed to an offense-based definition, is a well-known and influential approach (though not without criticisms) (Friedrichs et al., 2018). According to Craig and Piquero (2017), the definition emphasizes that financial crime committed by privileged members of society who

The Gender Gap in White-Collar Crime: A Multi-Country Study of Women Offenders in Economic Crime.
Maryam Kamaei, Petter Gottschalk, and Thomas E. Dearden (Authors)

misuse their legitimate access to money or resources to break the law is considered white-collar crime (Schnatterly et al., 2018).

It is important to consider the differences between men and women committing white-collar crime, as differences in opportunities, motivations, and willingness likely exist. The research question we pose in this chapter is: Why do women only account for 6% of white-collar crime inmates in Norway when half the population is female? Using a stage model, this chapter shows how gender influences the likelihood of being arrested and convicted for white-collar crime. This chapter provides a potential response to the research question. The model provides an organized structure for the research literature's explanations.

The reason for the model is to show and make sense of how normal sentiments recorded in theoretical considerations can predict the decreasing female division from overall public part to imprisonment portion. Friedrichs (2009) states that society's perception is that men make up the vast majority of those involved in all forms of criminal activity, including white-collar crime. The model supports Messerschmidt's (1997) claim that gender is a significant predictor of criminal activity, as males outnumber females. The fact that Norway ranks as the world's second most gender-equal nation, after Iceland, Sweden, and Finland, makes it an especially intriguing country to investigate in this context. This is in contrast to other common research locations, including the United States of America (51st) and the United Kingdom (15th) (World Economic Forum, 2018).

Norway is additionally of interest, since research recently assessed the discovery rate for middle-class crime is less than 10% (Gottschalk & Gunnesdal, 2018).

Both Friedrichs (2009) and Messerschmidt (1997) track down help in research by Steffensmeier and Allan (1996), who list various observational examinations in various nations in which men carry out undeniably more wrongdoing than women. Furthermore, Blickle et al. (2006) found that male criminals made up the majority of white-collar offenders in Germany.

This chapter focuses on two groups of students from business schools who took on the challenge of estimating fractions using the stage model. The first group consisted of middle-aged practitioners from the executive class. A young bachelor class comprised the second group. Investigations into financial crimes were the focus of both groups.

3.1 STAGE MODEL OVERVIEW

The stage model with the factors that influence and determine the proportion of women in prison is depicted in Figure 3.1. The five stages of the model fit the descriptions that follow.

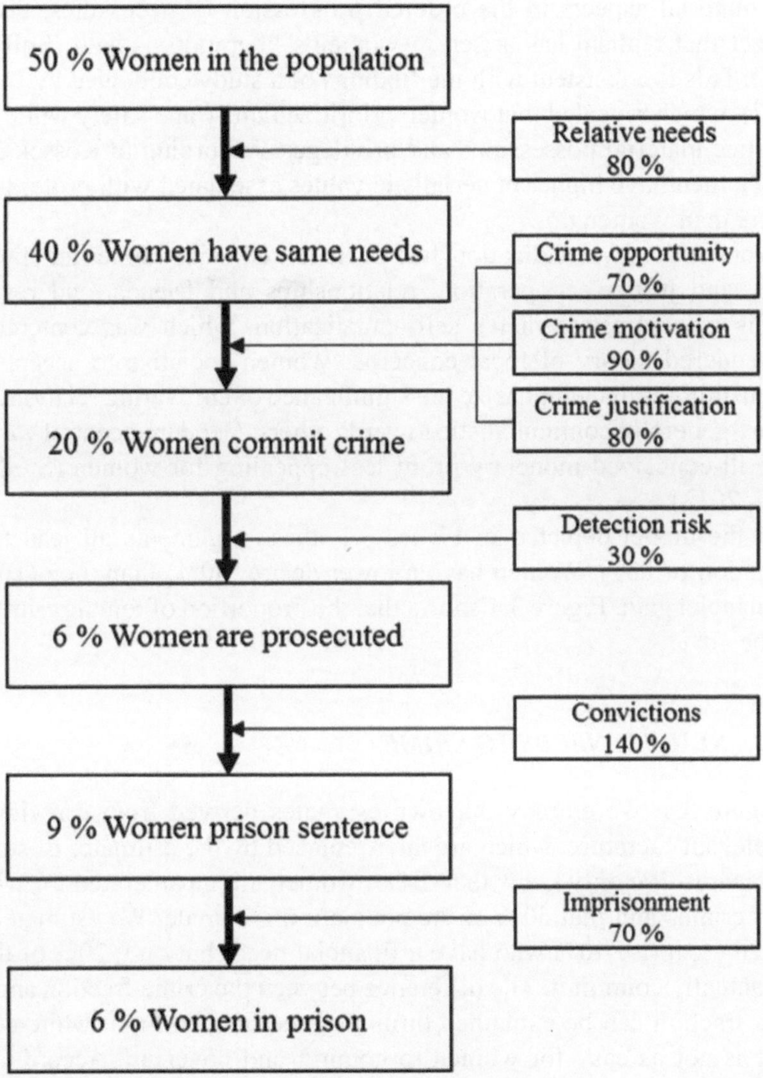

FIGURE 3.1 Full estimation for women and white-collar crime.

3.1.1 STAGE 1: FROM POPULATION TO NEEDS

Here we use Maslow's (1943) hierarchy of needs, starting with gender equality. However, female requirements have slightly different approaches to success. Financial crime is a less appealing option for women. This gender difference suggests that women focus on social aspects more than material aspects in the ordered progression of necessities, despite the fact that realism has arisen in women's liberation as well (Sullivan, 2012). This is consistent with the findings of a study conducted by Dodge (2007), which revealed that women prioritize family and safety while men prioritize material possessions and privileges. According to Kossek et al. (2017), men have higher materialistic values associated with professional careers than women do.

Women's self-actualization has been linked with home and family, equity and justice, cooperation, relationships and friends, and reward. This is in contrast to men's self-actualization, which was centered on the gendered theory of focal concerns. Women socialize to accept role responsibilities that emphasize the significance of cultivating relationships and are generally communalistic towards others. Gendered central worries make ill-conceived monetary profit less appealing for women (Steffensmeier, 2013).

In the model depicted in Figure 3.1, these arguments all lead to an estimation of 80%. Women have a lower desire (80%) than men (100%) for financial gain. Figure 3.1 shows that the proportion of female criminals will be 40%.

3.1.2 STAGE 2: NEEDS TO CRIME

In Figure 3.1, we employ our own estimates derived from a review of the relevant literature, which are later replaced by the estimates of survey participants. We only know that 6% of women are incarcerated for white-collar crimes and that 50% of the population is female. We estimate that women comprise 40% who have a financial need, but only 20% of those who actually commit it. The difference between the crime fraction and the needs fraction can be explained through three factors. First, white-collar crime is not as easy for women to commit and cover up. According to Haantz (2002), the lack of opportunity is the primary factor that accounts for only 17% of all convicted fraud committed by women. Aguilera and Vadera (2008, p. 434) state that "the presence of a favorable combination of circumstances that renders a possible course of action" is the definition of criminal opportunity. Women's general exclusion from male colleagues' social networks can partially explain the reduced opportunity to commit white-collar crime. This is shown by a study of Swedish female managers (Lindgren & Theandersson, 2000). According to research in The United States, female white-collar crime rises when women are invited to participate by men, but this is rare (Becker & McCorkel, 2011). In a similar vein, a study conducted in Australia found that women are less likely to engage in corruption (Bowman & Gilligan, 2008).

Second, women are not as motivated to commit and cover up white-collar crimes as men. According to feminist theory, women are more likely to be afraid of crime because they believe they are more susceptible to its consequences (Britton, 2000). Campbell and others (2001) argue that women are less likely than men to tolerate fear.

Finally, moral theory again explains why women are unable to justify criminal behavior (Bowman & Gilligan, 2008). Men may recognize gray areas in this situation, whereas women may perceive more black or white. As a result, activities that violate the law will be less able to be justified by women because they view them as black while men view them as gray. Women may develop greater self-control when they lack justification (Haantz, 2002; Holtfreter et al., 2010; Huffman et al., 2010).

3.1.3 STAGE 3: CRIME TO DETECTION

Our model's next component is the likelihood of detection in terms of the risk of detection when committing white-collar crime. In the model, we make the assumption that women have a 30% lower detection risk than men. According to Dodge (2007), ethics, morals, and social responsibility typically receive the most attention from women. It appears almost impossible for other people to simultaneously believe they are criminals. O'Fallon and Butterfield (2005), on the other hand, found that women and men are equally capable of unethical and ethical decisions. However, a greater proportion of women in parliament is correlated with a lower level of corruption (Dollar et al., 2021).

3.1.4 *STAGE 4: DETECTION TO SENTENCE*

It is clear that not all white-collar offenders are caught and sentenced. For our focus, we are looking for gender differences once more. It would appear that, in court, a greater proportion of prosecuted women are convicted rather than dismissed. As a result, we estimate that women make up 140% of sentences compared to men in our model.

One potential clarification for this orientation hole is because of a sensation of culpability. Women may perceive and feel more guilt for a crime, such as regret, shame, and depression (Hay, 2003). Keeping a secret is another reason, and women may prefer to be honest with their closest relationships. We have reached 9% of convicted women and 91% of convicted men at this point in our model.

3.1.5 *STAGE 5: SENTENCE TO PRISON*

The proportion of women in jail is the last stage in our model. We do not differentiate between prison and jail. There are 6% ladies and 94% men in prison. For what reason do we have 9% convicts but just 6% detainees among ladies? According to an empirical study of convicted white-collar criminals in Norway, women serve fewer and shorter sentences. We estimate that women serve 70% less time in prison than men to move from 9% of court convictions to 6% of inmates.

One possibility is that women are more likely to be offered alternatives to prison. Only 4% of men and 10% of women have alternatives to prison. Supernor (2017, p. 148) found "a lot more women were given community service than men" which they attributed to "the court systems [not wanting] to punish a woman in a way that would take her away from her family" and "women are considered homemakers for families."

Another reason is that women are more likely to be found guilty, but their prison sentences are typically shorter. Schanzenbach and Yaeger's (2006) empirical study demonstrates that women who are convicted receive shorter prison sentences.

3.2 BUSINESS STUDENT SURVEY

Bachelor's students in Norway can choose an elective course in financial crime and leadership at a business school. The subject matter of the course is white-collar criminals, whose motivations, opportunities, and willingness are crucial to comprehending crime. The course also focuses on fraud examination and detection. In class, students completed a questionnaire at the beginning of the semester. The questionnaire was completed by every student in the class. The scores on each scale ranged from one (strongly disagree) to six (strongly agree), with a score of 3.5 representing neither agreement nor disagreement with the statement. White-collar crimes are a common source of concern for respondents (4.6). Respondents accept that outer reviewers have the best capacity to distinguish wrongdoing signals (4.0), trailed by inner evaluators (3.9), tax agents (3.9), police officers (3.9), investigative journalists (3.7), and bank representatives (3.7). Infraction victims were deemed to have the lowest level of crime signal detection ability by respondents (2.8), followed by bankruptcy lawyers (3.1) and finally stock exchange clerks (3.5).

This study on the stage model for female white-collar offenders is relevant to business school students because many of them will engage in financial crime in the future. Some of them could become enticed to mishandle their situations to perpetrate middle-class wrongdoing, while others may be accountable for different monetary controls in jobs, for example, auditors and compliance officials.

Business school students responded in terms of their evaluation of relative orientation portions in a survey:

1. Comparison of women's and men's requirements for material status
2. Opportunities for women to commit financial crimes compared to those for men Comparison of women's and men's motivations for financial crime
3. Compared to men, women's ability to justify financial crime
4. Women's financial crime detection risk in comparison to men's
5. Comparison of women's and men's prison sentences for financial crimes Compared to men
6. women's atonement for financial crimes in prison
7. Respondents were also asked about their own gender, whether man or woman. Since the survey research took place during a lecture hour, the response rate is 100%.

3.2.1 STAGE MODEL RESPONSES

The 26 students in the executive class during the spring semester of 2019 are listed in Table 3.1. As shown in Figure 3.2, they estimate a relative need of 81%, criminal opportunity of 71%, criminal motivation of 62%, criminal justification of 10%, detection risk of 69%, convictions of 57%, and imprisonment of 45%.

Since we realize that the genuine detainment part is 6%, we need to address all appraisals appropriately later on in this section. In Table 3.1, some executive respondents believed that women have more opportunity, needs, motivation, detection, justification, and conviction than men.

There were 26 executive students in the class, with 17 women and 9 men. Gender differences in responses were surprisingly insignificant, according to our findings. The best contrast was with regards to probability of location. Men think women have a relative detection risk of 77%, while women think they have a relative detection risk of 65%.

TABLE 3.1 Executive Class Female Infraction Table

	N	Minimum	Maximum	Mean	Std. Deviation
Relative needs	26	15.00	200.00	81.4615	39.49606
Crime opportunity	26	10.00	150.00	71.3462	37.61802
Crime motivation	26	6.00	130.00	61.7692	33.51693
Crime justification	26	5.00	200.00	103.8462	53.12829
Detection risk	26	10.00	200.00	68.8462	42.07868
Convictions	26	10.00	150.00	57.1154	30.13878
Imprisonment	26	10.00	100.00	45.0000	28.60070

The executive group's correlation coefficients are shown in Table 3.2. There are various positive connection coefficients, including relative necessities essentially associating with wrongdoing inspiration, detection risk, convictions, and detainment. According to this statistical result, there is less of a correlation between men's and women's motivation for crime, detection risk, convictions, and imprisonment when there is less of a difference in material needs.

The results for a bachelor class are shown in Table 3.3. The bachelor class consisted of students between the ages of 22 and 40, whereas the executive class consisted of people working in both private and public organizations. Overall, single male students find no distinction among people in regards to needs that unadulterated realism can cover, as the need might arise in Table 3.3 are precisely 100%. In addition, a relative percentage of 92% of bachelor students suggest a minor gender difference

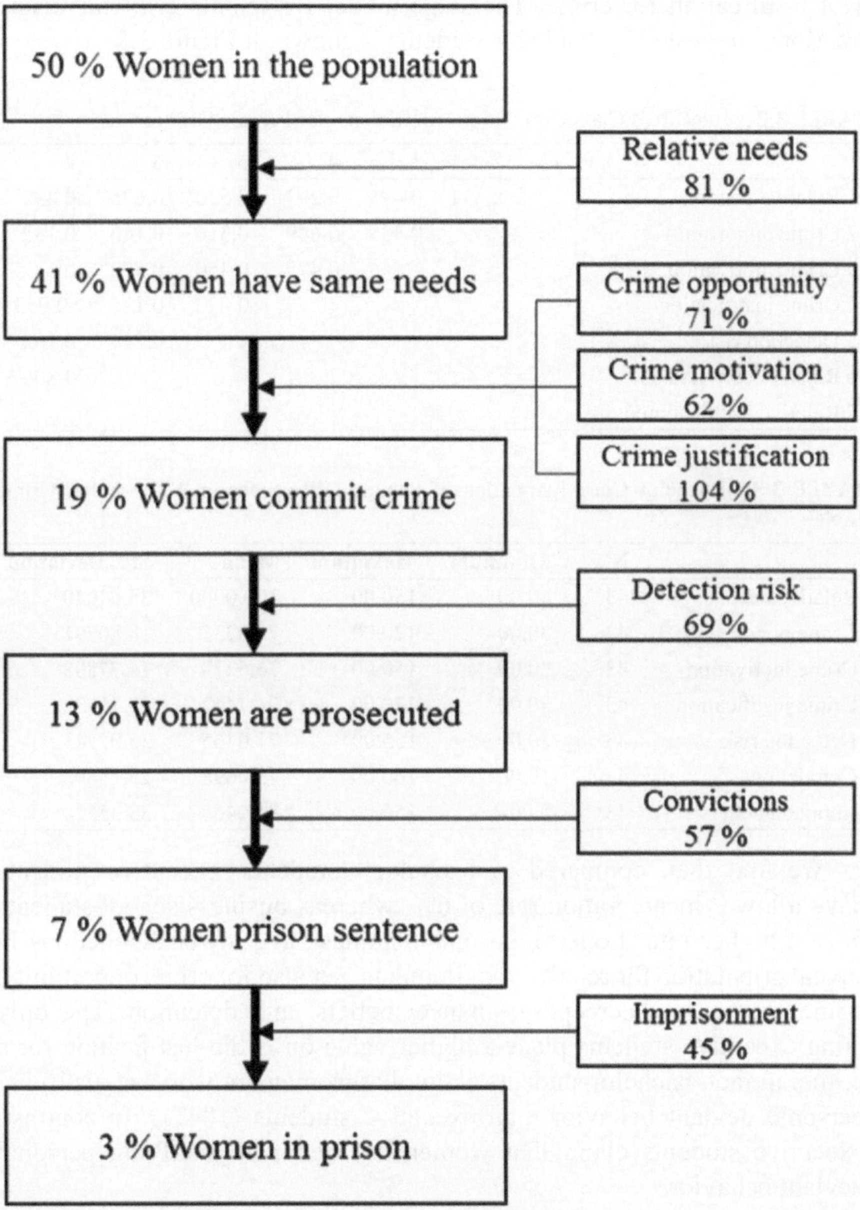

FIGURE 3.2 Executive class female infraction estimates.

as a justification for crime. The stage model for female criminals using fractions suggested by bachelor students is shown in Figure 3.3.

TABLE 3.2 Executive Class Correlation Coefficients for Female Differences

	1	2	3	4	5	6	7
1 Relative needs	_	0.371	0.495*	0.293	0.520*	0.675**	0.490*
2 Crime opportunity		_	0.439	0.649**	0.316	0.146	0.132
3 Crime motivation			_	0.475	0.450	0.578*	0.677**
4 Crime justification				_	0.022	0.125	-0.053
5 Detection risk					_	0.215	0.163
6 Relative convictions						_	0.806**
7 Relative imprisonment							_

TABLE 3.3 Bachelor Class Estimation of Female Differences in White-Collar Crime Table

	N	Minimum	Maximum	Mean	Std. Deviation
Relative needs	43	40.00	150.00	100.0000	35.64040
Crime opportunity	43	30.00	120.00	78.0233	18.80791
Crime motivation	43	30.00	150.00	76.6279	24.77808
Crime justification	43	30.00	170.00	91.7442	29.31528
Detection risk	43	10.00	155.00	71.0465	35.07743
Convictions	43	10.00	100.00	75.0698	25.15608
Imprisonment	43	0.00	150.00	71.0465	33.35520

We find that, compared to bachelor's students, executive students have a lower incarceration rate of 6%, whereas business school students have a higher rate. Lone ranger understudies have lower distinctions in sexual orientation for relative requirements, yet also for crime opportunity, crime motivation, perception chance, beliefs, and detention. The only thing executive students place a higher value on is the justification for a crime. In fact, bachelor students claim that women are worse at justifying personal deviant behavior than executive students (104%). In contrast, executive students claim that women are better at justifying personal deviant behavior.

Female bachelor students made up 30 of the respondents, while male students made up 13 of the respondents. Female bachelor students, like executive students, believe that men and women have a lower detection risk.

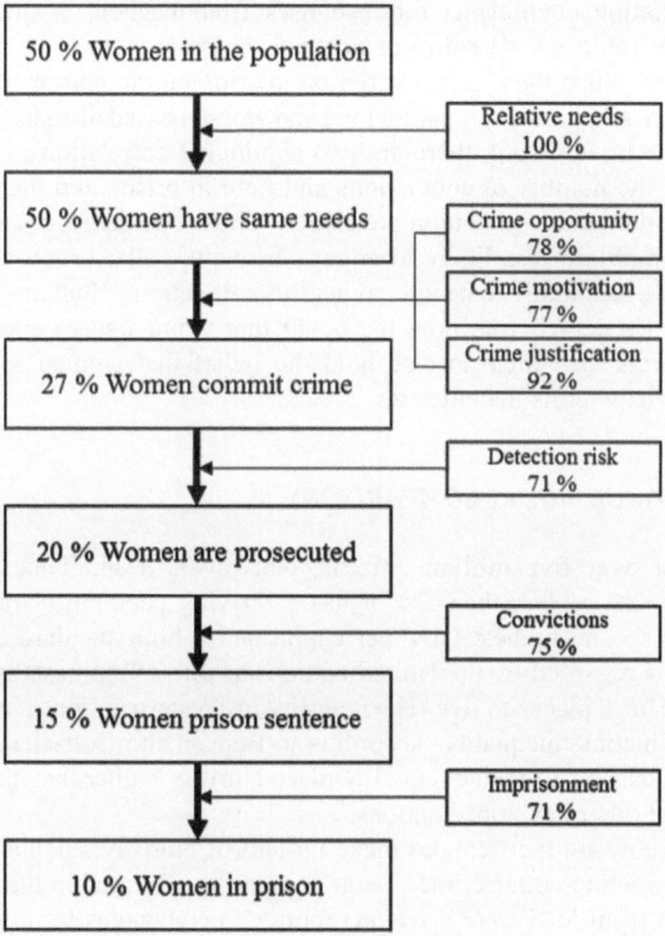

FIGURE 3.3 Bachelor students' estimation of female differences in white-collar crime.

TABLE 3.4 Bachelor Class Correlation Coefficients for Female Differences

	1	2	3	4	5	6	7
1. Relative needs	–	0.129	0.179	0.193	0.198	0.275	0.068
2. Crime opportunity		–	0.003	–0.013	0.119	0.198	–0.097
3. Crime motivation			–	0.472**	0.166	0.171	0.207
4. Crime justification				–	–0.180	0.250	0.164
5. Detection risk					–	0.294	0.190
6. Relative convictions						–	0.671**
7. Relative imprisonment							–

Correlation coefficients for responses from bachelor's students are shown in Table 3.4. We do not observe the same pattern as executive students in which there is less variation in criminal motivation, detection, conviction, and imprisonment for men and women based on assumed material needs. In Table 3.4, there are two significant correlations, indicating that both the number of convictions and time in prison and the variation in motivation and justification are shared. Those bachelor's students who think women are less likely to engage in white-collar crime also think women are less likely to be able to justify their actions. Students pursuing a bachelor's degree who hold the belief that women serve even shorter prison terms than men do also hold the belief that women serve even shorter prison terms than men do.

3.2.2 STAGE MODEL COMPARISONS

With just over five million citizens, Norway is a small nation. With a jobless rate of less than 3%, it has a thriving economy. Norway has Europe's second-highest GDP per capita and a high standard of living. Norway is regarded by the United Nations as one of the best, and sometimes the best, places to live. The majority of Western nations have higher levels of income inequality. According to Benson and Gottschalk (2015), several measures of gender equality place Norway higher than the United States and other developed nations.

We are aware that females make up half of Norway's population and 6% of the white-collar crime prison population. To explain the stepwise reduction from 50% to 6%, we incorporated percentages from the literature into the gender model in the literature review. Two groups of business students were asked to estimate the differences in women offenders for our empirical study. While estimates from executive students indicated that 3% of women were in prison, estimates from bachelor students indicated that 10% of women were in prison.

We have corrected the estimates of executive and bachelor students in Table 3.5 to show that 6% of women are in prison. We multiplied each estimate for executive student responses by 1.088. We multiplied each estimate for bachelor student responses by 0.921, the seventh potential for the fraction of 6% to 10%.

TABLE 3.5 Adjusted Female Differences Based on Six Percent Incarceration

	Theoretical Estimates	Executive Class Students	Bachelor Class Students	Average Percentages
1. Relative needs	80%	88%	92%	87%
2. Crime opportunity	70%	77%	72%	73%
3. Crime motivation	90%	67%	71%	76%
4. Crime justification	80%	113%	85%	93%
5. Detection risk	30%	75%	65%	57%
6. Relative convictions	14%	62%	69%	90%
7. Relative imprisonment	70%	49%	65%	61%
8. Female fraction in prison	6%	6%	6%	6%

In Table 3.5, the most glaring disparity relates to relative convictions. We hypothesized, based on Hey (2003), that female defendants receive more severe convictions because they may perceive and feel more guilt for a crime, such as regret, shame, and depression. As a result, it's possible that women confess more readily. Slyke and Parcels (2013), notwithstanding, support the understudy reactions as they recommend that ladies in middle-class offenses benefit from tolerance at the sentencing phase of law enforcement framework handling.

The detection risk section of Table 3.5 contains yet another significant discrepancy. Women have a low detection risk, according to the literature (Dodge, 2007; Dollar et al., 2001; O'Fallon & Butterfield, 2005), but it could be higher than our estimate of 30%. 75% and 65% of executive and bachelor students, respectively, believe that the gender difference in detection likelihood is not that significant.

Based on this chapter, significant avenues for future research exist. Based on the literature reviewed, the focus on the reasons why women participate in white-collar crime differently tends to dispel gender stereotypes. Women are portrayed as ethical, moral, socially responsible, less materialistic, and more self-reliant, according to stereotypes. These implicit assumptions were reflected in the survey's design, which differentiates between men and women in regards to needs, opportunities, motivation, justification, detection risk, relative convictions, and imprisonment. Students rated women in relation to men in response based on such apparent stereotypes. These characteristics may be challenged theoretically and empirically by subsequent researchers. Interviews with female inmates and professionals working in the criminal justice system, as well as watching trials, are examples of empirical methods. Moreover, it may be advantageous to extend the techniques and tests to create explicit understandings of distinctions in sexual orientation to look at how more extensive cycles and power designs can respond to the why-question of female participation in white-collar crime.

In conclusion, this chapter offered a speculative explanation for why women make up 50% of the Norwegian population but only 6% of the white-collar crime prison population. The chapter has developed a stage model framework to investigate the attrition of women in the commission and conviction of white-collar crime based on factors like opportunity, motivation, and justification. The chapter then moved on to compare stage models created from survey results with two university courses who came to different estimates (3% and 10%) and stage models created from existing literature. In pedagogical contexts, the presented models and data can be used for discussion.

In a country like Norway, where males make up 94% of the white-collar prison population, the fact that women make up only 6% of the population is certainly intriguing. Because Norway is the world's second-most gender-equal nation, behind only Iceland, which is a smaller country, the country is especially interesting to study. The low likelihood of female offenders being caught is one of the main explanations that emerge from the literature and empirical surveys of business school students. According to the last column of Table 3.5, the relative detection risk is 57%. Table 3.5 shows that relative imprisonment is the second-largest difference between men and women, with women experiencing a relative incarceration length of 61% longer than men for the same offense. The ability of male and female criminals to justify their actions is the area where there is the smallest difference in Table 3.5.

CHAPTER 4

Gender Stage Model Utah

Utah's white-collar crime registry includes 71 female offenders and 191 male offenders. This chapter presents an application of the dataset to a stage model suggested for female offenders. While 50% of the population in the state is women, the fraction of female offenders is 26.5%. The stage model suggests relative needs, relative crime opportunity, relative crime motivation, relative crime justification, and relative detection risk are factors that can explain why the conviction fraction is lower than the population fraction. This chapter compares Utah results to Norwegian results, where the fraction of female inmates in Norwegian prisons is 6%.

The previous chapter offered a discussion as to the potential reasons why 50% of the Norwegian population is female while women constitute only 6% of the prison population incarcerated for white-collar crime. The research presented several perceptions in the existing literature that help describe women's involvement in white-collar crime. These perceptions resulted in a stage model that explores the gender differences and attrition of women engaging with and being prosecuted for white-collar crime. A percentage of offenders filter out at each subsequent stage of the criminal justice process based on selection bias that occurs between each stage.

The research in the previous chapter compared the stage model generated literature with the results from a survey provided to business students. The estimates showed different rates, 3% and 10%, with regard to incarceration rate, while the real incarceration rate in Norway is 6%.

White-collar criminals use their privileged positions in public and business organizations to commit financial crimes by abusing their access to systems and resources to carry out and conceal their deviant acts (Benson & Simpson, 2018; Dearden, 2016, 2017, 2019; Engdahl, 2015; 2017 by

The Gender Gap in White-Collar Crime: A Multi-Country Study of Women Offenders in Economic Crime.
Maryam Kamaei, Petter Gottschalk, and Thomas E. Dearden (Authors)

Gottschalk & Tcherni-Buzzeo; Logan et al., 2019; Sutherland, 1939, 1983). Galvin et al. found that this is a narrow definition that they have extended in 2018, where they incorporate a wide range of peaceful wrongdoing with monetary intentions. We use the offense-based definition of white-collar crime rather than the offender-based definition in this chapter (Goossen et al., 2016; Piquero, 2018; Piquero & Schoepfer, 2010). The fact that anyone can commit fraud on the Internet is one argument for the offense-based perspective. Eight decades ago, Sutherland (1939) created the term "white-collar crime" (Geest et al., 2017). Another argument is to take into account the diverse nature of contemporary white-collar crime (Onna, 2020). Men and women do not have the same opportunities, motivations, or willingness to commit white-collar crime, according to previous research (Benson & Harbinson, 2020; Daly, 1989a, b; Galvin, 2020; Goulette, 2020; Harbinson, 2020; Klenowski et al., 2011; Ndrecka, 2020).

In this part, we apply the stage model introduced in the past section to information from Utah's Middle Class Wrongdoing Wrongdoer Vault (Utah Principal Legal Officer's Office, 2020). There are 71 female offenders (26.5%), 191 male offenders (71.3%), and 6 unknown offenders in the dataset. Due to the fact that females received shorter prison sentences than males, the percentage of 26.5% females is comparable to 9%, 7%, and 15% females in the Norwegian study—not the 6%, 3%, and 10% mentioned earlier.

4.1 STAGE MODEL OVERVIEW

Stage models with discrete levels serve to assess and evaluate a variety of phenomena (e.g., Röglinger et al., 2012; Solli-Sæther & Gottschalk, 2015). The previous chapter applied the concept of stages to explain the stepwise change in gender fraction from the national population to the prison population. Figure 3.1 illustrated the stage model with factors that seem to influence the fraction of women in prison. There are five stages, which we repeat here. However, our search for evidence for the stage model later in this chapter restricts itself to stop at the fourth stage of convictions, as the Utah dataset is only concerned with convicted offenders and not incarcerated offenders.

4.1.1 STAGE 1: POPULATION TO NEEDS

We start with the assumption that Maslow's (1943) hierarchy of needs is similar for both men and women. However, slightly different means may apply to the achievement of female needs (Benson & Gottschalk, 2015). If this is the case, financial crimes may be a less enticing option for women. Prior research has found that women emphasize social dimensions more than material objects (Sullivan, 2012). This is consistent with other research that shows that women prioritize family and safety while men prioritize material goods and privileges (2007). Furthermore, men tend to use their careers to focus on materialistic opportunities (Kossek et al., 2017).

In a Canadian study, Dodge (2007) showed that women's self-actualization was linked to family and home, justice and equality, team and cooperation, friends and relationships, and fame and reward. Men, in contrast, were linked to money, income, privileges, power, status, and authority.

Overall, these arguments lead the previous chapter to a relative estimate of 80% in the model. Thus, with roughly 50% women in the general population, the relative fraction is 40% for women's desire for financial gain as illustrated in Figure 3.1. This estimate is derived from an interpretation of the research literature briefly mentioned above. However, two independent groups of business students presented their own estimates for relative needs of 81% and 100% respectively, resulting in 41% of women having the same needs, and 50% of women having the same needs as men. The group of business students who suggested 100% implies that there is no real difference in material desire among men and women to exploit possibilities and to avoid threats.

4.1.2 STAGE 2: NEEDS TO CRIME

The model in Figure 3.1 estimated that while 40% of the people who have a need for gain from financial crime are women, only 20% of the people who commit financial crime are women. We estimate this by considering the change from needs to crime. This reduction comes through three factors. First, as mentioned previously, women do not have the same opportunity. This extends to white-collar crime, where the workforce is often discriminatory, leading to differences in positions and opportunities to commit white-collar crime (Braaten & Vaughn, 2019; Chan & Gibbs, 2020; Dearden & Gottschalk, 2021). Some scholars argue that this difference in opportunity is the main reason why women only commit 17% of fraud (Haantz, 2002). Aguilera and Vadera (2008, p. 434) suggest that this criminal opportunity may exclude women because of a smaller or different social network. They simply do not have the same combination of circumstances that allow them to exploit the business or fiduciary (Chan et al., 2010; Ullman & Siegel, 1993). This is supported by a study conducted in the United States which found that women commit more white-collar crime when they are invited by men (Becker & McCorkel, 2011).

In a similar vein, a study conducted in Australia found that women are less likely to participate in corruption schemes (Bowman & Gilligan, 2008). This is consistent with a straightforward experiment that we frequently carry out in front of various audiences in which the question is: who would you bribe? You want to construct a new home on land that the state has designated as recreational property, such as a picturesque shoreline. In the municipality, you can bribe either a male or female official. Your application can be approved by both of them. Taking into account all of the viewers, the vast majority always vote exclusively for men. Practically nobody would pay off a female authority.

Women may not be as motivated to commit and cover up white-collar crimes as men. One interpretation of feminist theory asserts that women are more likely to be afraid of crime because they perceive themselves as being more susceptible to its potential consequences (Britton, 2000). Campbell and others (2001) argue that women are less likely than men to tolerate fear.

Furthermore, women may not have the same mindset to be able to justify their crimes as suggested by moral theory (Bowman & Gilligan, 2008). These differences between men and women often lead to men feeling comfortable when realizing desires in "gray zones" (Gottschalk & Glasø, 2013; Gottschalk & Smith, 2015). Therefore, women will have a more difficult time justifying their actions when they are borderline illegal or unethical. Given the complexity of regulation and law, this may lead to more crime committed by men.

While relative crime opportunity is 70% in Figure 3.1, two groups of business students estimated 71% and 78% respectively. Relative crime motivation was 62% and 77% by business students compared to 90% derived from the brief literature review above. Business students estimated relative crime justification at 104% and 92% compared to 80% in Figure 3.1.

4.1.3 STAGE 3: FROM CRIME TO DETECTION

Women may be less likely to be detected when committing white-collar crime than men. The previous chapter assumes that the detection risk for women compared to men is 30% because of a lack of signal detection. Signal alertness, signal intensity, pattern recognition, and signal experience determine signal detection (Szalma & Hancock, 2013). According to Dodge (2007), ethics, morals, friendships, and social responsibility typically garner the most attention from women. It may appear nearly impossible for others to simultaneously believe they are criminals. Other scholars found that women and men are equally capable of making unethical decisions (O'Fallon & Butterfield, 2005). Based on the brief literature above, the two groups of business students suggested a relative detection risk of 69% and 71%, respectively, as opposed to 30% in Figure 3.1.

4.1.4 STAGE 4: DETECTION TO SENTENCE

How many white-collar offenders are detected and prosecuted and ultimately face conviction by the courts? Consistent with the work above, we are focused on the differences between genders. The model in Figure 2.1 estimates 140% as the relative sentencing fraction for women compared to men. This suggests that women are relatively more likely to receive a guilty sentence than men.

The general suggestion here is that women are more likely to experience feelings of guilt, regret, shame, and depression. Another reason is that women are more likely to want to be honest. A third reason might be that women wish to get the case over with, while men prefer to defend themselves in court. These elements are speculations since we had a difficult time finding relevant references in the research literature.

At this stage in the model, 9% are women and 91% are men. The two groups of business students suggested 57% and 75% in relative convictions, which means that they do not believe that a larger fraction of prosecuted women are convicted in court as suggested in Figure 2.1. Student responses were quite opposite as the students believe that a larger fraction of prosecuted men face conviction in court compared to women. Resulting from their estimated conviction rate, the business students end up with a fraction of 7% and 15% of women who receive prison sentences, while the model in Figure 2.1 suggests 9%. The Utah data that we will return to later in this chapter shows a 26.5% female offender fraction among white-collar criminals.

4.1.5 STAGE 5: SENTENCE TO PRISON

The last stage in the model in Figure 3.1 was the fraction of women in jail. Here we utilize jail as general incarceration and do not make a distinction between jail and prison. There are 6% women and 94% men in jail in Norway for white-collar crime. Why does Norway have 9% convicts but only 6% inmates among women? The general consensus is that women serve both fewer and shorter sentences compared to men. To move from 9% court convictions to 6% prison inmates, the estimate is that women only serve 70% of the incarceration time compared to men.

This difference in incarceration time could have several explanations. On face value, it likely means that the sentences themselves deserve less time, and are considered less severe (Schanzenbach & Yaeger, 2006). However, the court system could also be sentencing more women to alternative sanctions than men. 10% of women have the opportunity of alternatives to prison, but only 4% of men have the opportunity of such alternatives.

4.2 UTAH OFFENDER REGISTRY

Utah's White-collar Crime Offender Registry provided us with the information we needed (Utah Attorney General's Office, 2020). In 2015, this online registry, known as HB 378, was approved by the Utah Legislature. The registration requirement applies to Utah residents who have been found guilty of a white-collar crime in the second degree or higher. According to the White-collar Crime Registry, HB 378, 2015, theft by deception, securities fraud, fraudulent insurance, unlawful dealing of property by a fiduciary, communications fraud, mortgage fraud, and money laundering are included in the categories of crimes that are outlined in the statute. Unless a person is convicted three or more times, in which case they remain on the registry for the entirety of their lives, most people spend 10 years on the registry for each offense.

We transcribed each offender from the registry into a dataset in order to create a white-collar offenders database. We were able to get information about 268 offenders and their crimes from the registry website. The following demographics were gathered: birth date, height, weight, color of eyes, and color of hair. The date of the convictions, the type of offense, the court's location, the target, and a summary of the offense were all included in the information. We were also able to determine the offender's gender and age from the registry data.

In order to identify target groups, we categorized white-collar crime. For instance, when a middle-class wrongdoer commits tax avoidance, the objective is society. The bank and, ultimately, other bank customers suffer financial harm when a fraudster commits bank fraud. The victim of embezzlement by a white-collar criminal is the employer. The competitors of an offender who receives a bribe become potential victims.

Assuming that crime is different for men and women, we looked at a variety of targets and explained why men and women choose different targets. For instance, bank extortion could prompt serious results contrasted with theft. According to Gotttschalk and Tcherni-Buzzeo (2017), employers may not report a detected offender to the police because they do not want the public's attention, but banks may take action. Then, we could argue that female criminals favor embezzlement more because women are more concerned about the consequences.

4.2.1 STAGE MODEL ESTIMATES

The Utah White-collar Crime Registry dataset includes 71 female offenders (26.5%), 191 male offenders (71.3%), and six unknown offenders (2.2%). To better understand the differences in male and female offending rates, we consider the stage model. Prior to considering stage one, we established a baseline demographic difference. In Utah, there are fewer females, with an estimated 49.6% (U.S. Census Bureau, 2019).

4.2.1.1 STAGE 1: POPULATION TO NEEDS

To consider the first stage, we examined the amount of money stolen from females compared to males. Using the summaries from the cases, we considered the dollar amount that victims lost. As not all crimes reported financial dollar amounts, there were only 17 crimes analyzed. 4 female offenses, 11 male offenses, and 1 unknown gender had dollar amounts for their crime. On average, female white-collar offenses averaged $30,260, whereas male white-collar crime averaged $509,916 as listed in Table 4.1. Though based on a small sample size, we found that females stole, on average, only 6% of what males averaged.

A study of 405 white-collar offenders in Norway obtained a similar result in terms of difference in crime amount. While male offenders caused a crime amount of 57 million Norwegian kroner ($6.3 million), female offenders had a crime amount of 9 million Norwegian kroner ($1 million). In the Norwegian sample, females stole 7% and males stole 93% of the total money (Benson & Gottschalk, 2015; Gottschalk & Glasø, 2013; Gottschalk & Smith, 2015).

TABLE 4.1 Gender Differences in Amount Stolen

Amount Stolen	Females	Males
Average	$30,260	$509,916
Median	$31,500	$55,000
Min	$14,140	$4,000
Max	$43,900	$4,000,000
Standard Deviation	$12,181	$1,141,181

The fact that women have fewer opportunities than men likely accounts for some of the gender gap. However, given the substantial and significant differences, where men in the United States steal 16 times as much, and men in Norway commit crime six times as much, there must be other explanations as well. We suggest that female needs in the hierarchy suggested by Maslow (1943) to a lesser extent are achievable by money.

Based on the 6% amount for women compared to men, we assume that most of the difference finds its cause in other factors such as opportunity. However, we speculate that some of the difference finds its explanation in relative needs that we estimate to be 80%.

4.2.1.2 STAGE 2: NEEDS TO CRIME

In order to examine the second stage, we considered the circumstances of white-collar crime. As there is no direct measure of opportunity, we considered the circumstances that lead to opportunity. We considered the nature of specialized access (Cohen & Felson, 1979). Opportunity increases with more access to privileged information. The authors examined each case summary and coded whether the offender had specialized access through a perceived legitimate organization. This access was to information, money, or accounts and resulted from the course of their job, occupation, or position. For example, a bank teller or accountant would have access to accounts and money that a non-employee would not have access to. Conversely, an offender who commits a Craigslist fraud by pretending to send a product does not have specialized access. We reason that females will commit less white-collar crime because they have less access to this form of convenience. We argue that the specialized access position increases opportunity for easy targets.

We coded each situation using the description of the crime. If the role included access because of position or perceived position, we considered this specialized access. Typical examples included employees or business owners with access to information. Examples that had no access were often frauds or cons, in which the offender pretends to have legitimacy through trickery or manipulation. Our data revealed that females might utilize positions of specialized access more often than males. Overall, females used their specialized access in 52% of situations (37/71) and males used their specialized access in 40% of situations (76/191). This means that females utilized specialized access 30% more than males. Relative crime opportunity thus becomes 130%. We have no way of estimating relative crime motivation and relative crime justification for the Utah offenders. Therefore, we determine both without influence at 90%.

4.2.1.3 STAGE 3: CRIME TO DETECTION

For this stage, we consider that certain victims are least likely to report. These might include known victims, such as family, friends, and acquaintances. Overall, females were less likely to target known victims at 11% (24/213). Males targeted known victims more often at 20% (114/573). With this evidence, contrary to expectations, we found that females were more likely to face reporting since they target known victims to a lesser extent compared to males.

Our exploration at this stage is concerned with the objective determination by orientation. In some cases, the offender could be convicted of more than one offense. We included up to three casualties, which was consistent with the maximum number of casualties per offense in the actual library. Gender differences in the selection of targets were significant ($\chi 2=75.4$, $p=.001$). Females were less likely to target friends, acquaintances, or investors when we looked at the Chi-square effect cell by cell. They were more likely to target their employers, healthcare providers, and random people. Table 4.2 in the next chapter shows target selection and gender.

While the target perspective suggests that the detection risk for women is higher than for men, a number of other issues point in the opposite direction. In particular, the kinds of crime committed by males seem more relevant to the police. For example, money laundering of proceeds from traditional criminal activity is more frequent among male Utah offenders than among female Utah offenders. Furthermore, male offenders were frequently filing false statements, such as filing fraudulent personal injury claims, filing vandalism claims, filing fraudulent insurance claims, filing and receiving money based on fraudulent bills of sales, filing student loan applications, and filing multiple claims to multiple insurance companies. We assume that the detection rate is quite high when offenders file claims where the receiver of the claim is reluctant to pay. Female offenders did not file claims. Their crimes included more forging, such as presenting forged pharmacy receipts, forging signatures, and forging title documents, where we assume that the detection rate is lower.

A content analysis of the text elements in the Utah data illustrates that words like "forge," "prepare," and "steal" were more frequent among female offenders. These words appeared in 15% of female cases and only 6% of male cases. Words like "file," "launder," "sell," and "solicit" are frequent among male offenders. These words appeared in 21% of male cases but only 6% of female cases. Content analysis assumes that language reflects how people understand, think, and act (Bell et al., 2018; Duriau et al., 2007; Krippendorff, 1980; Patrucco et al., 2017; Saunders et al., 2007). Our interpretation of text elements in the Utah database suggests that male offenders were likely engaging in traditional deviant activities that traditional law enforcement know well.

4.2.1.4 STAGE 4: DETECTION TO SENTENCE

As listed in Table 4.2, the female fraction is 29% after stage 3. We know that the female fraction after stage 4 is 26%. Therefore, we simply calculate the relative conviction rate at 90%. We were unable to examine certain elements of this model, including motivational elements and conviction/sentencing data. Although we obtained disparate numbers and unexpected findings (e.g., females leveraging specialized access more often and offending against known offenders less often), the end result was similar to the proposed model as listed in Table 4.3. In consideration of just the first three stages, we end with 14% as opposed to the 29–27% expected.

TABLE 4.2 Estimation of Female Fraction of White-Collar Crime in Utah

Stage	Percent Female	Current Likelihood
0 Population	50%	50%
1. Needs	80%	40%
2. Crime	105%	42%
3. Prosecution	70%	29%
4. Conviction	90%	26%
5. Incarceration	–	–

4.2.2 COMPARISON UTAH NORWAY

The state of Utah in the United States of America has a population of 2.3 million, while Norway has a population of 5.4 million. They are similar in size and standard of living. However, they are also different on a number of measures. Utah scores high on religious measures, with more than 50% of the population saying they attend religious services at least once a week (Pew Research Center, n.d.) compared to an estimated 5% in Northern Europe, including Norway (Brenner, 2016). In addition, Utah is conservative whereas Norway seems quite liberal. These differences in populations provide increased generalizability of the stage theory, albeit in different percentages.

TABLE 4.3 Comparison of Estimates and Survey Results

Relative Gender Factors Females Versus Males	Sample Utah	Theoretical Literature	Survey 1 Norway	Survey 2 Norway
Relative needs	80%	80%	88%	92%
Crime opportunity	130%	70%	77%	72%
Crime motivation	90%	90%	67%	71%
Crime justification	90%	80%	113%	85%
Detection risk	92%	30%	75%	65%
Relative convictions	70%	140%	62%	69%
Relative imprisonment	90%	70%	49%	65%
Female fraction sentenced	26%	9%	7%	15%
Female fraction in prison	–	6%	6%	6%

Table 4.3 compares the Utah sample results to the Norwegian survey results and makes suggestions for theoretical literature. The only known facts are 26% female offenders in Utah and 6% incarcerated women in Norway for white-collar crime. It is interesting to note in the table that,

while the theoretical literature suggests a relatively smaller fraction for female offenders at each stage, except for the conviction stage, the Utah data suggests crime opportunity as the only exception from declining female fraction in the stage model.

Despite limited data, we see vast differences in the money amount stolen by female and male offenders. Males steal significantly more through white-collar crime than females. This pattern held for both the Norwegian and Utah sample. We consider this an effect of relative needs.

We examined opportunity by considering specialized access. Contrary to expectations, we found that females utilized positions of specialized access (Cohen & Felson, 1979) more often than males. This fit with our findings on target selection, where females were more likely to target employers and less likely to target other known acquaintances, such as family and friends. With this information, we conducted a content analysis that considered the actions taken by males and females. The content analysis showed that females were more likely to conduct crimes such as forgeries and other thefts. Males were more likely to commit crimes such as money laundering and financial statement fraud. Thus, we found that the Utah sample contained more opportunity for females, though this opportunity may have amounted to smaller thefts (e.g., forgeries netting smaller payouts than investment swindles do).

Future analysis should consider the justifications utilized by white-collar offenders. The stage model considers this, though testing of these behavioral elements is difficult. Despite drastic differences between Norway and Utah, the Stage Model appears useful in considering the differences between males and females committing white-collar crime.

In conclusion, this chapter has presented research where we tried to find evidence for the stage model for the fraction of female white-collar crime offenders. Based on the Utah white-collar crime registry dataset, we found some support for stages that can explain the drop in the female fraction from the population via financial needs and magnitude of crime, to prosecution and conviction. Our attempt to identify the core reasons why the female fraction drops through the stage model did not quite succeed. This opens up for future research, where we suggest the exploration of datasets that are more comprehensive, if available for research at all.

CHAPTER 5

Women's Target Selection

The hypothesis that gender influences target selection in white-collar crime is supported. We argue, based on the convenience theory, that male and female criminals have different perceptions of convenience when considering alternative crime categories and alternative victim categories. The White-collar Crime Offender Registry in Utah provided the data we used. The registration requirement applies to Utah residents who have been found guilty of a white-collar crime in the second degree or higher. The statute HB 378 includes money laundering, securities fraud, deception-based theft, unlawful fiduciary property dealing, fraudulent insurance, mortgage fraud, and communications fraud.

White-collar crime is financial crime committed by high-ranking members of business and public organizations (Logan et al., 2019; Sutherland, 1983). Researchers like Galvin et al. (2018) have broadened this narrow definition, which includes all forms of financial nonviolent crime. In this review, we utilize the offense-based as opposed to the wrongdoer-based meaning of middle-class wrongdoing (Goossen et al., 2016; Piquero, 2018; Piquero & Schoepfer, 2010). The fact that anyone can now commit fraud on the Internet is one argument for the offense-based perspective. "White-collar crime" was first used by Sutherland in 1939, which was eight decades ago (Geest et al., 2017:544).

Nonetheless, as a glaring difference to the circumstances during the 1940s, when most monetary wrongdoing was far off for the typical individual, the opportunity structure for middle-class crime has essentially evolved in contemporary society. The peculiarity of monetary wrongdoing and fraud has become increasingly democratized due, among other things, to the expansion of the credit economy, the growth of the service sector,

The Gender Gap in White-Collar Crime: A Multi-Country Study of Women Offenders in Economic Crime.
Maryam Kamaei, Petter Gottschalk, and Thomas E. Dearden (Authors)

the rise of urbanization, and the development of the internet. "White-collar crimes" that do not require employment or particular skills are becoming increasingly common among the poor and disadvantaged, who have been disproportionately affected by the criminal justice system in the past and now.

According to research (Benson & Harbinson, 2020), female and male criminals do not share the same opportunities, motivations, or willingness to commit white-collar crime (Galvin, 2020; Goulette, 2020; Harbinson, 2020; Ndrecka, 2020). This part addresses the following research question from a slightly different perspective: In middle-class crime, how does gender influence target selection? Using the theory of convenience, this chapter investigates, both theoretically and empirically, how gender differences in convenience might influence the implicit choice of victim when committing white-collar crime.

5.1 FEMALE WHITE-COLLAR CRIME

Fraud, manipulation, and corruption are all examples of white-collar crimes committed by women (Dearden, 2016, 2017, 2019). The hypothesis of accommodation recommends that the overall comfort of elective activities decides decision-making while perpetrating middle-class wrongdoing (Braaten & Vaughn, 2019; Chan & Gibbs, 2020; Dearden & Gottschalk, 2020; Gupta & Gottschalk, 2022). According to the crime-as-choice theory, people commit crimes because they perceive them to be more convenient than other options. Convenience, as defined by Mai and Olsen (2016), is the state of being able to carry on with something without exerting excessive physical effort. Convenience, according to Farquhar and Rowley (2009), entails avoiding difficulties and pain as well as saving time and effort (Higgins, 1997). Convenience, as defined by Engdahl (2015), includes pain relief and problem resolution as well as efficiency of time and effort. Comfort is an advantage for a specific activity over elective choices. White-collar criminals use any means necessary to achieve their goals. According to Aguilera and Vadera (2008:434), "the presence of a favorable combination of circumstances that renders a possible course of action" is the definition of a criminal opportunity. This definition is consistent with convenience.

Robert (2006) asserts that historical research on gender and white-collar crime suggests that women were frequently victims rather than perpetrators. Research has made it abundantly clear that women do commit white-collar crimes, albeit in much smaller numbers than men (Daly, 1989a, b; Gottschalk & Glasso, 2013; Gottschalk & Smith, 2015). Researchers are beginning to take gender differences in white-collar crime into account (for instance, Benson, & Gottschalk, 2015; Benson & Harbinson, 2020; Galvin, 2020; Glasso & Gottschalk, 2013; Goulette, 2020; Klenowski, 2011; Ndrecka, 2020; Reese & McDougal, 2018). Gender differences in the nature of white-collar crime have received little attention, despite the fact that research on gender and white-collar crime is still in its infancy. Numerous criminological theories assert that criminals will select a strategy that best serves their interests. Convenience theory is the most prominent example of this concept. Given conventional contrasts in jobs and connections between sexual orientations, almost certainly, the decision of middle-class offenses is different depending on orientation. The selection of targets is one unexplored area. It is likely that criminals will choose the most convenient targets as well if they choose the most convenient crimes. We intend to investigate these distinctions. As a result, this is our research question: When it comes to white-collar crime, how does gender influence target selection?

It is common knowledge that offenders and victims frequently share a known connection rather than being complete strangers (e.g., Chan et al., 2010; Ullman & Siegel, 1993). Consider whether white-collar criminals have a similar pattern of victim-offender relationships in light of this connection. Second, we suggest that the offender's choice of victims may be influenced by their gender. A common misconception is that women are more likely to target friends or family because of traditional gender norms regarding work and relationships. Another common misconception is that men are more likely to target known victims, like partners in business or employers. The idea behind these suggestions is that women find personal relationships to be relatively easier, while men find professional relationships to be relatively easier.

According to feminist theory, women are more likely to feel vulnerable to the consequences of their actions, which is why they are more afraid of committing crimes (Britton, 2000). Consequently, ladies will choose targets where they anticipate less serious outcomes.

5.2 UTAH OFFENDER REGISTRY

We obtained data from Utah's White-collar Crime Offender Registry for the studies in this chapter and the one before it (Utah Attorney General's Office, 2020). The Utah Legislature approved this online registry in 2015, which was referred to as HB 378. Utah residents who have been convicted of a white-collar crime in the second degree or higher are subject to the registration requirement. Securities fraud, theft by deception, unlawful dealing of property by a fiduciary, fraudulent insurance, mortgage fraud, communications fraud, and money laundering are all included in the categories of crimes outlined in statute HB 378, according to the White-collar Crime Registry HB 378 (2015). The majority of people spend 10 years on the registry for each offense, unless they are found guilty three or more times, in which case they remain on the registry for the rest of their lives.

To create a white-collar offenders database, we transcribed each offender from the registry into a dataset. We managed to gather details about 268 offenders and their crimes from the registry website. We collected demographics such as birth date, height, weight, eye color, and hair color. The information also covered the type of offense, conviction date, court location, target, and a summary of the offense. Additionally, we determined the offender's gender and age at the time of the crime from the registry data.

To identify target groups, we categorize white-collar crime. For example, society is targeted by tax evasion. Bank fraud harms the bank and its customers. Employers are victims of embezzlement. Competitors of bribe recipients can become victims.

We could explain by returning to the various targets how males and females select targets, assuming gender differences in crime. Bank fraud may have more severe consequences than embezzlement. Employers might not report offenders to the police to avoid public attention, but banks are likely to take action. Female criminals may prefer embezzlement due to heightened concern over consequences.

5.2.1 CRIME TARGET SELECTION

Overall, the dataset contained 71 female offenders (26.5%), 191 male offenders (71.3%), and six unknown offenders (2.2%). We discovered that males are, on average, older than females when it comes to white-collar crime ($t(260) = 2.59$, $p = 0.01$). The average age of men was 43.5, while the average age of women was 39.1.

To help the convicted better understand gender-specific convictions, we included the first three white-collar crime convictions recorded on the registry. The type of conviction is significantly influenced by gender (p = 0.03, (7) = 15.5). We also conducted a Fisher's exact test, which was significant (p = 0.01) due to the low cell count in some columns. Although this was not a precise test, we examined the cell-by-cell Chi-square effects; Protection extortion, which was committed by men in 95% of all convictions, was the element that contributed the most to the overall chi-square value. In Table 5.1, convictions are listed by gender.

TABLE 5.1 Conviction by Gender in the Utah Database

Conviction	Gender		Total
	Male	Female	
Communications Fraud	69 (30%)	30 (36%)	99 (31.5%)
Insurance Fraud	27 (11.7%)	13 (15.5%)	40 (12.7%)
Money Laundering	14 (6.0%)	4 (4.8%)	18 (5.7%)
Mortgage Fraud	0 (0%)	1 (1.2%)	1 (0.3%)
Pattern of Unlawful Activity	30 (13.0%)	9 (10.7%)	39 (12.4%)
Securities Fraud	38 (16.5%)	2 (2.4%)	40 (12.7%)
Theft by Deception	43 (18.7%)	20 (23.8%)	64 (20.1%)
Unlawful Dealing with Property by a Fiduciary	9 (3.9%)	5 (6.0%)	14 (4.5%)
Total	230	84	314

*Percentages are within gender (i.e., column total).

The gender-based selection of targets is the focus of our research question. In some cases, the offender could be convicted of more than one offense. We included up to three casualties, which was steady with the greatest number of casualties per offense on the actual vault. Gender differences in the selection of targets were significant (χ^2=75.4, p=.001). When we examined the Chi-square effect cell by cell, we found that women were less likely to target friends, acquaintances, or investors. They were more likely to attack random individuals, healthcare providers, and employers. Gender and target selection are shown in Table 5.2.

A particular kind of victim is required for certain categories of white-collar crime. For instance, protections misrepresentation is innately going to include financial backers as casualties. At the same time, an offender could select victimized investors from particular groups, such as those who adhere to a particular religion (affinity fraud). To work on our investigation into the connection between crime classification, target determination, and orientation type, we explicitly focused on target choice within a specific category of middle-class crime. We were only able to examine three classes of crime in this way because there were few female offenders; that includes communications fraud, theft based on deception, and insurance fraud. Similar to the target selection section above, we included up to three victims for each crime.

TABLE 5.2 Target Selection by Gender in the Utah Database

Conviction	Gender		Total
	Male	Female	
Business Partners	6 (2.6%)	0 (0%)	6 (1.9%)
Buyers/Sellers via Classified Ads	4 (1.7%)	0 (0%)	4 (1.3%)
Clients or Customers	12 (5.2%)	2 (5.3%)	14 (4.5%)
Elderly	6 (2.6%)	0 (0%)	6 (1.9%)
Employees	1 (0.4%)	1 (2.6%)	2 (0.6%)
Employer	16 (7.0%)	29 (76.3%)	45 (14.4%)
Family Members	15 (6.5%)	4 (10.5%)	19 (6.1%)
Financial Institutions	15 (6.5%)	2 (5.3%)	17 (5.4%)
Friends and Acquaintances	33 (14.3%)	5 (13.2%)	38 12.1%)
Government Agencies	6 (2.6%)	1 (2.6%)	7 (2.2%)
Healthcare Providers	0 (0%)	3 (7.9%)	3 (1.0%)
Home Buyers/Sellers/Owners	11 (4.8%)	2 (5.3%)	13 (4.2%)
Immigrants and Non-English Speaking	1 (0.4%)	1 (2.6%)	2 (0.6%)
Insurance Companies	26 (11.3%)	13 (34.2%)	39 (12.5%)
Investors	28 (12.2%)	1 (2.6%)	29 (9.3%)
Members of a Specific Religious Group	3 (1.3%)	1 (2.6%)	4 (1.3%)
Minors	1 (0.4%)	0 (0%)	1 (0.3%)
People with Physical Issues and Disabilities	1 (0.4%)	1 (2.6%)	2 (0.6%)
People with Substance Abuse Problems	9 (3.9%)	2 (5.3%)	11 (3.5%)
Random Individual(s)	3 (1.3%)	6 (15.8%)	9 (2.9%)
Retailers	20 (8.7%)	5 (13.2%)	25 (8.0%)
Single People in a Dating Environment	2 (0.9%)	0 (0%)	2 (0.6%)
Small Businesses/ Small Business Owners	11 (4.8%)	4 (10.5%)	15 (4.8%)
Total	230	83	313

*Percent are within gender (i.e., column total)

What's more, to consider casualty contrasts, we gathered casualty classifications in the following way:

1. Among the known targets are: family members, friends, and acquaintances.
2. Included are workplace goals: Clients or customers, employers, employees, investors, retailers, and employees collaborating in business.
3. Among the organization's goals were: retailers, insurance companies, financial institutions, government agencies, and business owners.
4. The demographic targets included: Minors, the elderly, single people in a dating setting, people who follow a particular religion, people who buy and sell homes, people who provide healthcare, immigrants, people who buy and sell in classified ads, people who struggle with substance abuse, and people who have physical health issues.
5. The remaining target group consisted of random individuals.

32% (n=39) of communications fraud was committed by workplace targets, followed by 31% (n=37) by organizational targets. Significant differences were found between male and female targets ($\chi 2$ = 23.4(4), p= < 0.001). It appears that females are less likely than males to choose known or organizational targets over workplace or random targets. Gender differences in target selection for insurance fraud, theft by deception, and communications fraud are shown in Table 5.3.

41% (n=31) of robbery by trickiness convictions were committed against associations, trailed by work environment casualties (37%, n=28). There was a moderately significant difference between male and female target selection of 2 = 8.7(4), p=.07. The difference was also moderately significant (p=.05) according to the Fisher's exact test. It appears that female employees have chosen organizational goals less frequently. Table 5.3 depicts gender differences in the targets of theft by deception convictions.

Because insurance fraud mostly targets a specific kind of person, it is a one-of-a-kind crime. Naturally, insurance fraud is most likely to target insurance company victims as organizations (86%, n=49). For insurance fraud, there are no significant gender differences in target selection ($\chi 2$=3.2(3), p=.36). A Fisher's exact test was also performed due to the low cell counts, but there was no significant difference (p=.41).

TABLE 5.3 Target Selection by Gender and Crime

Target	Communications Fraud			Theft by Deception			Insurance Fraud		
	Male	Female	Total	Male	Female	Total	Male	Female	Total
Demographic	16	3	19	5	1	6	0	1	1
	(18.6%)	(9.4%)	(16.1%)	(10.2%)	(3.8%)	(8.0%)	(0%)	(7.1%)	(2.1%)
Known	19	2	21	3	4	7	2	0	2
	(22.1%)	(6.3%)	(17.8%)	(6.1%)	(15.4%)	(9.3%)	(6.1%)	(0%)	(4.3%)
Organization	31	5	36	25	6	31	28	12	40
	(36%)	(15.6%)	(30.5%)	(51.0%)	(23.1%)	(41.3%)	(84.8%)	(85.7%)	(85.1%)
Workplace	19	18	37	15	13	28	3	1	4
	(22.1%)	(56.3%)	(31.4%)	(30.6%)	(50.0%)	(37.3%)	(9.1%)	(7.1%)	(8.5%)
Random	1	4	5	1	2	3	0	0	0
	(1.2%)	(12.5%)	(4.2%)	(2.0%)	(7.7%)	(4.0%)	(0%)	(0%)	(0%)
Total	86	32	118	49	26	75	33	14	47

* Percent are within gender (i.e., column total).

According to our research question, "How gender influences target choice in white-collar crime," we discovered evidence to support gender differences in target selection. Women were more inclined to approach random individuals, healthcare professionals, and employers. They were less likely to target companions, other acquaintances, and financial supporters. In addition, females appear to be less likely than males to choose known or organizational targets as well as targets from the workplace or at random.

A Norwegian study of white-collar criminals finds support for female workplace target selection. When compared to men, embezzlement was significantly more prevalent among females. In contrast, they were significantly less involved in corruption. Limited opportunities and target selection may both play a role in the latter outcome (Benson & Gottschalk, 2015; Gottschalk & Glas, 2013; Gottschalk & Smith, 2015).

5.2.2 GENDER TARGET DIFFERENCES

Decisions regarding white-collar crime are influenced by gender differences. We find that objective determination is necessary for certain types of middle-class offenses, such as fraud.

Furthermore, we observe that orientation plays a role in the necessary context of target determination. This aligns with the convenience theory, which disregards the perspective of opportunity differences between men and women, focusing on factors like access to facilities, resources, and systems within an organizational setting for committing and concealing crimes (Benson & Simpson, 2018; Logan and colleagues). Various aspects of the opportunity structure, such as institutional breakdown due to corruption (Rodriguez et al., 2005), chaos resulting from lack of supervision and oversight (Bosse & Phillips, 2016), and disruption caused by criminal market dynamics (Goncharov & Peter, 2019), seem to affect male and female offenders similarly.

Women tend to talk about ethics, morals, and social responsibility the most, according to Dodge (2007). It appears almost impossible for other people to simultaneously believe they are criminals. O'Fallon and Butterfield (2005), on the other hand, found that women and men are equally capable of making ethical and unethical decisions. According to Szalma and Hancock (2013), our perspective of convenience holds that a lack of suspicion results in a lack of crime signal detection. When compared to male suspects, a typical employer will rarely suspect female employees of misconduct and crime.

The question, "Who would you bribe?" is a straightforward experiment we frequently carried out in front of various audiences. You are planning to build a new home on land that the state has designated as recreational property, like a beautiful shoreline. In the municipality, you have the option to offer a bribe to either a male or female official. Taking into account all of the audiences, the vast majority vote almost entirely for men. A female official would almost never be bribed.

White-collar crime victims aren't just targeted because men and women are more likely to be caught. The motivation, the circumstance, and the target all play a role in the justification of the crime. Interviewing male and female offenders about how they use neutralization techniques would be an interesting way to study gender. We do anticipate gender differences in denial of responsibility, injury, victim, condemnation, and appeal to higher loyalties when it comes to alternative targets for white-collar crime (Sykes & Matza, 1957).

In conclusion, our research question, "How gender influences target choice in white-collar crime," suggests that gender differences in target selection are supported. Females were more likely to target random people, health care professionals, and employers. They were more averse to target companions, different associates, and financial backers. In addition, females appear to be less likely than males to choose known or organizational targets as well as targets from the workplace or at random. We argued, employing the theory of convenience, that when considering alternative categories of crimes and victims, male and female offenders have distinct perceptions of convenience. The data we used was provided by the White-collar Crime Offender Registry in Utah. Utah residents found guilty of a white-collar crime in the second degree or higher must register.

Victims of white-collar crime aren't just targeted because men and women are more likely to be caught. The motivation, circumstance, and target all play a role in justifying the crime. Interviewing male and female offenders about how they use neutralization techniques could be an interesting way to study gender. When it comes to alternative targets for white-collar crime, we do expect gender differences in denial of responsibility, injury, victim, condemnation, and appeal to higher loyalties (Sykes & Matza, 1957).

CHAPTER 6

White-Collar Gender Gap

This chapter presents research on gender and the field to examine gender differences in Norway's white-collar crime. This part examines whether significant-level monetary wrongdoing in Norway is impartial or orientation-specific (i.e., generally male) as it is in the US. It is based on a content analysis of newspaper articles and court documents about white-collar crime cases that were significant enough to be covered by national media outlets. According to Benson and Gottschalk (2015), the review demonstrates that the orientation gap in middle-class wrongdoing in Norway is almost identical to that in the United States, despite the fact that orientation imbalance is significantly lower in Norway than it is in the United States. Women made up just 22 (or 6.7%) of the 329 people included in this study's newspaper reports. According to the study presented in this chapter, formal gender equality does not appear to increase women's involvement in white-collar crime. As per Avakian (2009), it offers little help for the liberation speculation (Holtfreter, 2015; Steffensmeier et al., 2013). Instead, it suggests that theories that focus on gendered focal concerns and gendered access to criminal opportunities are the most useful explanations for the gender gap in white-collar crime.

6.1 THE EMANCIPATION HYPOTHESIS

For criminologists, the significance of middle-class wrongdoing lies to some degree in its apparent distinctions from different types of wrongdoing along several perspectives. Among the most significant of these perspectives are the socio-segment backgrounds of the people who

The Gender Gap in White-Collar Crime: A Multi-Country Study of Women Offenders in Economic Crime.
Maryam Kamaei, Petter Gottschalk, and Thomas E. Dearden (Authors)

perpetrate these kinds of offenses, specifically class and orientation, as well as the connection between middle-class wrongdoing and real-world related, organizational, and economic activities. This section is concerned with orientation as a vital perspective of social definition by examining two competing explanations of the orientation gap in middle-class wrongdoing. As the economic and occupational fulfillments of women continue to advance in modern societies, it becomes essential to understand whether women are becoming more involved in middle-class wrongdoing due to their increasing access to more robust occupational positions. On the other hand, alternatively, as women move into upper-level management positions, their presence will lead to decreases in middle-class wrongdoing in organizations. Cumming et al. (2015) suggested the latter option, who found that orientation diversity on boards could work as a mediator for the frequency of fraud.

To start with, this part looks at one of the primary clarifications set forth to represent the nature and low pace of ladies' involvement in middle-class crime: gender isolation and imbalance in society and the workplace. Gender isolation and imbalance in the workplace, some have argued, limit women's access to opportunities to commit middle-class crime (Benson & Simpson, 2018; Avakian, 2009; Steffensmeier et al., 2013). Therefore, one could speculate that as gender equality increases, women's involvement in middle-class crime will become more similar to men's, especially if gender equality is reflected in better economic status and job opportunities for women (Benson & Gottschalk, 2015).

By and large, the possibility that greater gender communication will lead to increased female involvement in crime addresses the liberation theory (Lutz, 2019). This theory emerged during the 1970s in early research on gender and crime. In terms of traditional street crime, the theory has generally not found empirical evidence. Variation in women's involvement in street-level crime, whether analyzed longitudinally within one country or cross-sectionally across samples of countries, appears to be more associated with economic marginalization, access to potential opportunities for consumer crime, and the formalization of social control rather than gender equality.

Although the liberation speculation appears to be off-base concerning orientation and contribution in road wrongdoing, there are hypothetical purposes behind feeling that it very well might be more pertinent to ladies' association in middle-class wrongdoing. The major criminological viewpoints assume that work and economic stability will generally reduce rather than enhance the probability of crime because such circumstances apparently lead to reduced motivation and stronger stakes in conformity. Therefore, to the extent that greater workforce participation for women and improved economic status are indicators, gender equality shouldn't cause an increase in that attitude in traditional crime. Middle-class crime, however, is more likely to be directly related to occupational position and is committed mostly by individuals of significantly higher economic status than offenders in typical street crime. Hence, assuming the liberation of women will affect their involvement in any form of crime, it should be middle-class crime, particularly white-collar crime, that arises out of occupation and is committed in organizational settings.

In this review, we analyze women's involvement in middle-class crime in Norway. Norway is a particularly suitable country in which to explore the liberation theory regarding gender and middle-class crime, because the country ranks significantly higher than the US in terms of gender equality. Therefore, if greater gender equality does indeed lead to women's increased involvement in middle-class crime, it is more likely to be evident in Norway than in the US.

Second, this study also tests and expands on a competing theoretical framework and methodology presented in a recent study of women's involvement in high-level corporate scandals in the US (Steffensmeier et al., 2013). Drawing on data collected from middle-class crime prosecuted by the Corporate Fraud Task Force (CFTF), Steffensmeier and colleagues demonstrated that women were significantly underrepresented among the defendants in these high-profile cases, especially as leaders in cases involving multiple participants. In reality, women played minor roles and received lesser benefits in these high-level corporate crime instances. Furthermore, women's pathways into middle-class crime were not the same as those followed by men. To interpret these results, the researchers developed a sophisticated theoretical understanding that incorporates the concepts of gender-segregation and homosocial reproduction in criminal organizations, along with the theory of gendered core concerns proposed by Steffensmeier and Allan (2000). Sex-isolation and homo-social proliferation can lessen ladies' admittance to middle-class criminal organizations and consequently their admittance to middle-class criminal opportunities, while gendered central concerns lead them to have lower tastes for risk than men. Consequently, Steffensmeier and associates show that despite the fact that the liberation hypothesis would anticipate elevated levels of female involvement in middle-class crime, there are balancing forces at play in the workplace that restrict women's involvement in middle-class crime to some extent in the US. The question here is whether the pattern of women's involvement in middle-class crime that exists in the US can find replication in Norway.

Although this research doesn't have access to data of equivalent richness to that used by Steffensmeier et al. (2013), this study can address similar issues involving high-level middle-class crime in Norway. As detailed below, the study conducted a content analysis of reports in Norwegian newspapers regarding middle-class crime cases that were of enough significance and prominence to attract attention from these national news sources. The research question we address is whether high-level middle-class crime in Norway is gender-neutral or gender-specific (i.e., predominantly male) as it is in the US. Considering the greater gender equality in Norway, one could expect greater neutrality in middle-class crime here. However, as we show below, this is not the case.

6.1.1 GENDERED CONCERN AND ACCESS

One aspect of the paradigm of gendered focal concern states that socialization processes that emphasize the significance of social relationships and communalistic orientations toward other people lead women to typically accept nurturing role responsibilities. Ladies are remembered to have socially arranged qualities, otherwise called public characteristics, while men are remembered to have accomplishment situated attributes (otherwise called agentic characteristics) (Huang et al., 2020). Assimilation of social responsibilities helps women develop identities as caregivers (Steffensmeier et al., 2013). Additionally, the role of criminal or lawbreaker is incompatible with the assumed female identity because women's concern for beauty and virtue contrasts with the ugliness of criminal stereotypes. According to the theory of gendered focal concerns, women are less willing to take risks than men because they adopt identities based on beauty, virtue, and caregiving. Benson (when: 10) describes gendered central concerns as follows:

The gendered theory of focal concerns holds that there are sociological and social-psychological differences between men and women that have the effect of making it more difficult for women to engage in crime than men. Men and women have different focal concerns that organize how they behave and relate to others. Women are expected to fulfill nurturing role obligations, to be affectionate and caring toward others, and to approach relationships in a cooperative and sharing spirit. In contrast to the groups-oriented concerns of women, the focal concerns of men are shaped by an individualistic and competitive orientation toward life, an orientation that values autonomy, dominance, control, and risk-taking. Because crime tends to have injurious or exploitative effects on others, engaging in crimes runs counter to the nurturing and cooperative construction of the female role in society. This makes it more difficult for women to engage in and justify criminal behavior. Although the competitive and aggressive construction of the male role does not explicitly call for criminal behavior, it is more compatible with such behavior, especially for crimes that are financially oriented or motivated by a desire to get ahead in life or to protect what one has.

The focus on gender implies that women will commit fewer crimes. A model is research by Gupta et al. (2020b), who investigated the gender of chief financial officers (CFOs) and irregularities in financial statements. When governance is poor, they discovered that businesses with female CFOs have a lower risk of financial misreporting than comparable businesses with male CFOs.

The gendered focal concern does not necessarily only derive from individual identity. Social identity can influence gendered focal concern as well. According to the social identity perspective, once a person categorizes herself and identifies herself as a woman and thus as a member of a special group and gains both physical and psychological resources from the group membership, the group becomes an important source of pride and self-esteem. This increases the likelihood that group members – in our case women – are obliged and willing to conform to and protect the extant norms. The interpretation and identification processes interact. Women thus protect the established norms according to their experience and the value of being a woman (Huang et al., 2020).

A second component of the gendered central concern worldview proposed by Steffensmeier et al. (2013) is the manner by which orientation shapes admittance to criminal opportunities. Admittance to middle-class criminal opportunities can come to fruition in two ways: (1) by means of admittance to specific positions and (2) through admittance to informal networks. Firstly, specific positions and roles offer particular types of opportunities. For example, the opportunity to engage in bank fraud is more accessible to business leaders and professionals than it is to individuals who occupy different positions in society. Occupational gender segregation may limit women's access to the types of job positions needed to commit certain types of offenses. Complex forms of middle-class crime, such as the use of tax shelters, require access to organizational resources and jobs that provide advantageous opportunities may not be as available to women as they are to men (Holtfreter, 2005). However, if occupational segregation based on gender is reduced, the liberation hypothesis would predict a greater involvement of women in middle-class crime.

The second way that criminal opportunities can arise is through social networks. Some types of crime are group efforts that involve networks of people in reciprocal relationships. Individuals not connected to these networks have reduced access to criminal opportunities. For example, sophisticated white-collar crimes, such as bribing officials abroad through local agents, require trusted reciprocal relationships between at least three parties to effectively operate. Often, women are followers rather than leaders in crime, and they therefore represent less central nodes in networks. They tend to play subordinate supporting roles. The key players in a criminal scheme enter the network carefully among individuals who are known, loyal, competent, and male. Even when women attain high-status positions in organizations, male-dominated informal social networks will typically exclude them from participation in both legitimate and illegitimate activities (Abraham, 2020; Berdahl, 2007; Downing et al., 2019). If the exclusion of women from informal networks extends to illegal networks, this would explain lower rates of involvement in white-collar crime for women even when they hold the same occupational positions as men.

6.1.2 GENDER EQUALITY IN NORWAY

Norway is a small nation of approximately 5,000,000 people. Its economy is flourishing, and the unemployment rate is less than 3%. Norway is rich with the second-highest Gross Domestic Product per capita in Europe, and the vast majority of the populace enjoys a high standard of living. Pay disparity in Norway is lower than in the US, as the difference in pay between the lowest-level workers and corporate presidents is much smaller than in other market-based societies.

Norway ranks much higher than the US on various measures of gender equality. According to the Global Gender Gap Report of 2008, Norway ranked first in the world in terms of overall gender equality, while the US ranked 27th. The overall gender equality ranking is a combination of scores in four areas: economic participation and opportunity, educational attainment, health and survival, and political empowerment. Although Norway performed significantly better than the US in this regard, the differences were less pronounced in the area of economic participation and opportunity, where Norway was ranked sixth and the US twelfth. In the sub-categories of the economic participation and opportunity domain, Norway scored higher than the US in workforce participation, wage equality for similar work, and estimated earnings, but lower in terms of holding top leadership positions, such as managers, senior officials, and legislators.

Norway has worked energetically to address gender disparity in administrative roles in the working environment, especially in large enterprises. In 2003, Norway passed a regulation requiring that the boards of all public corporations have no less than 40% female representation. Although many in the Norwegian business community criticized the law, it has succeeded in changing the composition of corporate boards in Norway. Women now make up 40% of corporate board positions. However, even though female representation on corporate boards is exemplary compared to other countries, this does not mean that Norway has achieved total gender equality in the workplace, as the labor market is still somewhat gender-segregated. For example, women dominate in public sector jobs, with 48% of employed women in Norway working in the public sector compared to only 19% of employed men. Additionally, while women hold 55% of management positions in the health and education sectors, they represent a smaller proportion of high-level management positions in the private sector. In short, it would be incorrect to say that Norway has achieved complete gender balance. Therefore, we should not be surprised if women are underrepresented in high-level white-collar crime compared to men. However, the key issue is whether the level of underrepresentation among women is as pronounced in Norway as it is in the US. If the empowerment hypothesis is correct, women's involvement in white-collar crime should be higher than it is in the US, even though they may not have yet reached complete equality.

6.1.3 GENDER AND CRIME IN NORWAY

Crime is generally less of a problem in Norway than it is in the United States. In 2009, Norway had a homicide rate of 0.69 per 100,000 people, whereas the United States had a rate of approximately 5 per 100,000 people. In contrast, white-collar crime is a well-known issue in Norway as well as in other nations. Out of almost 400,000 wrongdoings that were accounted for to the police in 2005, a little more than 8,000 were undoubtedly middle-class violations, as per official measurements. According to Statistics Norway, these "financial offenses" include unlawful acts like theft, charge infringement, accounting violations, fraud, and breach of trust, as well as violations of different acts involving investments, marketing, securities, commercial banking, and taxation.

It is evident that, like their counterparts in the United States, Norwegian women are underrepresented in official crime statistics, despite the fact that a comprehensive examination of gender and all forms of crime in Norway is beyond the scope of this chapter. In 2005, 36,169 people were charged with a crime of violence against another person, and only 12% of those accused were women. The role that women play in economic crime may or may not be more apparent depending on the type of crime that is taken into consideration. For instance, only 5% of those accused of negligent bookkeeping were women, while 30% of those accused of embezzlement were women. Women accounted for approximately 22% of all those accused of economic crime. As a result, according to the number of offenses, white-collar crime appears to make up a small portion of Norway's crime problem, just like it does in the United States. Additionally, women appear to be underrepresented in a variety of offenses, including white-collar crime, as in the United States.

However, as emphasized several times in this book, the detection rate for women in white-collar crime seems to be far below that of male white-collar offenders, making female offending a challenging and important area of gender research. The remainder of this chapter explores whether women's under-representation in detected crime generally extends to white-collar crime.

The essential objective of this study is to see whether Norway's middle-class wrongdoing is sexually impartial or, on the other hand, assuming it is orientation-specific in a manner that is similar to that of the US. In this chapter, we look into the possibility that elite financial crime in Norway is gender-segregated in the same way that it is in the United States, where men rule. Since Norway is more gender-equal than the United States, at least in terms of official public policy, there should be less gender-segregation there if gender inequality is the real cause of the gender gap in white-collar crime. However, despite Norway's high female labor force participation, women are still somewhat underrepresented in higher-level management and leadership roles. Critically, regardless of whether ladies are in undeniable level management positions (Abraham, 2020), they might still be excluded from informal networks in organizations, including those that organize criminal schemes. It's conceivable that in Norway, homosocial reproduction and gender isolation in the workplace are limiting women's access to middle-class criminal opportunities similarly to how they are in the US. This would imply that, like in the United States, middle-class wrongdoing in Norway is more likely to be gender-specific (Benson & Gottschalk, 2015).

6.1.4 NORWEGIAN WHITE-COLLAR SAMPLE

The information comes from a content analysis of white-collar crime articles published in Norway's two largest financial newspapers: Finansavisen and Dagens Næringsliv. These are conservative-leaning business publications. Furthermore, insight about middle-class violations is habitually announced in the business-accommodating public everyday paper "Aftenposten," which is remembered for the review. Despite the fact that they truly do provide details regarding the issue of elite financial wrongdoing as a general rule, left-wing publications like "Klassekampen" seldom cover specific middle-class criminal cases. Naturally, there are potential drawbacks to evaluating women's involvement in white-collar crime using newspaper reports. Newspaper articles are not entirely objective and unrelated to the topic under investigation when used as a source of data. On the one hand, female criminals may become more well-known for their crimes because of their gender, which may make them more newsworthy than if men committed the same crimes. In this scenario, women's involvement in white-collar crime would be overestimated. A second scenario, on the other hand, might result in women being underrepresented. This could happen on the off chance that the sorts of cases that papers see as newsworthy (for instance, large, intense, ludicrous outrages) are bound to have men as the wrongdoers. The first scenario appears to be more problematic for the current study because the focus of the research is on women's involvement in high-level elite offenses rather than financial crime as a whole. Selection effects from the data sources could be the reason why the study finds a significantly higher participation rate among Norwegian women than in the United States.

From 2009 to 2012, a period of four years, Dagens Næringsliv, Finansavisen, and Aftenposten were examined daily to identify stories about white-collar cases and the people involved. If a person met the three requirements listed below, they were considered a white-collar criminal. First, he or she engaged in an offense with deliberate intent as part of a regular business activity-related professional activity. Second, the crime cost a lot of money or caused a lot of harm to other people. Thirdly, the offender was portrayed in the newspaper as having high social standing, a position of power, and access to organizational resources. In short, Sutherland's (1939; 1993) definition of white-collar crime is consistent with this approach. In addition to other well-known researchers on white-collar crime (Benson & Gottschalk, 2015; Craig & Piquero, 2017; Dearden & Gottschalk, 2021; Dodge, 2009; Friedrichs, 2009; Holtfreter, 2015; Langton & Piquero, 2007; Logan et al., 2019; Schoepfer & Piquero, 2006). As a result, the study focuses on crimes committed by respected and high-status individuals while working. Individuals employed in organizational settings were the victims of all of the offenses.

According to Barak (2007), "news-making criminology" refers to the deliberate efforts and activities of criminologists to interpret, influence, or shape the representation of newsworthy crime and justice-related events. An important method for comprehending white-collar crime is news-making criminology as a perspective on the theory, practice, and representations of crime and justice. However, Barak's research concentrated on the media's construction of criminal imagery. Facts in the form of quantitative numbers, names, and locations from newspaper accounts serve as research data for this study, which makes use of the media as a potential source of objective information. As per Consumers and Orrick (2002), research recommends that the media present a twisted picture of wrongdoing by zeroing in on fierce, exciting occasions that are abnormal for crime in the public eye. They assert that the media disproportionately focuses on conventional crime while ignoring the impact of corporate misbehavior and that coverage of corporate offenses is lacking. This line of reasoning not only acknowledges the possibility of bias in this research study, but it also supports our research design by pointing out that one important feature of our sample is that white-collar crime cases are frequently reported in the media.

Nevertheless, some forms of corporate crime, most likely those that are more prevalent, may continue to go unreported. The media, for instance, may be biased against small corporate crimes in favor of larger, more sensational crimes. Our decision to use newspapers as sources necessitates keeping two methodological considerations in mind:

- **Prejudice Brought on by Media Coverage:** White-collar financial crime only attracts attention from the media when it is sensational and possibly revealed and discovered by the media itself. As a result, there is no basis for the assertion that the sample is representative of white-collar criminals as a whole. Instead, there is a bias toward white-collar criminals because, for some reason, journalists and newspapers that cover their stories are particularly interested in them. As a result, news coverage is explicitly included on the list of characteristics that white-collar criminals possess, along with opportunities and positions of trust.

- **Errors in the Press Coverage's Data:** The majority of newspaper articles contain errors. Factual errors may include the offender's name, age, sentence, crime type, and year, among other things. In addition, there might be too much emphasis placed on the sensational aspects of both crime and criminal activity. Anyone who has ever read a newspaper article about oneself will be aware that the presentation contains errors or, at the very least, false impressions. Several newspaper stories about the same case in different media were reviewed based on investigative research to reduce the possibility of error. In addition, in the majority of cases, we obtained court sentences to examine both the factual and narrative aspects of the crime.

It is essential to note that Norwegian journalists enjoy respectability due to their honesty and seriousness. Undocumented, sensational stories are reported by very few, if any, newspapers. In fact, none of these newspapers have been found in Norway during our investigation of white-collar financial crime. In the financial press, some journalists have developed sophisticated methods for investigating criminal cases using robust and open methods.

The media in other countries might find a very different public vision compared to the media in Norway, which enjoys and deserves public trust. For example, in the U.S., "it now appears clear that some prominent columnists and commentators placed the trust at risk by accepting substantial fees from Enron" (Rosoff, 2009, p. 515). Furthermore, Knottnerus et al. (2006) argue that deviance at Enron could be difficult to detect because of special rituals that were an important part of corporate culture. The press, needless to say, depends on public trust (Pontell & Geis, 2007).

In Norway, the media coverage of white-collar crime in firms is typically according to the institutional perspective suggested by Graf-Vlachy et al. (2020, p. 43):

> Scholars in the tradition of institutional theory emphasize the role of the news media as an important part of firms' institutional environment. Scholars' underlying assumption here is that providing institutional and cultural accounts within which the appropriateness and desirability of actions can be evaluated. affects impression formation and the legitimation of firms. Moreover, these scholars assume that to arrive at their assessments of firms and firm actions, the media apply institutional logics held by their audiences and, thus, exert influential institutional pressures on firms.

The ongoing review's example is tantamount to, however not indistinguishable from, the high-profile middle-class cases analyzed by Steffensmeier et al. (2013) since it just incorporates cases that were of adequate reputation or newsworthiness to collect paper inclusion. Specifically, there are three manners by which the example varies from the Steffensmeier (2013) test. In the first place, dissimilar to Steffensmeier et al., we only included cases that resulted in arrests and convictions, involved arraignments as the reason for their example, most of which brought about captures and convictions. Second, official indictments provide extensive documentation of the characteristics of their cases, so Steffensmeier and his colleagues had access to more extensive data. Steffensmeier had the option to create a more extensive picture of each case and the roles played by the various participants by combining this data with case-related reports from the Securities and Exchange Commission, trial testimony, documents, and various online materials. The content analysis of Norwegian newspapers forms the majority of our research. However, to verify the information presented in the newspaper articles, a review of various court documents resulting from defendants' convictions was necessary. Relying solely on news reports can be risky due to their tendency to distort or exaggerate the roles played by female co-conspirators to make stories more sensational by portraying women as more involved in the crime than they actually were. Therefore, if our findings differ from those of Steffensmeier et al. (2013) regarding women's roles, we must be cautious when interpreting the significance of these findings. Additionally, unlike Steffensmeier et al. (2013), the mix of offenses in each case in our sample is different. Specifically, the majority of our cases involve instances of tax fraud. This difference highlights the strengths and weaknesses of our study. On one hand, our study is not a direct replication of the Steffensmeier study due to the different mix of offenses, and any variations in results may be due to methodological differences between the two studies. However, we can explore whether the findings of the Steffensmeier study can be extended to a broader range of white-collar crimes by examining a different set of offenses.

Finally, our findings may not be generalizable to the larger population of white-collar cases that are not detected or prosecuted because our investigation is restricted to cases that resulted in incarceration. However, due to this characteristic, our study is comparable to the majority of American research on gender and white-collar crime, which relies heavily on official records (Holtfreter, 2005; Steffensmeier et al., 2013).

In addition, our investigation will, at the very least, provide insight into the gender distribution of criminals who hold high-level positions and are convicted. It will be possible for future researchers to ascertain whether the patterns that we observe among offenders in convicted cases extend to cases in which offenders are able to avoid conviction for some reason.

The three papers noted above were liable to audit from 2009 to 2012 to recognize stories providing details regarding instances of middle-class wrongdoing. We identified 329 white-collar criminals out of the 162 cases found during the reporting period. 60% (98) of the 162 cases involved just one person; The total number of people involved in the other 64 cases ranged from 2 to 16, with an average of approximately 3.5 per case. 50 of the 64 cases with multiple offenders involved all-male groups, while 14 of the cases involved mixed-gender groups. Groups were not all female.

Information about each case and the people involved was entered into research coding from newspaper reports. With respect to the people engaged with the offense, we coded their orientation and their word-related position. There were three types of employment positions: middle level (professionals like attorneys and investors), top level (chairpersons and chief executives), and bottom level (accountants and bank clerks, for example). We coded whether each offender worked in the private or public sectors because the Norwegian labor market is gendered and women are more likely than men to work in the public sector. We also recorded the individual's leadership or follower roles in the offense. The descriptions in newspaper articles about the crime and the person's role, as well as the case descriptions in court documents, were used to determine whether a person was a leader or a follower. A leader, for instance, would be someone who was the head of a business and oversaw the actions of others who were involved in the crime. A follower would be someone who, for instance, fits the description of an accountant who assists others in preparing fraudulent tax returns. Steffensmeier et al. (2013) three-fold typology of roles (leader and follower) is more comprehensive than our two-fold typology.

We coded the type of offense, the size of the criminal network involved in the offense (if it was not a standalone offense), and whether the organization or the individual(s) was the primary beneficiary to determine the nature and scope of each offense. Corporate crime is the first, while occupational crime is the second. The four categories of offense types include fraud, theft, manipulation, and corruption. The term "fraud" refers to situations in which the perpetrator or perpetrators induce others to take adverse action based on false or misleading information, and the victim's action is the result of the false or misleading information. Examples include subsidy fraud and bank fraud, in which the perpetrator misrepresents an item's value in order to obtain a bank loan or additional government subsidies. The illegal acquisition of another person's or an organization's valuable property is referred to as theft. Employee embezzlement and theft of intellectual property are typical examples. In cases of manipulation, the offender alters parameters to achieve a more favorable outcome for themselves. Normal models are tax avoidance and cartel arrangements, where the controller dodges assessments and gains benefits from cost fixing. Last but not least, corruption is the illegal taking and giving of unjustified benefits in the hope of being reciprocated. Bribing procurement officers to secure a contract and bribing municipal officials to secure a building permit are two examples.

6.2 RESULTS FROM GENDER RESEARCH

Our findings are presented in three stages. To begin, we investigate whether Norway's white-collar crime is gender-neutral or gender-specific. Then, we look at the differences between women and men in terms of the nature and roles they play in white-collar crimes. Last but not least, we investigate the significant topic of criminal organizations and women.

Norway's white-collar crime is not gender-neutral, as shown in Table 6.1. Instead, men rule, just like in the United States. Only 22 (6.7%) of the 329 people in the data set are women. The proportion of women in the U.S. data sets analyzed by Steffensmeier et al. (2013) is strikingly similar to this percentage, likewise centered around high-profile individuals. However, we note that the proportion of women is lower than in studies that focus on financial crime in its more common form. This book discusses, for instance, Utah's white-collar crime registry, which includes 191 male offenders and 71 female offenders.

The gender results of the current Norwegian study suggest that, at least when it comes to high-profile white-collar crime, Norwegian women seem to be just as involved as American women. In spite of the fact that our information doesn't allow us to decide if Norwegian ladies are engaged with lower-level monetary wrongdoing in a similar way as ladies in the US, the figures detailed above from Statistics Norway would suggest that this is the situation. For instance, in Norway in 2005, women were charged with 22% of all economic offenses.

A measurement of women's participation in high-level organizational positions is required to determine whether women are over- or under-represented in high-level white-collar crime. Their opportunities to commit criminal acts must be compared to their rate of involvement. According to Reimann (2012), women hold approximately one-third of high-level positions in the private sector and more than half of management-level positions in the public sector in Norway. As a result, the fact that women make up only 6.7% of white-collar offenders suggests that their participation in crime is significantly lower than their access to opportunities to commit high-level elite offenses.

TABLE 6.1 Descriptive Statistics for Norwegian Sample

Characteristics	(N)	%
Gender of Criminal		
Male	307	93.3
Female	22	6.7
Crime Type		
Fraud	151	45.9
Theft	24	7.3
Manipulation	95	28.9
Corruption	59	17.9
Occupational Level		
Top level (chairperson, CEO)	95	28.9
Middle level (attorney, investor)	151	45.9
Low level (accountant, bank clerk)	83	25.2
Sector of Organization		
Private business	304	92.4
Public agency	25	7.6
Beneficiary of Crime		
Corporate entity	41	12.5
Individual or individuals	288	87.5
Role in the Offense		
Offender as leader	192	58.4
Offender as follower	137	41.6

However, we cannot establish that the gender gap is 6.7% versus 50% or 33% in crime participation versus elite participation. As emphasized several times in this book, the rate of detection is likely lower for female offenders compared to male offenders. Nevertheless, we conclude that there is a gender gap, but not in the magnitude of available numbers. Please recall that the Norwegian estimate of a relative detection probability of 30% for women versus men, which resulted in an estimated 9% probability of detection for men and an estimated 3% estimated probability of detection for women in Norway. Gottschalk and Gunnesdal (2018) in their expert elicitation found a probability for men of 10.5%

and 6.5% for women in Norway. Please keep in mind that the amount of money involved in white-collar crime may also play a role in the assumed and estimated gender gap in crime detection. In the Norwegian example concentrated by Benson and Gottschalk (2015), the typical monetary addition from wrongdoing was lower for female guilty parties than for male wrongdoers. The typical financial increase for ladies in first-class wrongdoing was 9,000,000 Norwegian kroner, which is somewhat less than 1,000,000 US dollars. The typical monetary increase for men was 50 million Norwegian kroner, which is around 5,000,000 US dollars. As a result, male offenders committed more than five times as many crimes as female offenders did.

Fraud is the most frequent financial crime by white-collar convicts in Norway, followed by manipulation, corruption, and theft. Most convicts were in the middle-level white-collar positions such as chief financial officer, procurement manager, and sales director. Far more convicts come from the private sector than from the public sector. There are more leaders than followers in crime, which reflects that many offenders were on their own when committing financial crime.

Having laid out that ladies in Norway find less portrayal in high-profile middle-class wrongdoing cases contrasted with men, the following task is to contrast their experiences in these offenses with those of men. Similarly, in Table 6.2, we compare women with men concerning the types of offenses they commit, the number of people involved in their offenses, the primary recipient of the offense, the sector of the economy in which the offender is employed, the individual's occupational position, and the individual's role in the offense.

White-collar crimes committed by Norwegian men and women are distinct from one another. Nearly 60% of female offenses (59.1%) were misrepresentation offenses, contrasted with less than half (45.0%) of male offenses. While nearly one out of every five men were involved in corruption, there were no women involved. Considering our past conversation on the corruption scenario, where almost all respondents would pay off the man as opposed to the woman, this outcome surprises no one. However, given that both taking a bribe and receiving one is illegal in Norway, there may have been instances of female bribers.

The primary beneficiaries of the offense (an organization or an individual) and the economic sector (public or private) in which the offender was employed did not show any significant gender differences, as shown

TABLE 6.2 Involvement in White-Collar Crime by Gender

Characteristics	Men (N)	Men (%)	Women (N)	Women (%)
Crime type	–	–	–	–
Fraud	138	45.0	13	59.1
Theft	22	7.2	2	9.1
Manipulation	88	28.7	7	31.8
Corruption	59	19.2	0	0.0
Occupational level	–	–	–	–
Top level (chairperson, CEO)	92	30.0	3	13.6
Middle level (attorney, investor)	142	46.3	9	40.9
Low level (accountant, bank clerk)	73	23.8	10	45.5
Sector of organization	–	–	–	–
Private business	283	92.2	21	95.5
Public agency	24	7.8	1	4.5
Beneficiary of crime	–	–	–	–
Corporate entity	39	12.7	2	9.1
Individual or individuals	268	87.3	20	90.9
Role in the Offense	–	–	–	–
Offender as leader	180	58.6	12	54.5
Offender as follower	127	41.4	10	45.5

in Table 6.2. Regardless of gender, the vast majority of crimes were committed by workers in the private sector for personal gain.

Based on their individual characteristics and the nature of their illegal activities, men and women held distinct occupational positions. While only 23.8% of men held such positions, 45.5% of women held low-level positions like bank clerks or accountants. Certainly, compared to just 13.6% of women in the example, almost 33% of men held high-level positions in their organizations. Ladies were likewise more probable than men to be adherents, true to form (45.5% versus 41.9%), however the thing that matters is plainly not critical.

We likewise examine women's roles in middle-class criminal organizations, as displayed in Table 6.3. 15 of the 22 women who made up the sample were part of criminal groups or cases that had more than one person involved. As checked, the women involved with criminal associations

TABLE 6.3 Offense Characteristics for Groups and Solo Offenders

Characteristics	**Group Male (N)**	**Group Male %**	**Group Mixed (N)**	**Group Mixed %**	**Solo Male (N)**	**Solo Male %**	**Solo Female (N)**	**Solo Female %**
Sample size	50	78	14	22	91	93	7	7
Crime type	–	–	–	–	–	–	–	–
Fraud	18	36	10	71	41	45	3	43
Theft	2	4	1	7	10	11	0	0
Manipulation	15	30	3	21	34	37	4	57
Corruption	15	30	0	0	6	7	0	0
Co-conspirators	–	–	–	–	–	–	–	–
Small group (2–4)	44	88	9	64	–	–	–	–
Middle group (5–7)	3	6	4	29	–	–	–	–
Large group (8+)	3	6	1	7	–	–	–	–
Beneficiary of crime	–	–	–	–	–	–	–	–
Corporate entity	8	16	2	14	8	9	0	0
Individual(s)	42	84	12	86	83	91	7	100

were all in mixed-sex social groups. There were no all-female networks, so the majority of men were in networks that were all male. This finding is identical to Steffensmeier et al. (2013) who found conspiracies in data from the Corporate Fraud Task Force (CFTF) of the United States.

Indeed, mixed-gender groups made up 25% of the CFTF sample and 22% of our sample's total criminal networks. There was no significant difference among genders in terms of the number of individuals involved in the organization. The mixed-sex groups had an average size of 3.7, while the all-male groups had an average size of 3.5.

The majority of Norway's white-collar criminal networks are small, with only two to four people involved, as shown in Table 6.3; however, this was more so for all-male groups than for mixed-sex groups. The offense characteristics differed little between the all-male and mixed-gender networks. The mixed-gender networks were more likely to be involved in extortion offenses compared to the all-male networks, which were more likely to commit offenses of manipulation or corruption.

In both all-male and mixed-gender networks, as well as for single offenders of both sexes, the individual or individuals involved were the primary beneficiaries of the offense, not a corporate entity. Last but not least, about equal numbers of men and women committed crimes on their own. As indicated by Benson and Gottschalk (2015), female guilty parties represented a similar level of solitary wrongdoers as male guilty parties.

6.3 GENDER SEGREGATION IN CRIME

Because it is always connected to legitimate professional and organizational activities, white-collar crime is a reflection of social stratification in society (Benson & Simpson, 2018; Sutherland, 1939, 1983; Steffensmeier et al., 2013). Society has long been familiar with gender stratification in criminal activity, including white-collar crime (Holtfreter, 2005). One of the primary stratification fault lines in all societies is gender stratification in crime. Indeed, it has been argued for a considerable amount of time that workplace gender inequality and segregation limit women's opportunities in white-collar crime (Benson & Simpson, 2018; Dearden & Gottschalk, 2021; Dodge, 2009). However, while all societies exhibit some gender stratification, it is not uniform. Women outperform men in a number of health, educational, political, occupational, and economic outcomes in some nations (Hausman et al., 2008). To put it another way, there is a difference between countries in the gender gap. The charming chance that ladies' degree of crime may systematically shift couple with this variety in the orientation gap is raised. Through an examination of ladies' association in high-level elite economic crime in Norway, one of the least gender-segregated countries in the world (Benson & Gottschalk, 2015), we decided to investigate this possibility in the study presented in this section.

Contrary to what some may have anticipated, there is no evidence that gender equality is associated with an increase in the number of women involved in white-collar crime. That is, in any event, when we expect that there is without a doubt a recognition gap among female and male wrongdoers, the related result in an examination between Norway and the US should be the same. Just a supposition that the identification risk is different in Norway and the US would impact our outcomes. We do not, however, have any evidence to support such an assumption at this point in our research.

The design of the study presented in this chapter served to investigate the possibility of greater gender equality associated with increased occurrences of white-collar crime by women. White-collar crime in Norway is just as gender-segregated as it is in the United States, despite the fact that Norway has a much more gender-equal society than the United States. In Norway, the vast majority of high-level offenders are men; among those who have been identified, less than 1 in 10 are women. In the Norwegian sample, there were no all-female criminal groups, and less than one in four groups were mixed-gender. In a nutshell, the majority of criminal networks in our sample (78%) were entirely male. Brickey (2006) and Steffensmeier et al.'s observations of these figures are strikingly similar to one another (2013) about criminals and crimes in the United States. Therefore, women's involvement in white-collar crime is virtually identical in Norway and the United States, despite the gender-based differences in social stratification. Indeed, Norway's gender distribution is strikingly comparable to that of the United States, like their counterparts in the United States. According to Steffensmeier et al. (2013), Norwegian women are more likely than men to be involved in low-level forms of financial crime. However, this disparity is not as pronounced for those who engage in high-level forms of financial crime.

The speculation that orientation isolation in the public eye and the working environment represents orientation isolation in middle-class wrongdoing can make sense of the orientation hole in wrongdoing is projected into uncertainty by our finding that orientation and middle-class wrongdoing seem, by all accounts, to be so similar in Norway and the US. Norway has taken extraordinary steps to advance orientation equality throughout society overall and in the workplace. Regarding women's access to economic opportunities, the nation ranks sixth in the world. In fact, women currently hold at least 40% of board memberships on corporate boards, and an estimate states that they hold approximately 35% of management-level positions in the private sector (Reimann, 2012), with more than half of these positions in the educational and health sectors. In short, executive boardrooms and corner offices on the top floor are not just for men in Norwegian business. Instead, women make up nearly half of the seats at the table in the boardroom or behind the executive desks. Women, on the other hand, made up less than 7% of the white-collar criminals in our sample. This finding makes it abundantly clear that the absence of female offenders must be attributed to something else in addition to a lack of access to opportunities in the workplace.

The most conceivable translation of our outcomes would seem to come from the gendered central concerns and gendered access to criminal opportunities framework advanced by Steffensmeier et al. (2013). This book demonstrates the importance of Steffensmeier's interpretation by utilizing key elements from the theory of convenience, which posits that female offenders have less motivation, less opportunity, and less willingness than males. In contrast to the two other dimensions of motive and willingness, which align with the gendered central concern, the dimension of organizational opportunity in the convenience theory partially reflects the emancipation hypothesis and, consequently, gendered access to criminal opportunities. According to Steffensmeier and Allan's (1996) gendered theory of central concerns, women embrace role responsibilities that highlight the importance of nurturing social relationships and communalistic orientations towards others through socialization. By internalizing these responsibilities, women cultivate lifestyles as caretakers. Due to their identities, they are less inclined to take risks than men and less willing to harm, exploit, or betray others. In summary, the similarity of Norwegian women to women in the United States in terms of their personalities and identities could be one possible explanation for the apparent low level of female involvement in white-collar crime. Norway could be compared to several states in the United States, such as Connecticut, which seem to share similar demographics, climate, standard of living, and democratic institutions.

In the 1970s, a women's liberation movement in Norway focused on issues like equal pay, abortion rights, and long maternity leave for the mother and father. Norway has a long history of feminist concerns. The nation has made extraordinary advances in pushing gender balance ahead in a wide range of spaces, for instance by complete kindergarten inclusion in the country. At the smallest level, couples who enter into partnerships and have children typically expect one another to be financially independent and to contribute similarly to their joint standard of living. These changes may not have affected Norwegian women's sensitivity to risk and willingness to harm others in pursuit of their own personal interests. We note that Norwegian ladies' protection from these male inclinations and ways of behaving is a positive improvement according to the point of view of society in general.

Concern for victims of white-collar crime is one area that we haven't looked into for future research. The following frequency of victims is shown by the Norwegian database that is utilized in our investigation. The employer whose organization suffers a loss is the most common victim category. The revenue service, financial institutions, customers, and vendors are less frequently harmed. We have yet another influencing factor that has the potential to explain the gender gap in white-collar crime in our gender perspective of gendered focal concerns, in which women accept the role of feeling empathy for victims while men may not feel sorry for victims.

Gendered admittance to wrongdoing open doors is as yet a significant clarification for the orientation gap in middle-class wrongdoing in Norway. According to the theory of convenience, this is consistent with the absence of opportunities for organizational growth. Only 14 of the 64 criminal network cases in our sample involved women. We believe it plausible that there were no women identified or available to join the criminal networks because many of the criminogenic businesses have large national and international operations. Instead, we believe that gender inequality persists in Norway's access to opportunities in white-collar crime. Norwegian and other Scandinavian countries' research demonstrates that like their partners in the US, ladies struggle with accessing male-dominated informal communities. King et al. cite as one reason (2010) is that women are underrepresented in high-ranking positions, which causes gender discrimination (Triana et al., 2019) and being excluded from networks dominated by men.

Women, on the other hand, are skeptical of the way men tend to run businesses, such as when it comes to bonuses based on goal-oriented management, where achieving goals can have great consequences while failing to achieve them can be catastrophic (Jonnergrd et al., 2010). As appears to be the case in the U.S. (Benson & Gottschalk, 2015), we anticipate that all-male groups in social networking, which are sometimes referred to as “boys clubs” in Norway, also extend to criminal networks. Women in Norway are simply less likely than men to be invited to and interested in participating in criminal networks.

The generous welfare state and liberal social and economic policies of Norway are world-renowned. Women’s health, education, employment, and political participation are all explicitly addressed in many of these policies. Even though it’s not perfect, Norway has done a great job of promoting gender equality compared to the rest of the world. This is shown by the fact that it ranks first in global gender reports and lists of the best places to live. Therefore, one would anticipate that gender equality would result in an increase in female involvement in white-collar crime in Norway. However, our findings regarding the proportion of women involved in elite financial crime in Norway are strikingly comparable to those observed for women in the United States, which, it goes without saying, takes a significantly different stance on social inequality than Norway. Consequently, we might reason that orientation disparity and in this way absence of liberation, to the extent that the peculiarity connects with admittance to the work market and different assets, is certainly not a significant hotspot for causality of the orientation hole in middle class wrongdoing. Of course, the gender gap is about more than just having formal access to resources, where resources can be used for good or bad things. It also has to do with socialization practices and gendered expectations in society.

If this conclusion is true, it has some good news for the United States. First of all, it suggests that just because women are closer to being equal to men in social, economic, and political arenas does not necessarily mean that they will also begin to act like men when it comes to the tendency toward white-collar crime. Even though it is too early to say for sure, it is possible that as more women take on leadership roles in business, they will be able to effect changes that reduce elite crime. For instance, when both genders are represented on the board, criminogenic behavior among board members decreases in businesses. Similarly, Dollar et al. (2001) found that across a wide range of nations, corruption was lower when women were more represented in parliament.

Our review, similar to all others, has systemic limits and leaves a ton of inquiries regarding orientation and middle-class wrongdoing unanswered. We close with a short conversation of four of these constraints and the potential for resulting research they address.

First, as we have mentioned numerous times, we are aware of the possibility of selection bias in our findings when we rely on newspaper accounts of convicted criminals. Unfortunately, Norway's crime statistics do not include white-collar crime. Nonetheless, in light of the fact that we accept that the uncommonness of ladies would make episodes engaging as reports, that's what we trust assuming that there is predisposition, it would lead us to misjudge the extent of ladies associated with significant level first-class wrongdoing in Norway (on the side of the liberation hypothesis). In a nutshell, we have no reason to believe that any cases involving women in which a high-ranking elite member was convicted of a crime were overlooked by the Norwegian media. In this way, we accept it is sensible to make the determination that the impacts of test selection bias should be negligible given that we found such a small percentage of female wrongdoers and that our findings are consistent with those of surveys conducted in the US that used a different sampling methodology.

However, we acknowledge that our findings may have been influenced in some way by selection bias. Theoretically, it is also possible that the Norwegian media will favor protecting female suspects who are being tried in court. For instance, after reading newspaper articles on a daily basis for a number of years, one gets the impression that incidents involving naming, blaming, and shaming women are more common than those involving male white-collar offenders. It certainly appears that many media outlets wait longer when the case involves a woman rather than a man, without having classified and counted instances of anonymous coverage of defendants versus naming defendants. Women, on the other hand, are more likely to be identified by the Norwegian media only after the investigation and prosecution have concluded, if at all. This is in contrast to the situation in which men are typically identified by the media as soon as suspicion and detection are raised. However, because we immediately searched for and located names whenever cases were covered in the media, this gender disparity in media treatment has not affected our results. The low proportion of women in our sample could only be caused by Norwegian media reporting on women in a chivalrous manner, ignoring them. This possibility and determining whether or not it is a significant issue may inspire future research.

Second, because we are concentrating on cases that have garnered enough attention from national newspapers, we may have overlooked less common female offenders. Women may be more likely than men to engage in high-level forms of white-collar crime at a lower level. According to Haantz (2002), females account for 17% of the individual fraudsters reported by victims of fraud in the United States.

Compared to women, a higher proportion of men reported a non-zero likelihood of committing an offense. It was determined that the disparity of 35% for men and 26% for women was statistically significant. According to Reed and Rorie (2002), this is consistent with the expectation that women will report fewer intentions to harm than men.

In subsequent studies, it should be investigated to see if the apparent similarities between the United States and Norway in terms of gender and white-collar crime extend to less serious forms of these crimes.

Notwithstanding, since we stay faithful to the central meaning of middle-class wrongdoing in the wrongdoer-based viewpoint, this ongoing review excluded common economic wrongdoing by a wide range of individuals. For example, while Chief fraud using the Web is a significant type of economic crime (Galvin et al., 2018), it does not qualify as a white-collar crime in our study because the perpetrators do not have legitimate access to the property or resources.

Thirdly, women hold 35 to 50% of high-level corporate positions in Norway. Despite this, we found that only 13.6% of the women in our sample held senior positions in their companies. This suggests that women are less likely than men to be involved in high-level financial crime for some reason. However, it is impossible for us to determine the specific number of high-ranking positions held by women in the organizations investigated in this case. A more precise company-based estimate of female versus male opportunities for elite financial crime would be helpful if there are gender-based differences in how responsive individuals are to criminal opportunities.

At long last, countless countries with changing levels of orientation imbalance and female support in middle-class wrongdoing would be expected for the liberation speculation to be genuinely tried. The hypothesis investigates the connection between female involvement in crime and gender inequality as a whole, using legitimate access to professional resources as its foundation. Each of these two concepts is capable of evoking characteristics that are familiar to the general public. Future research that provides a cross-national comparative analysis using countries as the unit of analysis may ultimately validate the emancipation hypothesis regarding gender and white-collar crime (Benson & Gottschalk, 2015).

Despite these flaws, the current section adds new experiences. Steffensmeier et al. were put to the test and improved upon in this chapter. A significant point of view on gendered admittance to middle-class criminal open doors (2013) to an example from outside the US and gave the main hypothetically upheld relative investigation of elite wrongdoing and orientation. In a similar vein, the results indicate that the emancipation hypothesis regarding the connection between variations in gender inequality across societies and variations in women's involvement in white-collar crime does not appear to be valid. All things considered, the findings here suggest that the theories of gendered central concerns and gendered admittance to criminal open doors offer a better chance of making sense of orientation and middle-class wrongdoing.

It may seem like a contradiction in terms to deny the emancipation hypothesis on one side and accept the gendered access to criminal opportunities on the other side. In the context of relatively favorable opportunities as discussed in the first chapter of this book, as well as gendered access rather than just emancipation, it is obvious that emancipation does not guarantee gendered access. While emancipation to some extent is required to enjoy gendered access, it does not guarantee such access, as discussed in this chapter. Emancipation is thus a necessary but not sufficient premise to succeed for women in white-collar crime.

CHAPTER 7

Gender Perspective on Corruption

In the sample of convicted women in Norway presented in the previous chapter, there was nobody convicted of corruption. Both being a briber and being a bribed person are illegal roles in Norway. As discussed in the previous chapter, women tend to miss or avoid membership in male networks in the elite in society, both networks with legitimate activities and networks with illegitimate activities. Corruption must involve at least two persons or entities to work. Often, there are at least three persons in the network, such as a briber, a bribed person, and an agent connecting the two parties. The case study in this chapter tells the story of a female offender who collaborated with a male offender to gain access to bribes. To obtain illegal building permits in the municipality, corruption was required. However, applicants for building permits did not want to bribe a woman, as they were uncertain of her intentions. They felt safer and expected success when they bribed a man in the same department for building permits in the municipality. After receiving bribes, the two municipal officials shared the gain. In this case study, it is not obvious who the leader was and who was the follower.

The strength of guys in basically all types of wrongdoing is perhaps one of the most deeply grounded observational routines in criminal science. However, the gender gap in criminal activity varies depending on the type of offense. Men are more likely than women to commit violent direct contact predatory street crimes like murder and robbery, while women are slightly more likely to commit minor property crimes like shoplifting. The orientation hole in wrongdoing extends to middle-class wrongdoing. Lack of opportunity and women's aversion to risk could be reasons for gender differences in white-collar crime. The gender gap in white-collar

The Gender Gap in White-Collar Crime: A Multi-Country Study of Women Offenders in Economic Crime.
Maryam Kamaei, Petter Gottschalk, and Thomas E. Dearden (Authors)

crime varies by offense, just like it does with street crime. The fact that a female official in the building permits department of the Norwegian city of Drammen was involved in corruption came as a surprise. She admitted that several builders had offered her bribes. Women's involvement in corruption is not surprising when convenience theory and gender theory are applied to the gender model. As was discussed in previous chapters, the lack of suspicion toward female managers is linked to the lack of detection.

7.1 INTERNAL CORRUPTION INVESTIGATION

The sample size for this case study had increased to 405 convicted white-collar criminals in Norway between 2009 and 2015, with 8% being women. Bank fraud, employee embezzlement, tax evasion, and other financial crimes were typically brought against the female defendants. There were no allegations of corruption against them. Kindly review that we in different crowds have habitually posed the accompanying inquiry: Who would you bribe to get a building permit for your new home in a recreation-regulated area, like a public beach? A female or male executive officer in your municipality with the same authority and power? The response from the man is more than 95%, while the response from the woman is less than 5%.

As a result, when a female executive officer in the Norwegian city of Drammen was accused of corruption in 2016, it came as quite a surprise. The city's control committee hired global professional services firm Deloitte (2017) to conduct a private internal investigation of the building permit department.

We address the following research question in this chapter: How likely is it that female corruption offenders will be discovered? We are unable to provide a clear answer based on the case study. Nonetheless, we can use gender theory, opportunity theory, and convenience theory to discuss gender differences that are important to understand when studying financial crime committed by white-collar criminals. However, we can conclude that women face a significantly lower risk of detection than men do.

In the municipality of Drammen, Mette Cranner (age 58) was in charge of building permits. Before entering public service, she was an architect and ran her own architecture firm that eventually failed. She began accepting bribes from construction firms, landowners, and homeowners because her private expenses were significantly greater than her income. She admitted to being corrupt (Tommelstad & Quist, 2016).

The control panel in the district gave the order for Deloitte's survey, which basically manages authoritative conditions in regards to rules and guidelines. Deloitte needed to consider that there was a police examination happening in equal. Misrepresentation analysts from Deloitte gathered information through record examination, interviews, and a survey of 58 structure cases, which the two guilty parties had handled criminally in the structure license division.

The structure license division is important for city planning, building regulations, and development projects, including architecture and cultural heritage, urban renewal, the city's real estate, and environmental protection related to urban development. Environmentally friendly urban development is a major focus in many areas.

All 58 building permit cases that were examined were related to the corruption case identified by the region and reported to Deloitte for investigation. Therefore, the researchers did not randomly select cases from the building permit office's portfolio. The violations of legal standards, procedures, and regulations identified by Deloitte (2017) resulted from the review of building permit cases, verified information through interviews, and document analysis.

The basis for the investigation was the arrest of two employees at the structure license division in the winter of 2016 and their subsequent corruption charges after the region discovered significant deviations and reported the two municipal officials to the police. The Deloitte (2017) investigation primarily focused on organizational issues. Investigators did not uncover any additional criminal offenses in their review. Three suspicious incidents reported directly to Deloitte were handed over to the police for further investigation.

As per the report of examination by Deloitte (2017), huge shortcomings over quite a while existed in administration, leadership, control elements, quality assurance, and internal audits in the division responsible for building standards and permits. These shortcomings and deficiencies have led to violations of legal standards and internal procedures that should ensure sound case handling work in the Drammen region. Several aspects revealed by Deloitte regarding permit applications raise concerns about misconduct.

7.2 CONVENIENT CORRUPTION OPPORTUNITY

One of the most well-established empirical regularities in criminology is that men are more likely to commit almost any kind of crime. However, the gender gap in criminal activity varies depending on the type of offense. Men are more likely than women to commit violent direct contact predatory street crimes like murder and robbery, while women are slightly more likely to commit minor property crimes like shoplifting.

White-collar crime also suffers from the gender gap in crime. Lack of opportunity and women's aversion to risk are two potential explanations for gender differences in white-collar crime. The gender gap in white-collar crime varies by offense, just like it does with street crime. Fraud, manipulation, and theft were all committed by women in the Norwegian sample, but there was no corruption.

In 1996, Steffensmeier and Allan proposed a gendered theory of female criminal behavior. The following components and their interactions are the primary focus of the theory:

1. **Gender organization:** Moral development, gender norms, and social control

2. **Factors of Nature:** Differences in appearance, sexuality, and affiliation

3. **Criminal Open Doors:** Access to skills, criminal associates, and settings, and sexism in the criminal underworld.

4. **Criminal Behavior by Gender:** White-collar heinous crime is avoided by women. Models are insider-exchanging, price fixing, restriction of exchange, unloading of harmful material, fake item trade, payoff, and official corruption, as well as enormous-scale legislative wrongdoing.

5. **Reason for the Offense:** The context of the offense, which refers to the characteristics of a specific offense, is a major factor in many of the most significant differences between offenses committed by men and women. It could be the setting, whether the crime was committed with the help of others, the offender's role in starting and committing the crime, the type of victim, the relationship

between the victim and the offender, whether a weapon was used, the severity of the injury, the value or type of property that was destroyed or stolen, or the goal of the crime.

6. **Motives Behind the Crime:** Tastes for danger, the possibility of shame or embarrassment, self-control, and weighing the risks and benefits of crime.

Psychopathy, for example, is a personality disorder that affects some white-collar criminals. Psychopathy can indicate a lack of fear, antisocial behavior combined with a high need for social attention, immunity to stress, egoism, and self-centered impulsivity (Blickle & Schütte, 2017).

These six factors can interact with one another in gender theory. Gender organization and criminal preference, for instance, influence criminal motivation (Steffensmeier & Allan, 1996, p. 478):

> Gender norms, lack of physical strength, moral and relational concerns, and social control all contribute to gender differences in taste for risk, likelihood of shame or embarrassment, self-control, and evaluation of the costs versus rewards of crime, which in turn limit female willingness to participate in crime subjectively. Opportunity and motivation are distinct, but they frequently coexist, as when opportunity increases temptation. Being able tends to make one more willing, just like being willing increases one's chances of being able in legitimate business. Female criminals, like males, gravitate toward activities with the fewest risks, are within their capabilities, offer a satisfactory return, and are easily accessible.

The strong link between opportunity and white-collar crime among women is one important message from gender theory. The opportunity structure is inadequate if, for instance, women in public office are not receiving bribes.

Hierarchical open door is an unmistakable trait of middle-class wrongdoing that shifts with the people who are associated with wrongdoing (Michel, 2008). As a means of meeting needs, an opportunity is appealing (Bucy et al., 2008). White-collar criminals have the opportunity to commit economic crime and conceal it in seemingly legal business activities thanks to the organizational dimension. White-collar crime is a crime that requires special access.

According to the opportunity perspective, opportunity is a major factor in criminal behavior. The point of view accepts that people settle on decisions to engage or not participate in wrongdoing based on the accessibility and appeal of criminal opportunities. Situational crime prevention theory seeks to identify the factors that influence the distribution and attractiveness of criminal opportunities and suggests strategies for reducing them. The hypothesis predicts that diminishing the attractiveness of criminal opportunities will lead to decreases in wrongdoing (Ceccato & Benson, 2016).

People who are at the top of a corporate hierarchy—or pretty much any hierarchy, for that matter—have a lot of authority, avoid being challenged by others, demand results, and are used to getting what they want. As a result, elite members' various acts of dishonesty and illegality appear to be convenient for the criminals. They believe that if they were at a lower level in the power structure and believed that they were expected to lead by example and produce ethical outcomes, they would be able to disregard some of the reservations they would have. Greed, self-importance, immunity to criticism, getting one's way, and fear of falling are all factors that contribute to the facilitation of white-collar crime within an organizational setting. An offender is in a position to emphasize the importance of one's position in an organization's hierarchy, as well as the pressure to achieve results and the ability to cover one's tracks, assign blame to others, or insist on deniability. White-collar criminals typically employ a variety of rhetorical tactics to imply to subordinates that they have not committed any wrongdoing.

Aguilera and Vadera (2008, p. 434) stated that "the presence of a favorable combination of circumstances that renders a possible course of action relevant" was the definition of a criminal opportunity. According to Haines (2014), when individuals and groups are able to engage in unethical and illegal behavior with the assurance that they will not be caught or punished, opportunities for crime arise. White-collar crime can be committed at the community, business, and individual levels. At the community level, control systems may not exist, and financial crime may target entire industries. This could be seen in the construction industry, where cartels and undocumented work are common. Another example could be tax collection agencies that are unable to locate and control accounting data from businesses. Therefore, this establishes a climate wherein tax avoidance can happen with little risk of being discovered and penalized.

According to Huisman and Erp (2013), the five characteristics of a criminal opportunity are as follows: i) the amount of effort required to commit the crime; ii) the perceived dangers of being discovered; iii) the consequences of the offense; iv) the circumstances that may encourage criminal behavior; and (v) the offense's justification and mitigation. When Wikstrom et al.'s situational action perspective (Kroneberg & Schultz, 2018) conceptualize lack of self-control as well as lack of deterrence on the axis from (2) to (3), making a distinction between three stages: (1) perception of action alternatives (legal alternatives, illegal alternatives), (2) process of choice (habit, rational deliberation), and (3) action. The latter items are included in the convenience willingness dimension. The goal of the situational action perspective is to incorporate personal and environmental explanations into a situation. In 2020, Kleinewiese incorporated groups into the situational action theory (SAT).

Based on previous research on social cohesion in groups, such as team spirit or esprit de corps, it is reasonable to assume that an individual will be more likely to recognize the group if it is cohesive. According to SAT, the moral standards of the group and deterrence ought to have an effect on the causation of crime by becoming a part of the environment. Based on this application, it appears that SAT is a useful method for explaining how groups affect crime.

At the business level, morals and rules can be missing, while monetary wrongdoing is a clear business practice. A model here is endowment misrepresentation, where ship organizations report lower traffic numbers to guarantee greater government moves. Another model is internal receipt misrepresentation, where the accounting department lack oversight over who has management privileges to support what invoices.

At the individual level, greed can prevail, where the business has no appropriate response to monetary wrongdoing. A model here may be law firms where partners misuse money in client accounts. Another model is corruption, where the bribed individual receives money from the bribing individual, without anyone noticing on either side.

Benson and Simpson (2018) proposed that the hierarchical opportunity to commit white-collar crime manifests through the following three characteristics: (1) the offender has legal and legitimate access to the premises and systems where the crime is carried out, (2) the offender is geographically at a different location than the victim, and (3) criminal acts appear to be legitimate business. This is starkly different from street crimes like violence and theft, where the offender has no legal access, the offender is at the same location as the victim, and the offense does not appear to be legitimate. An important distinction between white-collar crime and street crime is that while white-collar criminals conceal their crime but do not hide themselves, street criminals do not conceal their crime but hide themselves. Street crime is usually highly visible, while street criminals are not always easy to identify. White-collar crime is often not visible, but white-collar criminals are not difficult to trace.

Middle-class wrongdoing doesn't occur secretly; it happens at work. The workplace is the setting for wrongdoing. McKenndall and Wagner (1997) describe the opportunity created by organizational and environmental conditions that facilitate rather than prevent the commission of crimes. For example, in the case of corruption, both the briber and the recipient are linked to a work environment. The briber typically uses company funds to pay, while the recipient receives the money personally because his organization is attractive to the bribing party.

The hierarchical aspect of work addresses the wrongdoer's potential for wrongdoing. Through work, ownership, position, relationships, and information, the wrongdoer can exploit their connection with the organization to commit financial crimes. As a sales manager, the individual can offer incentives, and as a procurement leader, the individual can receive kickbacks. As a finance manager, the individual may engage in embezzlement by manipulating accounting figures, and as a chief accountant, the individual can manipulate accounting to facilitate tax evasion. As a CEO, the individual can sign fake contracts or request fraudulent valuations that lead to bank fraud by asking the bank to finance future income from contract partners and real estate sales. There are numerous opportunities for financial crimes by executives and others involved in businesses. Examples of others include administrative managers, lawyers, auditors, bank managers, board members, boat dealers, car dealers, event organizers, committee members, management consultants, regional managers, entrepreneurs, investors, mayors, medical professionals, parliament members, nursery owners, property developers, real estate agents, shipbrokers, stockbrokers, and tax consultants.

Middle-class wrongdoing amazing opportunities happen through the three qualities described by Benson and Simpson (2018). The valuable opportunities are highest for top executives and other members of the elite in society. Similar to convenience theory, the three qualities make it comfortable, easy, and convenient to commit financial crimes to solve a problem or respond to a challenge. It may be quite common and therefore convenient for middle-class elite individuals to conceal crimes in the flow of legal activities, and thus provide crime with an outward appearance of legitimacy in a legitimate business (Pickett & Pickett, 2002).

A criminal is made by opportunity; it is sometimes stated. If the availability of legal opportunities to solve problems and take advantage of possibilities deteriorates, while illegal opportunities thrive and seem convenient, then middle-class individuals will become less reputable. If fraud, theft, manipulation, and corruption find completion easily and conveniently in the endeavor, while decent alternatives are invisible or difficult to implement, then opportunity creates a wrongdoer.

Hierarchical chance for financial wrongdoing relies upon scholarly and social capital that is accessible to the possible middle-class criminal. Scholarly capital is knowledge concerning grasping, understanding, reflection, ability, and expertise. Social capital is relations in various hierarchical and transactional exchanges. Social capital is the amount of real and potential resources available for middle-class individuals by virtue of their position in formal and informal orders, organizations, and systems (Adler & Kwon, 2002). Formal as well as informal power implies influence over resources that can be used for crime.

White-collar criminals are often not the only ones who commit financial crimes. They may collaborate with others both internally and externally. If internal crime cooperation is present, participation may be more convenient for all parties. The hierarchical opportunity is strengthened in an environment where crime is accepted. If there is external criminal cooperation, it may again be easier for everyone to participate. External factors, such as those who accept bribes or submit fake invoices, establish a relationship with the internal actor through a code of silence.

When a crime is committed on behalf of a business, the organizational aspect of white-collar crime is especially apparent. According to Trahan (2011), there is a difference between white-collar criminals who engage in financial crime on behalf of their employer and those who do so for personal gain. The first type is corporate crime, while the second type is occupational crime. Instances of corporate wrongdoing incorporate control of monetary figures for tax avoidance and outlandish government endowments, payoff to acquire contracts, misleading advance applications to get credit in banks, and tax evasion in assessment asylums to enlist protections clients. Since they occur within the company and to the benefit of the company, crimes committed by corporate entities demonstrate the organizational anchoring of crime (Bradshaw, 2015).

Corporate crime is frequently hidden by a group of individuals to improve business conditions, whereas occupational crime is important to hide by the individual to enrich themselves by abusing corporate resources (Hansen, 2009). As a result of position and trust in the organization, crime is committed in both instances, preventing accountability, control, and monitoring.

7.3 LACK OF OFFENDER SUSPICION

Women generally receive less suspicion than men do in the workplace. In general, the environment will make women less dangerous. To the degree wrongdoing is identified, a lady isn't thought of or treated as the principal suspect. She is either seen as a criminal supporter or as a criminal victim in a common criminal investigation when more individuals are involved in the crime. Identification risk connects to general reasons why women – to a far lesser degree than men – experience conviction for middle-class crime, namely females generally avoid convictions of crime when compared to males.

Potentially, ladies are more intelligent hoodlums than men are. Once more, when we do a trial in a group of people, most agree with this assertion. One justification for relative quickness is that ladies might will quite often stop crimes before it is past the point of no return. They are savvy and controlling, and often help their will through indirect ways. Ladies are a consequence of a childhood and considered the more fragile orientation in society, and therefore need to resort to alternative ways of getting things done. It might seem that they just get things done and do tasks that are indeed important for the organization to achieve, while men just do what they would like to do. Ladies corner areas where they appear innocent, like attention, health, and the environment. Ladies will often talk about ethics, protection, and social responsibility. It is extremely difficult for others to think that they are criminals. Therefore, the detection rate for ladies will be lower than for men. The fact that ladies talk about ethics is supported by a study conducted by Evade (2007). She refers to her Canadian study where 94% of all companies with a board of directors with at least three female members had established guidelines for conflict of interest. In companies with only male board members, the percentage was 68%. Studies like this can help confirm that women, more broadly than men, are concerned that the company should follow rules and policy lines to build and maintain a good reputation.

Some make a distinction between morals and being moral. Research by O'Fallon and Butterfield (2005) shows no distinction between women and men when it comes to making ethical and unethical decisions. Dollar et al. (2001), however, found that a higher proportion of women in parliament is associated with a lower level of corruption. However, the perception rate can play a role here. Research findings that women are more engaged with ethics and demonstrate stronger moral views than men are also confirmed in earlier studies.

A lower relative detection rate can also be explained by the tendency that white-collar crime only captures economic crimes of a significant scale. This leads to a smaller female share, as the typical amount in female crime tends to be lower than the average amount in male crime. Additionally, women may be more adept at avoiding detection and attention, remaining silent, and preventing crime at an earlier stage. A relatively low detection rate could also occur because authorities and researchers misunderstand female roles in crime and tend to view women as victims of crime. Women often present themselves as victims by claiming to be victimized by men.

Then again, men have a tendency to be the orientation that takes risks at high risk, and as a result, individuals around them more easily identify them. They can also seek attention because they like to display their material success. The police also contribute to the low perception of women. We can compare this with different types of crime. When the police respond to a family situation due to domestic issues, the main suspect is usually the man, and the police resolve the case by removing the man from the situation. If the police find documents in the home, they will assume that they belong to the man.

From a historical perspective, we may observe that society has embraced a culture where it is more common for men to be criminals. The confirmation bias can explain this phenomenon, where people tend to try to confirm what they already suspect they know. When there are few convicted women, then there should be fewer female criminals. When there are fewer female criminals, the police will focus on male criminals. When female criminals are not of interest to the police, then fewer women will ever face conviction and imprisonment.

The fact that organizations treat doubt and recognition differently for women is yet another explanation for the generally lower identification part. It could be because the board, executives, and inspector are more likely to report instances of male misconduct and wrongdoing to the police. By placing the blame for wrongdoing on female representatives, one might be more afraid to make a mistake when it comes to segregation. In internal investigations, forgetting about female wrongdoing and focusing on male wrongdoing can generally be beneficial. Conventional examinations appear to be more appropriate for male suspects than for female suspects.

Men typically have a longer criminal career than women, despite the fact that some women may stop in time to avoid discovery at any point (Cauffman 2008, p. 126):

> On average, males tend to have longer criminal careers than females. Because it is difficult to assess when a criminal career is "finished," convincing evidence about the duration of criminal careers is sparse. A long-term study by Roger Tarling followed a sample of male and female offenders who were born in 1958 through age 31, finding that the average duration of offending was 4.9 years for females, and 7.4 years for males.

Prosecution follows the detection of a crime in our model. Be that as it may, at times this isn't true. Therefore, both the rate of prosecution in court and the rate of detection are gender-dependent. A company may decide not to pursue prosecution in the event of detection within the company. They might want to keep their reputation private and keep the public from losing faith in the business. Anecdotal evidence suggests that businesses only report 3 out of 10 serious financial crime cases to the police. When it comes to female-related business crime, this number is probably even lower.

Lastly, the fact that a female municipal official in the building permits department of the Norwegian city of Drammen was involved in corruption came as a surprise. She mentioned that a few builders had tried to bribe her. It's not shocking to see women involved in corruption when we consider convenience theory and gender theory in the gender model. The trust in female managers is related to the difficulty in detecting issues. Both male and female criminals from the municipality ended up in prison.

7.4 CRIME DETECTION ESTIMATES

At an executive seminar in the Norwegian Internal Revenue Service, a total of 57 participants were handed a questionnaire regarding the likelihood of detection depending on the kind of white-collar crime. Each crime type was formulated both for female and male offenders, starting with "she" and "he" respectively. As listed in Table 7.1, there were no gender differences. A potential explanation might be that respondents did not notice the first word in each sentence that indicated gender. However, it might also be the case that this group of respondents does not suggest any gender difference in terms of detection.

Table 7.1 also illustrates the likelihood for various kinds of crime, where corruption in Myanmar is least likely to be detected, while embezzlement in the tax revenue authority itself has the highest probability of detection.

White-collar financial crime falls into four broad categories: corruption, theft, manipulation, and fraud. The term "fraud" involves inducing others to take adverse action based on false or misleading information, leading to the victim's action. Commonplace models are bank extortion and sponsorship misrepresentation, where the fraudster distorts the worth of an item to get a bank credit, or the fraudster distorts exercises to get greater government endowments. The act of unlawfully taking someone else's or an organization's valuable property is known as theft. Examples include employee embezzlement and theft of intellectual property. In instances of manipulation, the wrongdoer changes parameters to gain a more favorable result for themselves. Tax evasion and cartel agreements, in which the manipulator takes advantage of price fixing while avoiding paying taxes, are typical examples. Corruption is the illegal exchange of unjustified benefits with the expectation of reciprocity. Examples include bribing procurement officers for contracts and bribing municipal officials for building permits.

The likelihood of fraud detection is 57% to 56% and 43% to 44% as listed in Table 7.1. The likelihood of theft detection is 75% to 76% and

TABLE 7.1 Likelihood of Crime Detection Depending on Gender and Offense Type

Probability of Crime Detection	Percentage (%)
She commits bank fraud by claiming that the customer is in the process of signing a major contract with the company	57
He commits bank fraud by claiming that the customer is in the process of signing a major contract with the company	56
She cheats the state for subsidies by claiming that the ferry company has little traffic along the coast	43
He cheats the state for subsidies by claiming that the ferry company has little traffic along the coast	44
She commits embezzlement in the tax authority by transferring receivables for dead persons to her own account	75
He commits embezzlement in the tax authority by transferring receivables for dead persons to his own account	76
She embezzles client funds in the law firm where she is a partner	59
He embezzles client funds in the law firm where he is a partner	52
She commits tax evasion by manipulating the accounts of the company	34
He commits tax evasion by manipulating the accounts of the company	38
She backdates the contract for a football player so that the club does not have to pay the transfer fee	49
He backdates the contract for a football player so that the club does not have to pay the transfer fee	46
She bribes an employee in the municipality to get a license to serve alcohol in her restaurant	34
He bribes an employee in the municipality to get a license to serve alcohol in his restaurant	31
She bribes a minister in Myanmar to get mobile licenses in the country	28
He bribes a minister in Myanmar to get mobile licenses in the country	28
As a municipal employee, she receives a bribe from a restaurant owner who wants a license to serve alcohol	35
As a municipal employee, he receives a bribe from a restaurant owner who wants a license to serve alcohol	32
As a municipal employee, she receives a bribe from a developer who wants a building permit	35
As a municipal employee, he receives a bribe from a developer who wants a building permit	36
She has committed financial crime in the past and does it again at work	54
He has committed financial crime in the past and does it again at work	58

59% to 52%. The likelihood of manipulation detection is 34% to 38% and 49% to 46%. The likelihood of corruption detection is 34% to 31% and 28% to 28% for bribers. The likelihood of corruption detection is 35% to 32% and 35% to 36% for bribed offenders. Offenders with recidivism have a detection rate of 54% to 58%. The most surprising result is the overall high detection probabilities. Other research has suggested detection rates of 5% to 10% for financial crime by white-collar offenders (Gottschalk & Gunnesdal, 2018).

CHAPTER 8

Norwegian Offender Cases

Scholars have emphasized the lack of case studies outside the United States for many years. As a result, six women who committed white-collar crimes and were later prosecuted and found guilty in Norway are discussed in this chapter.

8.1 EMBEZZLEMENT BY BANK EXECUTIVE

Bente Selvaag was a bank executive in the Oslo branch of BNP Paribas. She embezzled 13 million Norwegian kroner (about 1.3 million US dollars) over a period of nine years by means of 260 transactions to her own and family member accounts. She received a prison sentence of three years (Kleppe, 2011, p. 6):

> After starting in an employment position as a "troubleshooting girl" during the financial crisis in the 1980s, Selvaag gained, according to the fresh confession verdict, access to initiate transactions at the beginning of this century. Thereafter, the 59-year-old carried out 260 transactions for 'at least kr 13,670,000' of the bank's funds that she abused for her own and others' purposes. Bente Selvaag was an executive in the department for debt collection and follow-up on defaulting loans when she diverted millions to her and family member accounts through transfers to an interim account.

It was her position as a bank executive in the department for debt collection that Selvaag gained legitimate access to the bank's systems and accounts. She started on February 13, 2001, to move money out of the bank via transactions to a temporary account before moving the money to her

The Gender Gap in White-Collar Crime: A Multi-Country Study of Women Offenders in Economic Crime.
Maryam Kamaei, Petter Gottschalk, and Thomas E. Dearden (Authors)

own and family member accounts. She teamed up with an acquaintance, and together they designed system functionality and data features, which made it difficult for the bank to detect deviant transactions. It was only after February 25, 2010 – after nine years – that standard control schedules in the bank gave a sign. During those nine years, Selvaag had been able to steal 13 million dollars. After signal enrollment and location in the review capability, the bank revealed Bente Selvaag to the police where she confronted the charge of misappropriation, while simultaneously being quickly excused from her situation at the BNP Paribas. On December 16, 2011, nearly two years later, she received a three-year prison sentence from the Oslo district court. The judge emphasized that embezzlement that has a negative impact on the employer is a serious breach of trust.

The bank immediately terminated the employment of Selvaag at the stage of crime detection, and she has since returned the entire embezzled amount, which led to a somewhat milder conviction than the prosecution had suggested.

What specifically describes Bente Selvaag as an offender in the upper echelon in society was her position and access at BNP, which made it possible and convenient to commit substantial financial crime over a long period of many years. She enjoyed high social status. She resided in the best area in Oslo, near the ski jumping field Holmenkollen where numerous affluent Norwegians have their homes. She lived in a house worth at that time more than one million US dollars, which today would be more than two million dollars. The crime occurred in her professional position at the bank, and she enjoyed complete confidence and trust from the top management at the bank. Accordingly, she had convenient organizational opportunity to do what she did. The open door got both from her significant level position and from her genuine area of obligation inside bank activities. It was expected for her to approach frameworks and records to go about her business.

Bente Selvaag also had a network that enabled her to establish contact with her conspirator. Her network, in addition to family members, did not react when they received money in their accounts from her. She belonged to the elite in society, and she spent the embezzled money to finance the real estate at Holmenkollen. Her crime case popped up in the media, on TV, on the radio, on the Internet, and in the newspapers, which is one of the criteria in this book to define a person empirically as a woman in white-collar crime. The house on Dagali road 19 in Holmenkollen was purchased by Bente Selvaag and her husband Ivar Hagen in 2001 for six million Norwegian kroner. A few months later, in December 2010, Bente Selvaag realized that she would be prosecuted in court and decided to sell the property for 10 million kroner.

The amount of money involved, which is higher than average for female white-collar offenders, is one interesting aspect of this crime case. Women are usually a little more careful and take a little here and a little there, rather than 13 million in the same organization. Another interesting aspect is the duration of the wrongdoing, which must imply that there was no short-term motive to solve an acute financial problem, which typically characterizes much of what women do when they commit financial crime at work. A third interesting point is that Selvaag had a helper, which is unusual for women who don't follow criminal kingpins. Convicted females typically worked alone when they committed embezzlement and fraud. In those cases where a man and a woman work together in crime, then the man is kind of a criminal leader and the main actor, while the woman follows orders and follows them. This is evident in the Italian mafia, such as Cosa Nostra, where the role of women is to take care of communication between male offenders.

A fourth interesting aspect of this case is that detection occurred through regular control routines in the bank, despite the fact that deviance had taken place for nine years. Very few incidents of white-collar crime detection occur internally in organizations, especially not through regular control routines. When whistleblowers do not trust the internal whistleblowing procedure or the individuals assigned to follow up on reports from whistleblowers, they typically turn to the media.

A fifth interesting aspect is the quick refund of embezzled money. Selvaag sold her house for 10 million and somehow added several million to pay back 13 million in addition to interest rates. This is according to the court document in 2011 (Kleppe, 2011).

Bente Selvaag had an external helper. He (61) died. People called him the shotgun man because he frequently went crazy. For example, a woman (59) and her daughter (41) should at one point only put their garden furniture out and fix the garden. Then the woman's ex-husband showed up with a shotgun. It happened outside the family house on Nesøya, a peninsula close to Oslo. The ex-husband killed them both, and then he took his own life (Hansen et al., 2009).

Figure 8.1 represents the use of the comfort hypothesis leading to misappropriation by the bank leader. The thought process was individual out of potential outcomes. The open door depended on status and access to assets. The readiness depended on judicious decision.

Status is an individual's overall standing within a valued social aspect or their social status within a formal or informal hierarchical system. Status is the result of a subjective evaluation process, and it is the extent to which an individual is admired and respected by others (McClean et al., 2018). According to Akkar et al., high-status individuals enjoy greater respect and deference from those at the bottom of the social hierarchy, as well as power and influence over them (2020, p. 532).

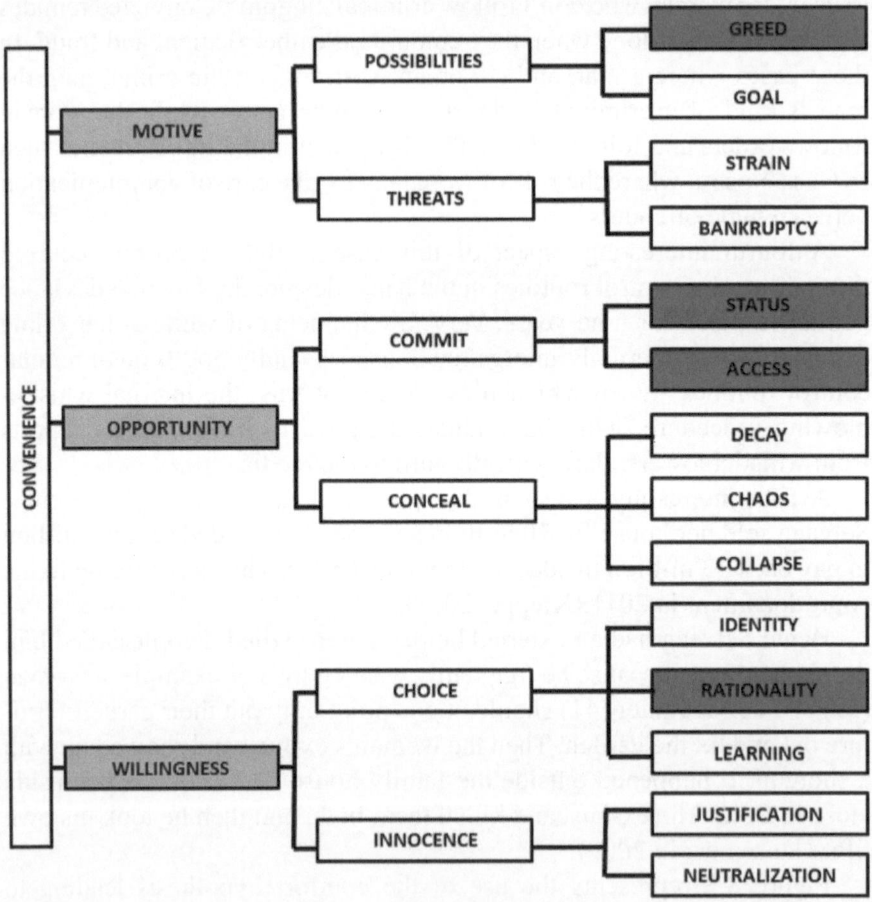

FIGURE 8.1 Convenience themes for Bente Selvaag.

In the eyes of others, status is a property that belongs to those who are regarded as having a higher social standing or rank in a pecking order based on a set of shared social attributes.

A person with a higher social status or rank enjoys numerous real advantages in their personal and professional lives. For instance, groups ask high-status actors for advice, pay them more, provide them with unsolicited assistance, and give them disproportionate credit for joint tasks. Our social ecosystem consistently rewards those with high status in a myriad of ways.

8.2 MANIPULATION BY ACCOUNTING EXECUTIVE

Gunn Fosse was the chief accountant at the ferry company Ofoten and Vesteraalen Dampskibsselskap (OVDS). Company ships sailed along the Norwegian coast with goods and passengers. The Norwegian government subsidized the company to make sure that ferries also visited small places inside fjords with goods and passengers. The fewer passengers and less goods reported by the ship-owner, the more subsidy the company received. The fraudulent scheme was thus to report fewer goods and passengers to receive more state subsidies for the operations of the company, which is a typical case of corporate crime.

Gunn Fosse was a typical accomplice in the crime. She was upset when she was the first defendant prosecuted in court. She quickly wrote an autobiography with the title "Mayday! The Captain's First in the Lifeboats" to express how unfair she found being prosecuted, especially since the top executives seemingly avoided prosecution.

Convicted white-collar offenders' autobiographies are a fascinating source of information regarding convenience in white-collar crime. Examples include Middelhoff (2017) in Germany, Kerik (2015) in the United States, Belfort (2008) in the United States, Benulic (2018) in Sweden, and Bogen (2008) in Norway. They all wrote their autobiographies while in jail for financial crimes committed in a professional setting. They were all members of the elite in society as chief executives in major organizations, such as a business enterprise, a police commission, a stockbroker, an energy supplier, and a sport sponsor, respectively. In our perspective of women as members of the elite in financial crime in society, an autobiography by Montella (2016) is particularly interesting, since she, as chief financial officer (CFO) at Lehman Brothers in the United States when the bank collapsed, never had to face charges by the criminal justice system.

The female chief accountant in Norway wrote her autobiography with help from a journalist. One of the book sections has the heading "Legal Roulette" (Fosse & Magnusson, 2004):

> The person who holds the belief that there is only one type of truth, the real and honest coming from the depth of the soul, has not met the justice goddess Justitia. Truth can be a complicated question. Justitia's weighing scale seems to choose to exempt from the fine-tuning calibration of the adjusting device, and might be as unreliable as an exhausted bathroom scale. When there is no evidence, then "the legal truth" is the judge's weight assessment for doubt and belief. This is a phenomenon occurring when you are sitting in the middle of the battlefield among lawyers. You get your credibility weighed and measured by people who do not know you as a person. During a few days in court, where the prosecutor is present to cast doubt on your motives and your fairness, the judges in the court turn to the legal truth to decide whether you speak true or false. The legal truth results from a so-called probability overweight. It is in reality nothing more than what we commonly call personal discretion or guesswork.

This statement by the defendant is interesting because many cases involving white-collar crime do not have clear facts supported by evidence. Also often lacking is a clear application of the law that obviously pertains to the facts. Both the lack of evidence and relevant laws make it plausible to argue that legal truth sometimes appears random. However, the claim of probability overweight is clearly incorrect. Since the criminal justice system in Norway is extremely concerned about injustice and errors in justice, courts quickly dismiss cases against potentially guilty individuals if there is any doubt at all.

The subsidy fraud lasted for a decade, from 1992 to 2002. Gunn Fosse was involved throughout this period. The police investigated her, the prosecutor charged her, and the court convicted her of fraud according to the Norwegian penal code. She admitted involvement in the crime but felt no guilt, as she had simply followed instructions from others. She applied the neutralization technique of appealing to higher loyalty (Schoultz & Flyghed, 2016).

Bjarne Øverås was the CEO at OVDS. The company had more than a 1,000 employees, and its headquarters were in the northern Norwegian city of Narvik. In 2003, the organization received media attention in an extortion case, where five current and former executives, along with the company itself, faced allegations of manipulating ship accounting to obtain larger funds from the Norwegian state. The Salten (2004) district court ordered the company to repay a significant amount of money to the state, and all executives were ultimately sentenced to prison. CEO Øverås received the longest prison term, with a sentence of three years and six months. Gunn Fosse, the chief accountant, had already been sentenced to two years and six months in prison. Controller Brre Simonsen and Chief Financial Officer Stig Lennart Nerdal each received a sentence of two years and six months. Jan Gustav Thygesen, the fifth executive, served nine months.

Figure 8.2 represents the utilization of the comfort hypothesis to control by the bookkeeping chief. Corporate crime was the white-collar offense, not occupational crime. She had the resources to commit accounting fraud that was reported to the subsidizing agency, which lacked appropriate control mechanisms. By neutralizing any feelings of guilt, she felt innocent. She employed the crime neutralization strategy of higher loyalties. According to Sykes and Matza (1957), expectations were met. The offender claims that the act was carried out in fulfillment of a moral obligation rather than out of self-interest. The criminal targets individuals with greater loyalty. People who believe they are in a predicament that needs to be resolved even if it means breaking a policy or law use this tactic. An employee may appeal to organizational values, hierarchies, or practices within the context of an organization.

8.3 CLINIC FRAUD SCHEME BY MEDICAL DOCTOR

Ragnhild Johanne Stuve was a medical doctor who worked at a private healthcare clinic in Haugesund, which is a city north of Bergen in Norway. The clinic rented expensive medical equipment from a vendor in Scotland. Some of the surplus from the rent returned to her since her brother owned the company in Scotland. By overcharging the Haugesund clinic from Scotland for rent of medical equipment, she had extra income returning to her from Scotland via the island of Guernsey and Moor Shipping to Haugesund. It was a convenient way of gaining illegitimate profit, at least as long as her brother did not get attention from the Norwegian criminal justice system in other matters.

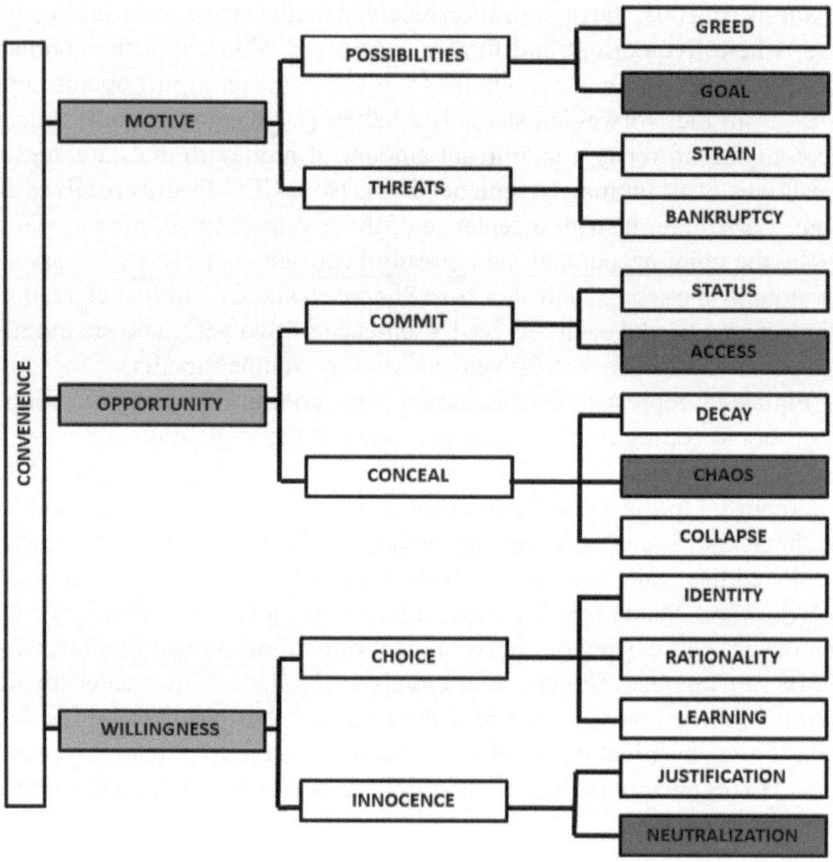

FIGURE 8.2 Convenience themes for Gunn Fosse.

However, her brother Tor Johan Stuve was a ship-owner who eventually went bankrupt with his shipping company, which drew the attention of the Norwegian police. Ragnhild Johanne Stuve claimed innocence both in the district court and in the Gulating Court of Appeals. Nevertheless, she was convicted and sentenced to eight months in jail for economic fraud. Both the district court and the appeals court found sufficient evidence that she had defrauded the medical clinic in Haugesund, for example by paying for equipment rental that had already been fully paid off and had no remaining value in the books. Sometimes invoices came from a firm in Guernsey that received the money, which was then transferred to Moor Shipping, a company controlled by her brother Tor Johan Stuve (Waal, 2010a).

Ragnhild Johanne Stuve claimed innocence, that is why she appealed the district court ruling. Gulating Court of Appeal had to address the following questions: Did she remove money from the clinic by means of a constructed contract with her brother Tor Johan Stuve, or was the intention in the contract acceptable? Were just the documentation and implementation that suffered from obvious weaknesses? According to prosecutor Anna Haugmoen Karlsen, the Norwegian National Authority for the Investigation and Prosecution of Economic and Environmental Crime (Kokrim) argued that the defendant could not treat the clinic's funds as if they were her own. The possibility that the physician Stuve had a narcissistic attachment to the clinic is an intriguing point of view. A distinct type of narcissism is narcissistic identification, in which the perpetrator perceives little to no distinction between oneself and the organization. The money from the business is personal money, which can be used however the narcissist sees fit (Galvin et al., 2015). While pomposity and expected deference have a place with the inspirational element of comfort theory, sympathy shortfall has a place with the eagerness aspect of comfort theory where the wrongdoer has a penchant for self-absorption (Nichol, 2019). The offender demonstrates unreasonable expectations for preferential treatment (Zvi & Elaad, 2018).

Prosecutor Karlsen meant in court that Doctor Stuve had committed tax evasion by transferring money abroad before it ended up in the hands of ship-owner Stuve and then returning to her. Karlsen also prosecuted that Doctor Stuve had committed fraud against the medical clinic in Haugesund. The clinic had paid for services that it never received or expected to receive. Økokrim was convinced that the money disappeared intentionally through money laundering on the island of Guernsey. Ship-owner Stuve had a myriad of companies in a complicated organizational structure in tax havens such as the island of Guernsey (Waal, 2010a).

Doctor Stuve said repeatedly in court that the intention behind the agreement was good, and that the agreement should ensure that the medical clinic got access to modern medical equipment. The fact that the new medical equipment never arrived was explained by the bankruptcy of ship-owner Stuve in the shipping company Tordenskjold. Due to the immense financial problems caused by the bankruptcy, her brother was not in a position to deliver according to the agreement with his sister. Doctor Stuve said in court that she trusted her brother 100% to provide access to the new equipment for the medical clinic in Haugesund. She mentioned that she never read the papers that he asked her to sign because she trusted him (Waal, 2010b).

According to the contract, the medical clinic should pay 125,000 Norwegian kroner (about 12,500 US dollars) every month to a Guernsey firm that the brother had established. The firm was set up to provide rental of laser equipment both to the sister's clinic and to other doctors and clinics. In that way, the clinic felt they had guaranteed access to new and modern equipment that the market demanded. Doctor Stuve admitted in court that the new and modern equipment never arrived at the clinic in Haugesund. Økokrim's Karlsen said in court that the prosecution considered the leasing contract a smokescreen, a defrauding scheme, and a shell cover for cheating with money from the clinic to avoid paying taxes (Waal, 2010b).

Tor Johan Stuve, the brother of Ragnhild Stuve, then faced charges of financial misconduct, serious fraud, and violation of accounting and tax laws linked to the collapse of the shipping company Tordenskjold (Kapital, 2010b). The next section in this chapter presents the case of Tordenskjold where another woman was involved.

Besides the fact that the court condemned Ragnhild Stuve to nine months in jail, she was also required to pay a fine of 250,000 US dollars and 2.5 million Norwegian kroner. She committed financial crime in an organizational setting where she had access to resources to commit and conceal wrongdoing, making her a white-collar offender. As a medical doctor in a private clinic, she belonged to the elite in the local community in Haugesund. She had a network with her brother, which made crime a convenient avenue for her. Her personal motive for fraud is unknown, but the convenient opportunity offered by her brother might have triggered her interest in defrauding the clinic and conducting tax evasion. Her willingness for deviant behavior might derive from the seemingly lack of a victim when she followed the fraud scheme designed by her brother. There is no indication in the case that her brother forced her to enter into the fraud scheme, or that the brother benefitted financially from the fraud.

Figure 8.3 illustrates the application of convenience theory to a fraud scheme by a medical doctor. The motive was individual greed. The opportunity was status and access to resources. The willingness was a choice based on identity and rationality.

A unique form of narcissism is narcissistic identification, in which the perpetrator perceives little to no distinction between themselves and the

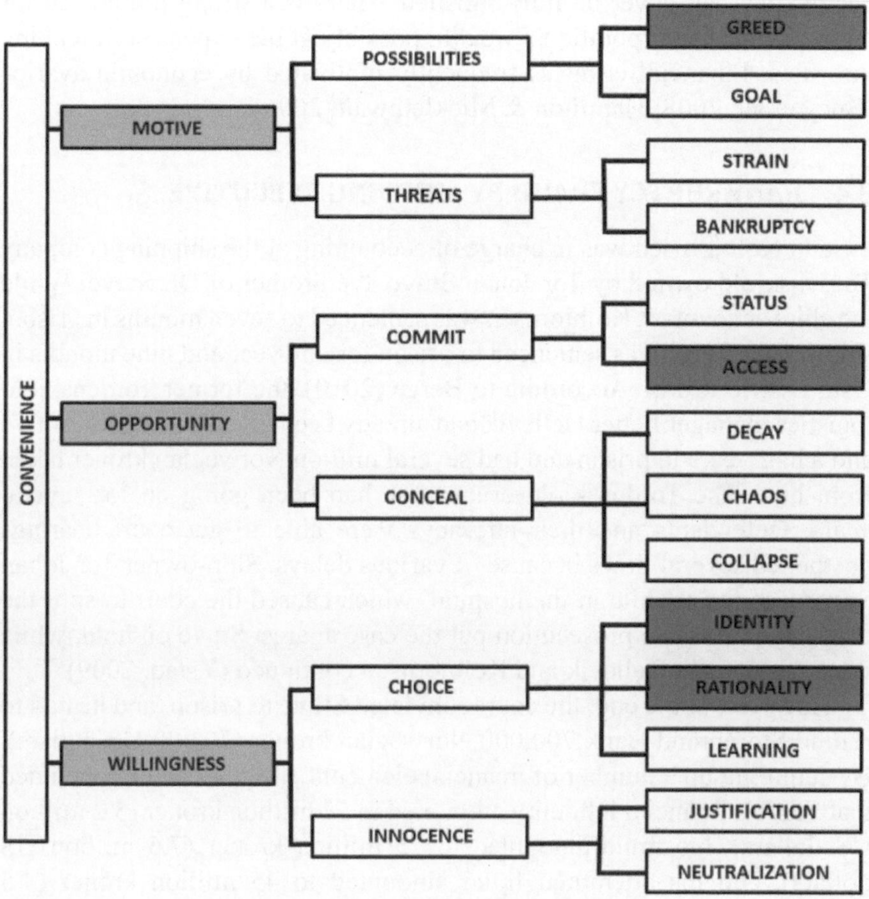

FIGURE 8.3 Convenience themes for Ragnhild Johanne Stuve.

organization. The money from the business is personal money, which can be used however the narcissist sees fit (Galvin et al., 2015). According to Nichol (2019), grandiosity and admiration fall under the motivational aspect of convenience theory, whereas empathy deficit falls under the willingness aspect of convenience theory and indicates a sense of entitlement on the part of the offender (Zvi & Elaad, 2018). The offender demonstrates unreasonable expectations for preferential treatment.

According to Goldstraw-White (2012), greed implies that the offender or the organization in question will never be content because they will always seek greater profits. Greed is a socially constructed set of needs and desires that can never be fully satisfied. There is a strong preference for maximizing the corporation's wealth, possibly at the expense of breaking the rules. Financial crime is frequently motivated by economic avarice (Bucy et al., 2008; Hamilton & Micklethwait, 2006).

8.4 BANKRUPTCY FRAUD BY SHIPPING EXECUTIVE

Susann Kolbjørnsen was in charge of accounting at the shipping company Tordenskjold owned by Tor Johan Stuve, the brother of Dr. Stuve. While the chief accountant Kolbjørnsen was sentenced to seven months in prison, ship-owner Stuve was sentenced to prison for one year and nine months in Oslo District Court. According to Berge (2010), the former Tordenskjold logistics manager Petter Hellevik had already been given a sentence of five and a half years in prison and had several million Norwegian kroner taken from him. The Tordenskjold crime case had been going on for several years. Defendants and their attorneys were able to get court hearings postponed several times because of various delays. Ship-owner Tor Johan Stuve was for a while in the hospital, which caused the court to split the case into parts. The prosecution put the case against Stuve on hold, while the cases against Hellevik and Kolbjørnsen continued (Ystad, 2009).

However, in the end, the court convicted Stuve to prison, and he had to refund Storebrand Bank 700,000 Norwegian kroner (70,000 US dollars). By summing up a number of financial elements, the prosecutor concluded that Stuve's financial infidelity amounted to 52 million kroner (5.2 million US dollars), his fraud amounted to 75 million kroner (7.5 million US dollars), and his attempted fraud amounted to 45 million kroner (4.5 million US dollars). However, the judge acquitted Stuve on most of the charges. The judge found Stuve only guilty of having conspired to fraud and infidelity amounting to the equivalent of 5.5 million US dollars.

The court cases against the shipping executives started when the shipping company Tordenskjold filed for bankruptcy. The fraudulent behavior occurred between 1997 and 2003, according to the Norwegian national authority for the investigation and prosecution of economic and environmental crime (Økokrim). In one of the fraud cases, Stuve and his shipping company defrauded another ship-owner for 60 million kroner. The other shipping company sued Tordenskjold, including Stuve, Hellevik, and Kolbjørnsen, and a district court decided that Tordenskjold had to return all the money (Hareide, 2006). Økokrim was of the opinion the ship management at Tordenskjold systematically defrauded the company for money for six years (Berge, 2010).

In addition to the three Tordenskjold executives Stuve, Hellevik, and Kolbjørnsen, their bank contact was also a defendant in court. Håkon Ingebrigt Roska, assistant bank manager at Finansbanken, which later became Storebrand Bank, was part of the same case complex. He received a jail sentence of seven months. Additionally, he had to compensate his former employer (Langberg, 2011).

Tor Johan Stuve graduated from the Norwegian School of Economics with a degree in business administration. He was active in the shipping and logistics group at the school. He invested in his first ship at the age of 26, in 1986. The court of appeals increased his prison sentence from one year and nine months to five years. On the other hand, Hellevik's sentence of five and a half years decreased to four years (Kleppe, 2012b). Clearly, the court of appeal considered Stuve, rather than Hellevik, to be the leader in the crime.

Susann Kolbjørnsen, the chief accountant, received a prison sentence of seven months plus two years' probation for violating the factoring pledge according to Norwegian penal code § 343, for accounting manipulation according to Norwegian penal code § 392, and for tax evasion according to Norwegian penal code § 371. What characterizes Susann Kolbjørnsen as an offender is, firstly, that she faced charges of fraud related to tax evasion and manipulation in accounting practices. Secondly, she committed these criminal offenses in her professional capacity as an executive at Tordenskjold. It was advantageous for her to have a significant position in the company, within a network where she held power and influence. Finally, she also had trust and legitimate access to resources to carry out and conceal the crimes. Due to Kolbjørnsen's high social status and belonging to the upper classes in society, the media extensively covered her case in their reports, focusing on her name and background. For instance, a newspaper featured on its front page the headline "Tordenskjold executives Tor Johan Stuve, Susann Kolbjørnsen, and Petter Hellevik are prosecuted for depleting companies, embezzlement, and serious fraud amounting to 100 million kroner."

The application of convenience theory to the shipping executive's bankruptcy fraud is depicted in Figure 8.4. Moral panic can result from exploring and exploiting illegal means of survival in the face of corporate collapse and bankruptcy (Chattopadhyay et al., 2001; Kang &

Thosuwanchot, 2017). In the current situation, the corporation's survival may become so critical that it cannot be ignored (Blickle et al., 2006). In order to recover from a crisis, fraud and corruption are sometimes seen as short-term solutions (Geest et al., 2017), where, when the crisis is over, the measures will come to an end. A crisis is a major threat to the organization that frequently has no clear cause, effect, or course of action (König et al., 2020).

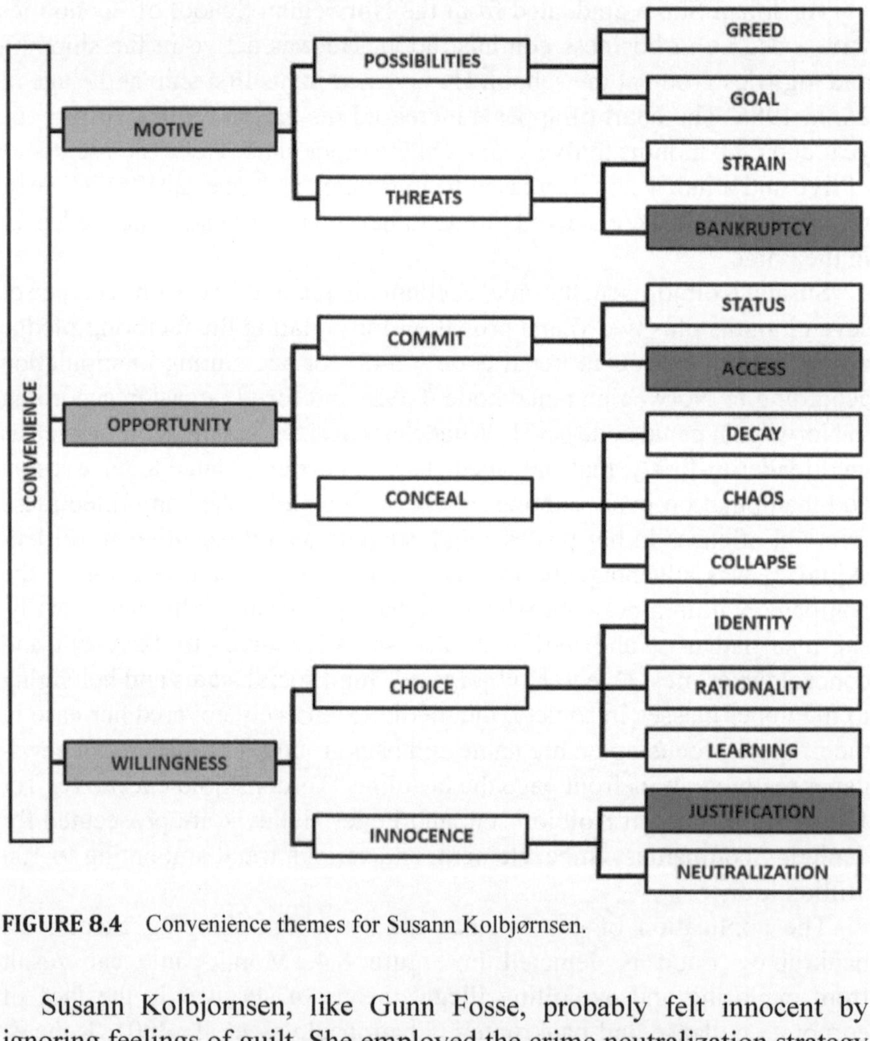

FIGURE 8.4 Convenience themes for Susann Kolbjørnsen.

Susann Kolbjornsen, like Gunn Fosse, probably felt innocent by ignoring feelings of guilt. She employed the crime neutralization strategy of higher loyalties. It fulfilled our expectations (Sykes & Matza, 1957). The offender claims that the act was done out of a sense of moral duty rather than self-interest. They target individuals with higher loyalty. Those who feel they are in a tough situation that needs to be addressed, even if it involves breaking a rule or law, tend to use this strategy. An employee might refer to the organization's values, hierarchies, or practices in such situations.

8.5 KINDERGARTEN FRAUD BY COMPANY OWNER

Nina Beate Tollefsen joined the cause when the Norwegian government guaranteed all parents with small children that their youngsters could expect admission to nurseries and kindergartens at subsidized prices in the country. It was part of the government's struggle for gender equality. To succeed with full coverage of kindergartens and nurseries all over the country, the government relied on private entrepreneurs to quickly build and run such service premises for children (Grindaker, 2011).

In fact, many more people than Tollefsen supported the national goal of providing all children with access to daycare. Soon, all kids could spend their days in a care facility close to their homes. Parents – sometimes the father, but more frequently the mother – deliver the child around 8 am, and pick up the child again around 4 pm, although most premises are open from 7 am to 5 pm. Sometimes grandparents pick up grandchildren, and they typically do it already around 3 pm to spend some time playing before handing the children over to their parents. Independent of the length of daily stay, the state has limited the monthly fee to no more than 3,135 Norwegian kroner (about 313 US dollars) per month. Most charge less, and the fee is lower for a number of groups, such as parents with several children in care premises, and parents with low income or disabilities.

It all works fine, except for one thing. The state does not allow childcare facility owners to make a profit. The owners should make sure to cover all their costs with the fee from parents, but they should not charge more than required to cover their costs. Therefore, what some of them do is to increase their costs artificially. They can increase their own salaries if they, at the same time as being owners, also work in the childcare as managers or in other relevant positions. They can increase the rent if they own the building. They can make private expenses look like childcare expenses. As a result, nursery and kindergarten owners have numerous opportunities for fraud in the professional setting (Grindaker, 2011).

The Norwegian national authority for investigation and prosecution of economic and environmental crime (Økokrim) charged Nina Beate Tollefsen and John Andrew McCracken with abuse of financial funds and fraud. The defendants were accused of overbilling their own companies with skyrocketing rent for childcare premises and in addition charging private expenses to the companies. Økokrim claimed in court that the married couple had swindled their daycare organization for 9.5 million kroner (950,000 US dollars).

By means of overbilling of premises rent as well as cash withdrawals, the couple had depleted their four childcare facilities in Oslo named Tusseladden, Stomperud, Sohaugen, and Opplandsgate, which all eventually went bankrupt. While the fraud was going on, one of the defendants also received disability pension and thus additionally faced charges of fraud against the social security agency for 800,000 kroner (80,000 US dollars).

The married couple owned several companies that operated childcare facilities in Oslo. The indictment was based on evidence that the couple, through fake invoicing of rent, cash withdrawals, and refund of private expenses, illegitimately charged the companies for 9.5 million kroner. The indictment covered a period of about six years, and the depletion of funding in the companies led to bankruptcies (NTB, 2012).

The indictment also charged the couple with social security fraud and conspiracy to commit social security fraud by providing misleading information. The couple kept secret that the husband, McCracken, had income that exceeded the monetary level and thus excluded the justification for social benefits from the state.

State prosecutor Espen Haug at Økokrim made the following statement about the case (Grindaker 2011, p. 13):

- This is a serious indictment in the sense that it has been committed financial infidelity against companies, which have received public funds to run kindergartens.
- We believe that the defendants have unlawfully taken away money so that it has harmed the operation of these kindergartens.

Tollefsen was sentenced to three years in prison, while McCracken, a white-collar criminal, was sentenced to two years and six months.

Tollefsen appears to have been the criminal's leader, but McCracken's role as a follower is unclear. According to Fehr et al., a follower has a belief in the morality of the leader's pressure, which can cause them to feel shame and guilt if they fail to support the leader (2015). Emotional regulation in leader-follower relationships was studied by Glas and Einarsen (2008) (Gottfredson et al., 2020). They discovered that, in contrast to expressing or faking positive emotions like enthusiasm, interest, and calmness, followers typically suppress negative emotions like disappointment, uncertainty, and annoyance.

Asker and Bærum district court included in their verdict confiscation of 4.5 million kroner (450,000 US dollars). The court deprived both offenders of the right to conduct business for five years and three years respectively. Again, there is a gender gap in seriousness where the court considered the female offense more serious than the male offense. Maybe the man with the English-sounding name was indeed a follower, and the woman with the Norwegian-sounding name was a leader. However, archival search has failed in exploring this possibility. The court sentenced them together to replace one million kroner to the bankrupt companies. Violations of the Norwegian penal law thus included bankruptcy crime, theft, and several types of accounting manipulation. Both were in the end convicted of social security fraud of 1.3 million kroner (130,000 US dollars) in Asker and Bærum district court (Asker Bærum, 2012).

The district court at Asker and Bærum wrote in their verdict about McCracken (Asker Bærum, 2012, p. 42):

> John A. McCracken has acknowledged criminal charges (negligence) for the matters. Based, among other things, on this acknowledgment, lack of accounting documentation, and the bankruptcy reports for the companies, the court finds it evidenced beyond any reasonable doubt that accounting in Stomperud Barnehage Ltd./NUF, Opplandsgt. Barnehage Ltd./NUF, Solhaugen Barnehage Ltd./NUF, and Tusseladden Barnehage Ltd./NUF in the period from January 2006 to the respective bankruptcy openings in 2007, was not updated in accordance with the rules in accounting legislation. Insufficient submission of supporting documents, inadequate accounting, and confusion in the companies' finances have made it difficult to process bankruptcy data and conduct auditing review. The circumstances, in isolation, constitute material breaches of the accounting act's rules. John A. McCracken as the formal and actual general manager of the companies intentionally committed the offenses.

This quote from a gender perspective is interesting. The man was the general manager, while the woman was probably the chairperson. Furthermore, the term Ltd. stands for Limited, which is a British abbreviation that is similar to Inc. in the United States, AG in Germany, and AS in Norway. Maybe the companies somehow had links to the UK where McCracken probably had a network of some sort.

Several years after his conviction in 2012 and following incarceration, McCracken emerged again in Norwegian media. Now he had taken the last name of Tollefsen as John Andrew Tollefsen. Although the court had deprived him of the right to conduct business for three years after release from prison, he had started a company offering summer camp to children. After a short while, his new company went bankrupt. He needed 750 registered children for financial break even, while only 10 children signed up for his summer camp (Krokfjord, 2017).

The married couple had astronomical private consumption compared to the average Norwegian. Their car fleet included Porsche 996 Carrera 4, Porsche 911 Turbo, BMW X3, BMW X5, Audi Q7, Mercedes ML63 AMG, and Mercedes S350. McCracken bought steadily new wristwatches of the type Rolex, Audemars Piguet, Omega, and Patek Philippe in the price range above 10,000 dollars. In 2005, the couple had a total debt of 31 million Norwegian kroner (Kleppe, 2012a), which is the equivalent of three million US dollars.

Nina Tollefsen attempted in court to say that she did not understand what was going on, and that she had trusted her husband. The court did not believe her and said in the verdict that even if the husband was the potential brain behind all wrongdoing, they had nevertheless cooperated closely and conspired in crime. Formally, Nina Tollefsen had her name registered as owner and chief executive in most of the companies, nurseries, and kindergartens.

The two offenders lived in a nice neighborhood outside Oslo in a mansion of considerable size. In 2020, they had moved to an apartment in Oslo. Nina Tollefsen was then chairperson and chief executive at a company named Pearl, which reported financial loss according to public records for registered organizations.

The application of convenience theory to the company owner's kindergarten fraud is shown in Figure 8.5. The motivation was individual avarice, just like Ragnhild Johanne Stuve. Status and having access to resources were the opportunities. The willingness was a rational and identity-based choice. Narcissistic identification is a type of narcissism that is similar to Ragnhild Johanne Stuve in that the perpetrator sees little or no difference between himself or herself and the organization. The business money is considered personal funds, to be used at the discretion of the narcissist (Galvin et al., 2015). Nichol (2019) categorizes grandiosity and admiration as part of the motivational aspect of convenience theory, while empathy deficit is linked to the willingness aspect of convenience theory, indicating a sense of entitlement on the part of the offender. According to Zvi and Elaad (2018), the offender displays unreasonable expectations for special treatment.

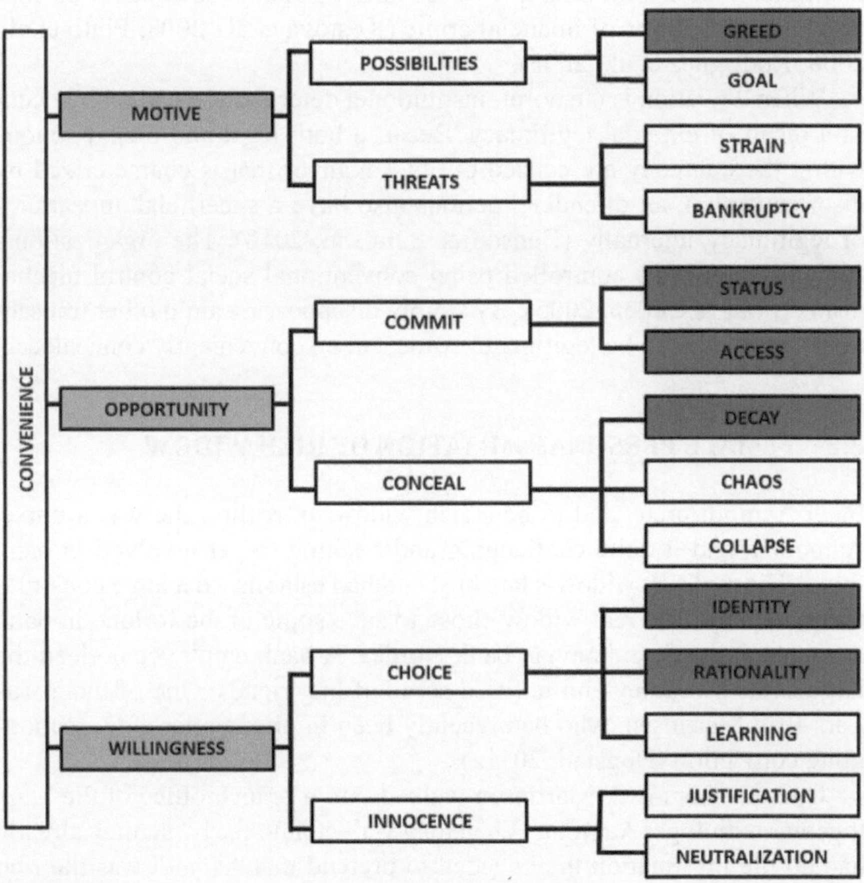

FIGURE 8.5 Convenience themes for Nina Beate Tollefsen.

Greed implies that the offender is never satisfied, as he, she, or the organization always wants more profit (Goldstraw-White, 2012). Greed represents socially constructed needs and desires that can never be completely covered or contented. There is a strong preference to maximize wealth for the corporation, possibly at the expense of violating the laws, rules, and guidelines. Economic greed is a strong motive for financial crime (Bucy et al., 2008; Hamilton & Micklethwait, 2006).

Nina Beate Tollefsen also had a convenient opportunity for the concealment of her offenses. Decay occurred in the form of institutional deterioration (Barton, 2004; Donk & Molloy, 2008). Institutions are the patterned, mutually shared ways that people develop for living together. Institutional deterioration improves conditions of convenience for corruption and other forms of financial crime (Kostova et al., 2008; Pinto et al., 2008; Rodriguez et al., 2005).

When deviation is the norm, institutional deterioration can easily occur as a result of external legitimacy. Because both legal and illegal actions within the company are carried out in a manner that is characterized by disorganization, an offender's actions also have a superficial appearance of legitimacy internally (Benson & Simpson, 2018). The organization's behavior cannot be controlled using conventional social control mechanisms (Pratt & Cullen, 2005). By simply disappearing amid other transactions that appear to be legitimate, crime can be conveniently concealed.

8.6 FEMALE PERSONAL IMITATION OF RICH WIDOW

Inger Aamodt pretended to be a rich widow. In reality, she was a nurse. Aamodt found it quite challenging and exciting to get involved in bank fraud. The real rich widow's late husband had established a large construction company. The real widow chose to save some of the fortune in bank accounts at the Scandinavian bank Nordea. A bank employee noticed the large sums of money and notified some of his friends. One of them was Lars-Erik Martinsen, who had recently been in prison after a drug smuggling conviction (Dugstad, 2011a).

One day Lars-Erik Martinsen walked into a branch office of the bank together with Inger Aamodt. When they walked into the bank, they already had all the information they needed to pretend that Aamodt was the rich widow. In the course of eight days, Martinsen and Aamodt were able to transfer 60 million Norwegian kroner (6 million US dollars) from the real widow's accounts to several accounts in Dubai. It was money that all belonged to the widow of the construction company founder. Her name was Randi Nilsen (Kapital, 2010a).

Since the bank fraud did not avoid detection, eight offenders ended up with convictions in the case. The sentence for Inger Aamodt was four and a half years in prison. The sentence for Lars-Erik Martinsen was four years and nine months in prison. Rolf Erik Fredriksen got a slightly more severe punishment of five years in prison. Fredriksen was the internal bank employee who detected the money and provided information about accounts to others in the network. There were people in the network on the receiving end in Dubai. Those people involved in the transfer and receipt of the real widow's money were Fakhir Munir (five and a half years), Usman Zahoor (five years and nine months), Edmond Thaqi (four years), Umar Zahoor (one year), and Sonia Rashid (one year and three months).

Sonia Rashid was the second female offender after Inger Aamodt in the network. She lived in Dubai and claimed that she understood the real widow wanted to buy property in Dubai. She refused to return to Norway to appear in court, so the Norwegian court sentenced her in absentia. She claimed that the money was gone and that she no longer had any control over it or any knowledge of where the money had disappeared.

The wealthy widow Randi Nilsen did not realize that criminals had emptied her bank accounts, first by 60 million kroner and then by 30 million. When the bank contacted her and inquired about the total transfer of 90 million Norwegian kroner (9 million US dollars) to Dubai, she said she had not noticed that any money was missing (NTB, 2011).

Nurse Inger Aamodt was on sick leave from her job. She stated in court that she only had a debt of 100,000 kroner. She disguised herself as the wealthy widow Randi Nilsen when she entered the Nordea branch office to transfer money to Dubai. Aamodt signed documents using Nilsen's name, allowing Martinsen from the bank to take over control of Nilsen's accounts.

Nurse Inger Aamodt said in court that she knew nothing about the bank fraud. However, some of her work colleagues recognized her in a picture from a surveillance camera in the bank. While she disguised herself as Nilsen, her colleagues were nevertheless certain that the woman in the picture was Aamodt. The judge trusted the witness statements and convicted Aamodt to prison.

Another piece of evidence against Aamodt was telephone contact between Aamodt and bank employee Rolf Erik Fredriksen at the time when the disguised Aamodt and Martinsen entered Nordea bank at Tveita in Oslo to approve disposition rights for Nilsen's accounts (Dugstad, 2011b).

The most important evidence against Aamodt was deleted photos that police detectives found on the computer belonging to Fredriksen. The photos showed a disguised Aamodt. One of the photos was on the falsified bank identity card that Aamodt used to obtain account authorization.

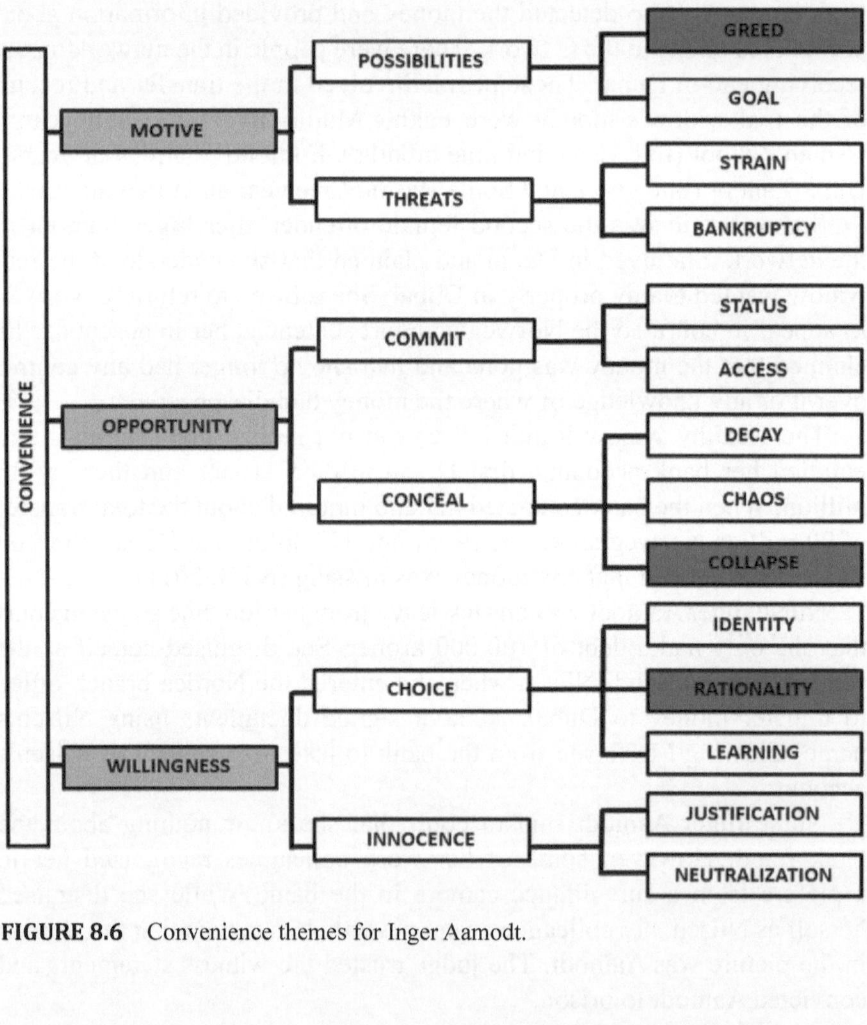

FIGURE 8.6 Convenience themes for Inger Aamodt.

Yet another piece of evidence against Aamodt, who denied involvement in the crime, was a recorded telephone conversation where Aamodt approved the transfer of a large amount of money from the offended Randi Nilsen's account to an account in Dubai. Aamodt and Martinsen had falsified the disposition rights for the offended Nilsen's account and registered Aamodt's phone number so that Aamodt could confirm transactions when the bank called her.

Figure 8.6 illustrates the application of the convenience theory to the personal imitation of a rich widow. The willingness of Inger Aamodt seems to derive from sensation seeking to experience adventure. It was a rational choice. According to Craig and Piquero (2017), some white-collar criminals' willingness to commit financial crimes is related to their desire for adventure and excitement. In addition to seeking exciting adventures and new, intense, and complex experiences, criminals also accept the legal, physical, financial, and social risks associated with these adventures. They attempt to avoid boredom by substituting thrills and adventures for routine activities like meetings. They despise monotonous situations and prefer risky and exciting activities.

Inger Aamodt was able to participate in a crime network (Goncharov & Peter, 2019; Nielsen, 2003) that potentially can conceal crime.

CHAPTER 9

Comparison of Iran and Norway

This chapter is concerned with women and white-collar crime. The general design is a comparative study of Iranian mafia and Norwegian offenders. White-collar crime is economic wrongdoing committed by privileged individuals in the upper social and economic elite in society. This chapter extends research on the gender gap among white-collar offenders. We suggest that the extent of gender equality determines or influences the fraction of female offenders. Traditionally, women represent a small fraction of convicted white-collar offenders. The gender gap has been explained by low female participation in privileged positions because of gender inequality. One empirical measure of the extent of gender inequality is the global gender gap index. In terms of gender equality in the country, Iran ranks 143 on the index for 2022, while Norway ranks 3 out of 146 countries. As a result, Iran and Norway are two extremes on the index, making a comparison study useful. A small sample of convicted offenders in Iran is compared in this chapter to a larger sample in Norway. Our results provide little support for the suggestion that the extent of gender equality can explain gender gap differences in white-collar crime rates. In addition to answering the research question – how do women and white-collar crime compare in Iran and Norway? – this chapter emphasizes research literature and news reports from Iran as little has been published so far about the phenomenon of white-collar crime in the Islamic Republic of Iran. The meat mafia, the sugar mafia, the tea mafia, and the steel mafia are all examples of white-collar crime in Iran. Primarily, "white-collar crime" refers to offenses committed by upper social and economic level individuals. The term was first coined by Sutherland (1939) and later applied by a number of scholars in their research (e.g., Gottschalk, 2022).

The Gender Gap in White-Collar Crime: A Multi-Country Study of Women Offenders in Economic Crime.
Maryam Kamaei, Petter Gottschalk, and Thomas E. Dearden (Authors)

Moreover, coined by Daly (1989a, 1989b), the term "pink-collar crime" refers to white-collar crime committed by women in the workplace. It is impossible to deny the significance of white-collar crime, particularly pink-collar crime, and the wide range of its effects on society's fundamental aspects. Therefore, significant attempts and cautious planning are required to monitor the committer's behavior in such crimes and their punishment (Simpson et al., 2022). In this chapter, however, we first examine whether white-collar crime in Iran and Norway is gender-neutral or gender-specific; subsequently, the differences between men and women in white-collar crime, and their roles in the crime are studied as well. The findings call into question the hypothesis that gender segregation in society and the workplace is the cause of white-collar crime rates because they indicate that white-collar crime rates are comparable in Iran and Norway. However, in terms of access to the labor market and other resources, the gender gap is not rooted in white-collar crime because of gender inequality; and Iran's women are likely to benefit from these outcomes. Therefore, white-collar crime in Iran is exemplified by the meat mafia, the sugar mafia, the tea mafia, as well as the steel mafia in Iran.

9.1 COMPARATIVE RESEARCH ISSUES

Economic crime committed by a person of respectability and high social status in the course of the offender's occupation is referred to as white-collar crime (Gottschalk, 2022). White-collar crime is defined as an offense based on the offender's social and occupational status. According to Sutherland (1983), white-collar crime is any illegal act that violates trust and responsibility for personal or organizational gain. Generally, in criminal science, middle-class wrongdoing types like extortion, defilement, and control are perceived as offenses perpetrated by powerful people in the work environment. In Iran, the term "deviant workplace behavior" refers to (Damghanian & Ghaleroudkhani, 2022, p. 158):

Negative behaviors like sabotage, tardiness without authorization, and theft are all examples of workplace deviance, which is the deliberate, malicious attempt to sabotage an organization by causing problems in the workplace. Anti-productive behaviors and deviant behaviors share a lot of similarities, and there are two categories of deviant behaviors: the deviant behaviors of an individual and an organization. The term white-collar crime is a criminological label that was first expressed by Sutherland (1939). Few jurisdictions have white-collar crime as a legal issue as the term "is basically a criminological term" (Mirkhalili & Khodadoost, 2017, p. 130). Rather, it is the underlying crime types that are subject to prosecution and conviction.

The term "pink-collar crime" was first used in the 1980s by criminologist Katie Daly to describe female employees in low- to middle-level positions like accountants, engineers, and managers who steal money from their employers. According to Kamaei and Abolhasani (2020), one of the most important aspects of white-collar crime is that Sutherland only considered men when it came to white-collar offenders 431):

> Sutherland's definition excludes women. Historically, women have been institutionalized through discrimination in customary laws and rights; they were prohibited from entering higher economic classes.

Historically, women were barred from entering higher economic classes because of institutionalized discrimination in customary law and rights according to Iranian researchers Kamaei and Abdolhassani (2020). Women in Iran face a set of legal and social barriers that limit not only their lives but also their livelihoods, resulting in gross economic inequality in their lives. Although women constitute more than 50% of Iranian university graduates, their labor force participation rate is only 17%. Iran is ranked 143 out of 146 countries on the Global Gender Gap Index 2022 in terms of gender equality. At the end of the index, Norway is ranked 3 as the third most gender-equality-oriented country. Equality is related to empowerment that reflects women's decision-making power (Noor et al., 2021). Hoodfar and Sadr (2010) discussed Islamic politics and women's quest for gender equality in Iran.

Ghaffari et al. argue that (2022, p. 1707), Iran is "a society with a strong conservative bent." According to Iran's strict Islamic laws, for instance, female bodies are not allowed in advertising. Government agencies must approve exceptions after reviewing each advertisement's design and narrative. Representative offices for censorship are located in all major cities by the Islamic Republic of Iran Broadcasting and the Ministry of Culture and Islamic Guidance. Furthermore, a study of the Gender Development Index and women's participation in Iran showed that the rate of women's economic participation increased in recent years; however, there is still a significant difference between participation rates of men and women. When examining "the index of gender development and increase in women's participation in Iran, it shows the rising economic participation rate of women, but there is still a huge difference between the participation rate of women and men" (Modarresi Alam et al., 2017, p. 111). Moreover, compared to men, the compliance of women is higher for various reasons. One of the most significant causes of men's higher rate of white-collar crime than women is the greater number of men in careers, particularly in operational and decision-making positions in organizations. In addition, it is generally accepted that women are more likely to engage in white-collar crime when they have more opportunities to engage in social activities. Dodge (2009), among others, addresses the issue, revealing that the greater the number of women in political, corporate, and economic positions, the more probable they are to be associated with middle-class wrongdoing. According to the background of the research on gender and white-collar crime, women are frequently the victims of white-collar crime and are rarely convicted (Robb, 2006). There aren't many significant criminological theories that include theories about white-collar crime. When explaining the statistics of crimes committed by women, some theorists, such as Pollock (1950), believe that official statistics show a lower number of crimes committed by women than is actually the case. This is because of the work that officials like judges and police officers do. According to Pollock (1950), women commit crimes at the same rate as men. However, women's criminal acts are frequently overlooked because few are willing to come forward (Jalilvand et al., 2017), and as a consequence of their relative difficulty, their wrongdoing remains hidden (Garrett, 1987). However, current research indicates that women are more likely than men to engage in white-collar crime, albeit at a lower rate (Daly 1989a, b; Benson & Gottschalk, 2015; Gottschalk & Glaso, 2013; Gottschalk & Smith, 2015; Holtfreter, 2015). Academics were encouraged to continue their research on gender differences in white-collar crime as a result of the findings (for instance, Benson & Harbinson, 2020; Dearden & Gottschalk, 2021; Galvin, 2020; Gottschalk & Gunnesdal, 2018; Goulette, 2020; Reese & Constantin, 2021; 2018 by Reese and McDougal; Ruhland & Selzer 2020; Stadler & Gottschalk, 2022).

While the gender issue in white-collar crime has been extensively discussed in the research literature, few scholars have empirically studied the gender gap. However, theoretical and anecdotal studies consistently claim that men are more likely than women to commit white-collar crime even when the latter group reaches higher social and career positions. Among empirical studies, Gottschalk (2012) found only 4% female criminals among white-collar offenders in Norway. This might be surprising, since Norway is an egalitarian society where the rights of men and women are almost equal. The country holds a low gender gap and ranks third on the Global Gender Gap Index.

At the other end of the index, we find Iran, which ranks 143 (out of 146 countries) in terms of the gender gap. The small sample of 19 white-collar offenders registered by Ghorchibeigi (2019) has only one woman criminal. As a fraction of all in the sample, the one woman represents 5%. Here we thus have the somewhat surprising result that the female fraction in a gender-equality country such as Norway has about the same female fraction of white-collar offenders as a gender-inequality country such as Iran.

The low fraction in Iran and other similar countries has traditionally been explained by gender-specific career and organizational positions, as well as the glass ceiling for women in organizations (Kolade & Kehinde, 2013). However, others have pointed to women's more law-abiding temperament and compassionate encounters in the criminal justice system compared to men. Moreover, some believe that women who reach higher positions in organizational structures are more likely to be noticed and controlled because of their uniqueness than their male counterparts, and they are less trusted in illegal activities.

The consideration of gender in white-collar crime thus represents evolving and challenging ground for study. Although there is literature on female offenders and their victimology, the data are inadequate. The male and female populations are somewhat equal in Iran and Norway, while gender equality and gender balance in the workplace are almost opposite in the two countries.

An interesting empirical finding relates to embezzlement, which refers to the unlawful misappropriation or misapplication of an asset that was entrusted to an individual (Ryan, 2021). Embezzlement involves the abuse of trust or fiduciary responsibility (Cardao-Pito, 2021). Paxton (2022) found that the statistics on pink-collar criminals are alarming: "According to the FBI, male embezzlers have increased only 4% since 1990, while pink-collar criminals have increased over 40% during that period." A similar finding is made in Norway, where the low female fraction of white-collar offenders is generally low, while the fraction of women embezzlers is quite high compared to men. It seems that embezzlement is the kind of financial crime that women mainly commit to the extent that they are involved in white-collar crime. Corruption, manipulation, and fraud seem to be less frequent among pink-collar criminals.

Sutherland (1939) was the first to define white-collar crime; however, there is considerable debate on the definition, which we shall address: "individuals of higher social classes are more likely to commit criminal behavior; and such behavior differs from the criminal behavior of the lower social classes in existing administrative procedures in dealing with offenders; however, administrative procedures are not very important in the cause of the crime" (Hammond, 2018, p. 40). Accordingly, the crime is defined by the position of the offender; nevertheless, it should be defined as a law based on a criminal act. For instance, under the laws of the Crown Prosecution Service in England and Wales, when a murderer commits murder, the act is defined as the illegitimate murder of a person with the intent to kill. Therefore, Sutherland's definition does not state which behaviors fall into the category of criminal acts, nor does it explain the aggregation of crime under this definition. In Sutherland's time, white-collar crime could easily be associated with men, as only a few women were found in high-status jobs, and their years of absence as criminals were attributed to lack of opportunity. However, since then, although the glass ceiling has been removed in many countries such as Norway, enormous changes have taken place as an increasing number of women are now found in senior positions in business, politics, and professional groups, and as entrepreneurs. It is often asked whether this has led to the emergence of a new white-collar female criminal: the pink-collar criminal. Could women at the top be more aggressive, dishonest, and ready to sacrifice ethics in pursuit of promotion and profit? (Croall, 2003). However, the question is also whether the white-collar crime definition should be changed.

In the study of white-collar crime, the main distinction is between the offender and the offense, and thus the criminal and the crime, where the former is characterized by high social and economic status, while the latter is characterized by illegitimate financial profit (Salimi, 2009, p. 239):

> The most important manifestations of white-collar crimes are: fraud, corruption (including bribery), employment offenses, consumer offenses, drug and food offenses, environmental crimes, cybercrimes, and customs offenses.

Secrecy is an important feature of white-collar crime; this means that the offenders do not disclose their illegal activities; rather, they attempt to legitimize and justify the acts. Moreover, white-collar offenders are opposed to blue-collar and dirty-collar ones, and are politically, economically, or socially influential, and they are likely to be distinguished "by their appearance, which is usually in the form of a dark suit, white shirt, and tie" (Salimi, 2009, p. 245). White-collar crime is a financial crime committed by those with privileged positions such as chief executives in business jobs and public organizations (Dearden & Gottschalk, 2021; Gottschalk, 2022). Moreover, white-collar offenders steal billions of dollars in largely undetectable ways: counterfeiting, embezzlement, and fraud, to name a few. White-collar offenders are "far more dangerous," and the consequences of the crime they commit are "wider than others" (Nasiri, 2014, p. 7); furthermore, these offenders straightforwardly "affect the national security of the country" (Monazamitabar, 2009, p. 141).

A pink-collar criminal is a female white-collar offender who abuses her job position to commit and conceal financial crimes such as embezzlement, corruption, or fraud for her benefit or that of her professional association (Daly 1989a, b; Gottschalk & Glasø, 2013; Hammond, 2018; Paxton 2022; Rohall, 2019). The pink-collar criminal belongs to the elite of society; she is a person with high respect and social status who has access to resources and commits and conceals a crime during her professional activities. White-collar crime is a financial crime committed by privileged individuals in a professional context in which offenders benefit from legitimate access to resources (Logan et al., 2019).

In criminology, however, the dominance of men in almost all forms of crime is one of the most consistent empirical findings (Benson & Gottschalk, 2015). The gender gap in crime is not uniform; it varies according to the type of crime as exemplified by embezzlement. Men are highly dominant in committing brutal street crimes that involve violence, such as murder or robbery, while women are more likely to commit minor financial crimes, such as shoplifting or embezzlement.

In Norway, Benson and Gottschalk (2015) reported that women constitute only 7% of white-collar offenders while the rest are all men. Moreover, Estrada et al. (2019, p. 145) argued that the gender gap in registered crime is narrowing; "the fact that men commit far more crimes than women is one of the main findings of criminological research." Similarly, Messerschmidt (2013) suggested that gender is an important predictor of criminal involvement because men dominate criminal acts. Holtfreter (2015, p. 422) found that "the gender gap in crime – the superfluity of men in all official seizure statistics – has narrowed in recent decades and is significantly lower for white-collar crimes." Consequently, as gender equality increases, women are expected to become more involved in white-collar crime; particularly if gender equality is reflected in the improvement of economic status and career opportunities for women.

Traditionally, the gender gap reflects recognized insights into white-collar crime. What makes gender studies even more stimulating is the potential gender gap in the way women are compared to men. According to a review of the research literature in Norway, Gottschalk (2019) estimated the relative detection risk for women versus men at only 30%, which indicates a 3% and 9% chance of detection for women and men, respectively; this is because Gottschalk and Gunnesdal (2018) found that only one in 11 white-collar offenders discovered in Norway is prosecuted and imprisoned. Consequently, when there is only a 9% chance for men, then there is only a 3% chance for women if the relative detection risk for women is only 30% (Gottschalk, 2019). However, one of the potential causes of hypothetical and estimated gender gaps in crime detection is the amount of money involved in white-collar crime. In the Norwegian sample studied by Benson and Gottschalk (2015), the average economic benefit from crime for female offenders was lower than for male offenders. The average economic profit of women in pink-collar crime was 9 million Norwegian kroner, which is slightly less than US$1 million. Furthermore, the average economic gain for men was US$50 million, which is approximately $5 million. Accordingly, the crime outcome for male offenders was more than five times higher than for female offenders.

In criminology, traditionally, white-collar crime describes work-related offenses committed by individuals in high positions. The offenders of these kinds of crime are called white-collar criminals. Sutherland's (1939, 1983) definition is abnormally based on the status of the offender rather than the offense committed. A murderer commits murder, an aggressor commits rape, and a fraudster is convicted of a crime in which a person uses deceptive means to deceive the other party and thereby seize another's property, the condition of which is financial gain. However, crime types are those that are defined as such by law; but should white-collar crime only include cases that are defined as crime or should it also include other prohibited non-criminal acts? Indeed, Sutherland suggested that white-collar offenses should include a range of behaviors, including criminal and administrative offenses. Newman (1958) suggested that the white-collar crime definition is so broad that it includes any crime committed during the career. However, not all theorists agree that white-collar crime is different from other kinds of crime. The general theory of crime emphasized that offenders (including white-collar criminals) are those who express antisocial behavior and do not conform to the norms of society. Moreover, their behavior may be explained by two causal principles (Gottfredson & Hirschi 1990). This general theory of crime predicts that white-collar criminals are both versatile (experienced) wrongdoers and as perverted as street-level offenders, they reject the motive (as a causal factor) and the white-collar-crime label to distinguish these offenders, including, street criminals.

Criminologists, among other researchers, deal with different types of white-collar crime to better define the types of offenses. However, it is suggested that white-collar crime seems likely to divide into two categories of crime committed in the workplace: crime committed in favor of (a) an employer from whom participants may gain personal benefit or avoid personal loss; and (b) oneself, to achieve personal gain or avoid personal loss. The former may be described as a corporate offense (e.g., the crime involves securities fraud). The latter may refer to a professional crime with a personal interest that is often labeled occupational crime (e.g., members of the legal profession include mortgage fraud, inflated expense fraud, or theft from clients' accounts). However, what is common in (a) and (b) is that these offenses are committed by individuals at the time or during their work for a profit. Furthermore, they cannot commit the crime without being present at work and having access to work resources; and what distinguishes it from street crime, which may include taking property from another, is place and location. While the street offender disappears from the scene while the crime is visible, the white-collar offender remains on the scene while concealing all traces of wrongdoing (Benson & Simpson, 2018).

A report by Corston (2007), who studied how women are treated in prisons, concluded that when women feel vulnerable (in family, personal, social, and economic matters), they are more likely to be in crisis and engage in criminal activity. For many prisoners, crime is a simple response to a crisis. However, the report showed that women commit different kinds of crime than men; "women usually commit acquired crimes and are less involved in violence and professional offenses" (Corston, 2007, p. 6).

White-collar crime, as research confirms, is a male-specific crime; in other words, most white-collar criminals are men. This specific feature is more prominent in societies such as Iran, where "women have traditionally had fewer opportunities to participate in economic and financial activities" (Ghorchibeigi, 2019, p. 234). In each society, the scope of white-collar crime is varied and expanded according to the existing economic and social conditions. Just a few years ago, nevertheless, there was a debate on the profits of billions by white-collar people from the Iranian economy, such as meat, sugar, and steel mafia.

The definition of mafia and white-collar people is more complete in the way that mafias are those who, by force of communication and more awareness, go the way of 100 years overnight and pocket billions in profit. Examples of these mafias in Iran are referred to in this research. As argued by Esfahani et al. (2022, p. 595) in the Iranian context, "the most important assets of any organization are employees that are loyal and satisfied." The importance of loyalty and satisfaction is certainly true as well for members of any mafia organization in Iran. The role of women in mafia organizations is typically to take care of legal activities as exemplified by the classical mafia organizations in Italy where women can be in charge of the legal garbage collection company in the city owned by the mafia, while men can be in charge of arms and drug trade. Very seldom, women in mafia activities can be identified, where an exception is the woman in Iran who led a network that stole sheep and smuggled them to buyers across the Persian Gulf (Bourse & Bazar, 2019).

9.2 IRANIAN MEAT AND SUGAR MAFIA

The existence of a meat mafia in Iran was mentioned in Iranian newspapers and cited by Bourse & Bazaar (2019):

> The existence of a "meat mafia," which is the source of much of the turmoil in meat markets, is the subject of an investigative report that was originally published by Iran Newspaper and was republished by the ISNA news agency. The newspaper claims to have seen documents indicating that one of the businessmen received more than EUR 35.5 million in subsidized currency. However, he distributed the product after calculating the prices based on the free-market exchange rate, thereby causing prices to rise by 92%.

In an interview with ISNA, Afshin Sadr Dadres, chief executive officer (CEO) at the Central Light Livestock Union of the country, commented on the meat mafia (Nikru News, 2022):

> He stated that hot meat should reach consumers at a price of 140,000 tomans per kilo, and said: "Meat mafias will not let the price of meat go down so that they can continue importing, and the some will eventually reach the eyes of the consumer."

The currency in Iran is rial where 10 rials are one toman. In 2022, one US dollar had an official exchange rate of 42,000 rials and thus 4,200 tomans. The kilo price cited above of 140,000 Iranian tomans is thus 33 US dollars. Similar to Afshin Sadr Dadres, Jalal Mahmudzadeh, vice chairman of the Agricultural commission had referred to the meat mafia two years earlier (Tabnak, 2019):

> After this comment, many media started research on rent in the import and distribution of imported meats, and this story of rent reached its peak in Paish program on Channel One TV on February 28, 2017. In this program, several exemplary entrepreneurs were present, and one of them made a stormy speech about the powerful red meat import mafia.

Meat is one of the basic goods that has been captured by the mafia in Iran for several years. When the price of meat became expensive and no institution or official could bring it back to its previous price, the discussion of the meat mafia became more prominent and the traces of the presence of white-collar offenders in the import and distribution of meat were felt more strongly. The first person who disclosed the most about the meat mafia was Nader Ghazipour, a member of parliament. Ghazipour has been a representative of the people of Urmia in the Islamic Council for two terms. He made revelations in the parliament about the increase in the price of chicken and meat. At that time, Ghazipour stated that the identity of the meat mafia is very clear and warned against the importation of flour by these persons, and claimed that he and his family are among the biggest bank debtors of the country and in the Agricultural Bank despite knowing about this matter (Akhbar, 2012).

Regarding the price of chicken, at the same time as the price of this product increased, it was opened to the hands of the mafia. Ghazipour continued his revelations and explained the story as follows (Quds, 2012):

> What I asked from the Ministry of Commerce, they said that they gave the soybean meal to the union instead of giving it directly to the farmers. The union also sold this soybean meal to the factory owners at a free price instead of giving it to the farmers. Previously, this price varied between 600 and 800, which suddenly increased to more than 1,700 and 1,900 tomans. That is, the men earned more than 1000 tomans per kilo.

Bourse and Bazaar (2019) reported that "Iranians (were) forced to forgo meat staples as prices soar":

> Common Iranians could anticipate a generous feast of meat stew or kabob no less than one time each week. In any case, with meat costs taking off to all-time highs, Iranians need to scale back their utilization in one more instance of falling expectations for everyday comforts as Iran's economy flounders under the tension of authorizations and bungle (…)
>
> The fast expansion in the cost of meat has been accused of different variables, including corruption, exploitation, and abuse of hard cash endowments allowed to shippers (…)

However, more damagingly, the falling value of the rial and the availability of foreign currency at an artificially low cost lured many traders into smuggling out livestock or imported food in large quantities to neighboring countries, where they found a lucrative market, causing shortages back in Iran. In countries such as Iraq, bootleggers could sell livestock and double their investment.

From a gender perspective, it is interesting to note that Bourse and Bazaar (2019) mentioned a woman:

> In one reported case, a group led by a quiet middle-aged woman took sheep from villages in the southwest of the province of Khuzestan, loaded them onto trucks, and smuggled them to slaughterhouses across the Persian Gulf.

Sugar is one of those products that always generates a lot of discussion and is also in the public eye. Like other mafias, the sugar mafia is secretive, meaning no names of this mafia are published, and they are unknown to the public (Quds, 2012). This is because no one has the ability to deal with mafias. However, once, the president mentioned the existence of the sugar mafia among the people of Qom. It was on one of the Thursdays of 2017 that 10 traders and importers of raw sugar raised the price of each kilo of sugar by 50 tomans in a meeting held to collude in the hoarding of this product.

At the end of 2021, the trade association of Iranian sugar factories had warned about the efforts of some brokers and middlemen to reduce the sugar import tariff to zero. Despite all these warnings, in the first two months of the year, to support national production, the amount of sugar imported into the country increased to 680 tons. People were confused.

In recent years, the name of a person named M.Y., or Mohammad Reza Yousefi, was used in circles as the Sugar Sultan of Iran. The case of Sultan sugar can be considered the most famous economic corruption after another 3,000 billion tomans corruption case. Some people called him M. Mohammad Reza Yousefi faced serious allegations of rent-seeking, land-grabbing, fraud, and bribery. Due to his major role in the buying and selling of sugar factories, and his influence in the import and export of this commodity, he was nicknamed the Sultan of Iran's Sugar by the media. After that, he was known by this name more than his real name. The accused, who was a simple employee of Karaj municipality until 16 years ago and did not have much property, but according to some, at the time of his arrest, he was the owner of property worth hundreds of billions of tomans.

According to Moj (2019), Mohammad Reza Yousefi was sentenced to 26 years in prison and ordered to repay 73 billion tomans. Some years earlier, Etemad (2011) newspaper had his name in the headline "Sultan Sugar of Iran died before the end of his sentence." He had been just a simple municipal employee, but he succeeded in taking over government lands and lands whose owners lived abroad, making billions in wealth for himself.

When sugar workers went on strike at an Iranian state-owned company, the workers blamed the sugar mafia (Anon, 2007):

> The workers claimed that a "sugar mafia" was operating in the country and had the government under its control. While many sugar-producing companies were facing bankruptcy, the private sector and the government were making significant profits from importing sugar.

Bazaar (2022) interviewed one of the major sugar distributors. He mentioned that dealers and mafia members sometimes caused disturbances in the market, taking advantage of such situations. The price of sugar could be characterized by fluctuations where the sugar mafia benefited from the ups and downs. In the neighboring country Pakistan, "the sugar mafia had threatened Prime Minister Imran Khan as well as the then DG FIA/Chairman of the Inquiry Commission, Wajid Zia, to stop the probe into the sugar scam" (Abassi, 2021).

9.3 IRANIAN TEA AND STEEL MAFIA

From the end of the 1970s and the beginning of the 1980s, strange things happened in the Iranian tea industry. The tea organization was dissolved, the smuggling of tea into the country increased, and the changes progressed to such an extent that since then there were whispers about the existence of a tea mafia in the country. The first spark was struck in 1982 by Tahmasab Mazaheri, the then Minister of Economy, when he exposed the 4-person case of the tea import mafia. He even went to Sri Lanka to prevent the illegal import of tea, and an agreement was signed with the authorities of this country regarding the legal import of tea to the country for mixing with domestic tea for consumption or export. But 3 months after returning from this trip, he was dismissed from the position of the Ministry of Economy, and naturally this case was also placed in an aura of uncertainty (Eghtesad, 2013).

However, in an effort to clarify the dimensions of tea smuggling into the country between 1995 and 2004, the Sixth Parliament prepared a research report on the country's tea industry. In this research and investigation, the liberalization of tea, tea smuggling, the quality of smuggled goods entering Iran, the type of processing of Iranian products abroad and their reimport as smuggling, tariff evasion, and dozens of other issues were investigated (GWW, 2009).

Iraj Nadimi, the then representative of Lahijan in the parliament, who was the designer of this investigation, has interesting words about this after six years have passed. He talks about the pressure of the mafia of power and wealth on the Ministry of Health (Lahig, 2010):

> The Ministry of Health used to prevent adding essential oil to tea, which in my opinion is an example of the pressure of the mafia of power and wealth, because under the title that essential oil is carcinogenic, they prevented that. The tea can be processed inside and thus they created two opportunities for themselves. One is the opportunity to sell to foreigners so that they can add essential oil and the second is the opportunity to

> import the type of tea with essential oil. Abbreviated names such as (A, C) and (A. L) ended well, so that it is not clear what is the matter of the tea mafia? A mafia that, according to Seyed Mohammad Gharavi, is one of the activists of the tea industry makes 250 billion tomans in profit annually.

Unfortunately, as argued by Tabnak (2010), the process of increasing the import of strategic products to the country was such that it set the stage for the increase of game brokers and the formation of large-scale mafias. Tea is another strategic product that was caught by the mafia. The first time was Tahmaseb Mazaheri who brought up the tea import mafia. At that time, Mazaheri disclosed the case of 4 people of the tea import mafia, but after his dismissal, the case of these 4 people is in a halo of ambiguity until now.

Steel is another profitable product that attracts the attention of many people, but currently steel is mostly in the hands of white-collar people who even elect the bosses. There are many economic benefits hidden in the various stages of iron ore extraction and its conversion into steel, and access to the country's virgin mines is one of the rents that the country's steel mafia has planned to dominate these resources in recent years.

Mashreqh news claimed that the violations in the 1,000 billion tomans tender and the way of selling the country's steel products are the most prominent violations by the steel mafia. It is also said that the violations in the country's steel sector have been supported by certain political currents on the one hand and influence in various departments of the Ministry of Industries on the other hand, so that the people appointed to key positions have a clear track record in financial and economic issues (Afkar, 2012).

However, with the rapid growth of white-collar crime, the millipede of corruption quickly penetrated the large areas of profit and threatened beneficiaries' securities; so that generations and decades may have to dissect the dimensions and complexity of white-collar aspects in Iran. However, there will remain unresolved issues, since white-collar crime in the country is not limited to embezzlement, bribery, fraud, or forgery of documents, as mentioned in classic textbooks. Rather, there is widespread corruption in profitable national resources and other areas such as oil, gold, land grabbing, forestry, seafaring, environmental degradation, food fraud, consumer rights abuses, and employment and customs violations (Sooreisrafil, 2017).

According to the Moj news agency, in late December and early January 2016, the news of the arrest of a super-debtor was reported. At first, the name of this person was mentioned as "R.D.," but with a little more detailed investigation, it was found that his exact name is Rasool Daniyalzadeh. After a short period of time, the officials of the judicial system confirmed the arrest of this person, and the spokesperson of the judicial system also stated that the investigation of his case has begun. In this regard, it was found that Daniyalzadeh has a large bank debt in his case, which some estimated to be more than 2600 billion tomans (Moj, 2019). According to the reporter of the legal-judicial field of the social group of the Young Journalists Club, Rasool Daniyalzadeh was convicted for the crime of forming a corruption network and was sentenced to 15 years in prison with a reduced sentence due to returning to the country after filing the case (Vic, 2020).

In all the Iranian newspapers cited, people like Rasool Daniyalzadeh (Iran's Steel Sultan) and the late Asadullah Asghar Oladi (Iran's Sultan of Dry Goods), Abbas Irvani (Sultan of Automobile Parts), Seyed Moein Barani Behbahani (Sultan of Porsche and Textiles), Bagheri Dermani (Sultan of Bitumen and Real Estate), Modalelha (Sultan of Sugar), Vahid Mazloumin (Sultan of Currency and Coins), Asadolah Asgaroladi (Sultan of Dry Bars), Khandan Garami (Sultan of Car Imports), Mohsen Ahmadian (Sultan of Petrochemicals), all of them are men and none of the perpetrators are women (Rooziato, 2020). Therefore, most white-collar criminals in Iran are obviously men. This matches the Norwegian sample of 329 people, which included only 22 female criminals and 307 male criminals (Benson & Gottschalk, 2015).

9.4 GENDER GAP RESEARCH METHOD

While there is substantial research published regarding white-collar crime in countries such as Australia, Germany, the Netherlands, Norway, the United Kingdom, and the United States, there is almost nothing regarding white-collar crime in countries like Iran. Therefore, the previous pages provided important insights into the Iranian situation that is characterized by a variety of mafia organizations. As documented, very few women can be found in the mafias in Iran. Women tend generally to play a very different role in mafia organizations compared to men, where women may be in charge of legal activities while men can be in charge of illegal activities (Grønningsæter, 2022).

As already emphasized in this chapter, women are generally less likely to commit white-collar crime labeled pink-collar crime. This difference was called the gender gap by Steffensmeier and Allan (1996). Gender gaps have always been a hot topic in discussions of women's crime. When it comes to criminal activity, women are distinct from men; they are treated differently, just like everyone else. Distinctions in sexual orientation and the connection between financial aspects, disparity, and wrongdoing over time were analyzed by crime analysts. Oakley (1974) and other feminist scholars criticized the methodology based on the masculine current and the application of objective determinism, which is a deductive or positivist approach. In addition, this is referred to as the paradigm argument.

Löschper (2000) argued that "crime is constructed and addressed through social discourses and processes of social interaction in control institutions; therefore, it is only a qualitative examination of the crime that makes sense" (Hammond, 2018, p. 49). An alternative way to investigate women's crime is a qualitative approach; because in this way, we can explain why women commit white-collar crime, not why women commit fewer offenses than men. For instance, Elliott (1952) argued that the formation of women's gender roles and socioeconomic factors may explain the low crime rate among women. Criminal statistics, which support the commission of less crime by women, have questionable credibility in this perspective, where reporting crime in the form of statistics should have three criteria that women's offenses often lack, namely: 1) to harm society; 2) hold a general nature; 3) involve the victim's cooperation with the law. However, women's offenses are more specific than men's. Moreover, victims of female offenders are often children, husbands, lovers, or family members. Compared to men, however, Hammond (2018, p. 50) found that "her criminality starts later, comes to a peak later and lasts longer than man's," and "double standards, modern sales techniques, and the social frustration of women's position in society contribute to the crimes."

Pollock (1950) posited that female crime was primarily sexually motivated, while male crime was largely economically motivated, with the exception of crimes of passion. He argued that women were given preferential treatment at every stage of the criminal justice system, arising in part from men's 'chivalrous and paternalistic regard for women,' allowing for fewer arrests, less prosecution, shorter sentences, and a lower rate of incarceration than male offenders (Virk, 2011, p. 104). Pollock (1950, p. 73) observed that:

> Female criminality deserves more research attention than it has received, regardless of how insignificant its numerical importance may appear based on criminal statistics taken at face value (.) The lack of scientific attention to the problems presented by women offenders is probably due to the recurrent observation that significantly smaller numbers of women come into contact with law-enforcing agencies than men (.)

Pollock (1950) also stated that "the issue of women's crimes has been ignored in research," and "the lack of scientific attention to the problems of female offenders is probably because women have less contact with legal institutions than men," as well as "women's crimes require further investigation, even if the number of female offenders is not statistically significant" (Hammond, 2018, p. 53).

The research method in the present study is descriptive-analytical. In this method, in addition to depicting what is, the researchers describe and explain the reasons for the existing situation and compare it with other conditions. Collecting information using library studies is a form of archival investigation. In this method, the literature and records of the problem or research subject are studied. As a result, the outcomes of the studies are recorded and stored using appropriate tools, such as receipts, tables, or forms, and at the end of the work, findings are classified and used. According to the research findings, the final analysis and conclusion, the last stage of the research was based on the library method. In library studies, collecting sources and data, legal books, opinions, and opinions of jurists, articles published in the journals of domestic and foreign reputable scientific institutions have been referred.

The Norwegian data are based on a content analysis of white-collar crime articles published in Norway's two largest financial newspapers: "Finansavisen" and "Dagens Næringsliv." These two publications are conservative business publications. This study also included the business-friendly national newspaper "Aftenposten," which regularly reports on white-collar criminals. In view of media reports, court archives were recovered for each sentenced middle-class guilty party. Benson and Gottschalk have looked at the data in these newspapers and court documents. This feature enables the Norwegian study to be comparable to Iranian studies and the cases under review because it is restricted to cases that have been successfully prosecuted (Benson & Gottschalk, 2015). From 2009 to 2012, the three aforementioned newspapers were looked at to find stories about cases of white-collar crime. Of the 162 cases found during the detailing time frame, we recognized a sum of 329 middle-class lawbreakers. 60% (98) of the 162 cases involved just one person. There were 64 people involved in other cases, ranging from 2 to 16, with an average of 3.5 people per case. Out of 64 cases connected with a crook organization, 50 cases were all-male organizations and 14 cases were mixed-gender organizations. No all-female network existed.

The subject of study in Iran, which was done by Ghorchibeigi (2019), is judicial documents that include 19 cases related to white-collar offenders in the city of Tehran, the capital of Iran. Judicial cases were filed by documents in the prosecutor's office or court and led to the issuance of indictments. The way of selecting these documents was in such a way that information was gathered by referring to the enforcement branches or criminal courts or investigation branches in many prosecutors' offices and courts in Tehran and by studying the aforementioned cases. The selection of studied samples has been completely purposeful. Firstly, the judges have been talking about the topic and context of the investigation, and secondly, the cases in question have been reviewed. The cases were studied in brief and if they were in accordance with the mentality and objectives of the research, they were studied in more detail.

The research method in most of the archival studies in Norway has been conducted by the field method, while the research method in this chapter is analytical and descriptive. Field research in certain subjects, especially in the case of women, faces many limitations. Due to several problems, it is not possible to interview white-collar criminals in Iran. Access to convicted white-collar offenders is difficult in Norway as well and outside the scope of this research.

9.5 GENDER GAP RESEARCH RESULTS

Overall, white-collar crime in Norway is not gender-neutral and, like in Iran, is dominated by men. Of the 329 individuals in the data set, only 22 (6.7%) are female (Benson & Gottschalk, 2015). This figure is surprisingly similar to the ratio of women in the Iranian data set that was analyzed by Ghorchibeigi (2019) with 1 out of 19 women offenders (5.3%). Therefore, the result of gender, at least concerning white-collar crime, shows that the level of participation of Norwegian women is quite similar to that of Iranian women. Although our data do not allow us to determine the importance of Norwegian women's participation in white-collar crime being lower than or equal to that of women in Iran; however, the figures reported from the Norwegian Statistics Center are proof of this claim. It should be noted that in 2005, women made up approximately 22% of all those charged with economic crime. In a study in Iran, out of a total of 19 cases examined, roughly 94% of the offenders were men and only one was a woman, who was an employee and responsible for the credit of a bank.

And the way she committed it was that because she was responsible for the credits of one of the bank branches and according to herself there was trust in her, the customers who paid their installments in cash, without doing the perforation, received the receipt, signed and sealed and took the deposited amounts for herself or if someone paid his installments late, she took the late amount for her own benefit and to hide the date of payment of the installments on or before the due date has hit. Even in one case, when the accused could not provide the amount required to collect the check issued by him, she claimed that "to protect his reputation" and "that I was sure that my wife would pay me within an hour" provides the amount of the check from the funds available in the bank.

Another point is that the accused expects the bank and the court to withdraw from the complaint and punishment due to her gender. Also, the accused is worried and scared about the punishment that is going to be determined for her and more widely about her fate after the conviction and stated:

> "I am a woman, and I am asking you to forgive me and forgive me for my faults and punish me financially."

This shows that the accused also believed that others did not think of her as a criminal because of her "being a woman" and did not think that she could commit embezzlement. She was very concerned so that she stated:

> "I made a mistake, like an unscrupulous and shameless person, I messed up the bank accounts and books. Have mercy on my husband, have mercy on my son, my husband doesn't know and if he finds out, he will get very angry and get a divorce."

The Iranian pink-collar offender had education at the same level as the 18 male convicts. She deposited the embezzled money at another credit institution in her brother's name without the brother knowing about it:

> "I deposited the education amount in an account with one of the financial and credit institutions in my brother's name and used it to pay my installments."

Similar studies also show that the share of women in relation to corporate and occupational crime is insignificant, although the share of bank embezzlement by women is much higher than other kinds of occupational crime. The results of one of the important studies in this regard (Kathleen Daly's study on gender and white-collar crime) are also consistent with the findings of this research, so that this research claims that: a) The contribution of women in organizational and corporate crime was insignificant, b) The share of women in all types of occupational crime has been insignificant (although in relation to bank embezzlement, this share was 50%), c) Women are less likely to commit crime in groups and are more likely to commit white-collar crimes alone, d) The average earnings from committing white-collar crime by women are lower than the amount of earnings from crime committed by men, and e) Women more than men refer to the issue of family financial needs as a motive for committing white-collar crime (Daly, 1989a, b).

Among the studied cases in Iran, "manipulating the invoices or forging documents" was the most common method of committing a crime, particularly at the level of occupational crime committed by employees (approx. 42%). Establishing a fraudulent company and agency is another fraudulent way of committing such crime (about 26%). Along these lines, the offenders incited the victims to invest by creating incentives for the victims (e.g., earlier or cheaper delivery). However, encouraging investment, false propaganda, abuse of organizational or legal authority, and pretending to influence administrative authorities are considered other techniques of deceiving the victims.

Among the 19 studied cases in Iran, 31.6% occurred in the public sector. The cooperative sector, and especially housing cooperatives, for various reasons, is another unsafe sector. In the public sector, nevertheless, the perpetrators were all employed in the financial sector or government agencies. Furthermore, other cases are those committed in the private sector (approx. 52.6%). In the private sector, finance employees and board members commit most offenses. However, "opportunity" (Benson & Simpson, 2018) seems to be the most influential factor in committing these offenses.

In conclusion, we challenged in this chapter the assumption that more gender equality will lead to more crime equality between women and men in society. We found no support for the suggestion that a country like Norway with a strong degree of gender equality will have a significantly larger fraction of female offenders labeled pink-collar criminals, and we found no support for the suggestion that a country like Norway with a strong degree of gender inequality will have a significantly smaller fraction of offenders labeled pink-collar criminals.

More interesting than shedding light on various white-collar mafia activities in Iran that cannot be found in Norway. We presented in this chapter valuable insights into the meat mafia, the sugar mafia, the tea mafia, as well as the steel mafia.

Our finding of no link between gender equality and the female fraction of white-collar offenses supports the focal concern hypothesis rather than the emancipation hypothesis. Gendered focal concerns can inhibit criminal behaviors in females in the corporate context (Steffensmeier et al., 2013). The focal concern hypothesis is concerned with gender differences in interests and priorities. The worldview of gendered central concern battles that ladies associate into tolerating sustaining job commitments that underline the significance of social connections and communalistic directions toward others. Women develop identities as caregivers as a result of the way these responsibilities are absorbed. Benson (2020, p. 10) defined gendered focal concern in this way:

> The gendered theory of focal concerns suggests that there are sociological and social-psychological differences between men and women that make it harder for women to engage in crime compared to men. Men and women have distinct focal concerns that influence their behavior and interactions. Women are often expected to fulfill nurturing roles, show affection and care towards others, and approach relationships with a cooperative and sharing attitude. On the other hand, men's focal concerns are influenced by an individualistic and competitive approach to life, valuing autonomy, dominance, control, and risk-taking. The nurturing and cooperative nature of the female role in society makes it challenging for women to justify engaging in criminal activities, which are often harmful or exploitative. In contrast, the competitive and aggressive

nature of the male role, while not explicitly promoting criminal behavior, may be more aligned with it, especially in financially motivated crimes or those driven by a desire for advancement or protection.

The gendered focal concern suggests that women will commit less crime. An example is research by Gupta et al. (2020), who studied chief financial officers (CFOs) in terms of gender and financial statement irregularities. When governance is poor, it was found that businesses with female CFOs tend to have a lower risk of financial misreporting compared to similar businesses with male CFOs. The focus on gender isn't solely based on individual identity but can also be influenced by social identity. From a social identity perspective, when a person identifies as a woman and part of a specific group, they gain resources and pride from this membership, boosting self-esteem. This leads to a greater likelihood of group members, in this case women, adhering to and safeguarding existing norms. The processes of interpretation and identification are intertwined. Therefore, women uphold established norms based on their experiences and the value they place on being a woman (Huang et al., 2020).

9.6 IRANIAN MAFIA CONTEXT TERMINOLOGY

The term "mafia" has been used in this chapter to describe organized crime within meat, sugar, tea, and steel fraud in Iran. The term is chosen since it is commonly applied in the Iranian context within the country. As much more is known about the white-collar crime context in Norway (e.g., Benson & Gottschalk, 2015; Dearden & Gottschalk, 2021; Gottschalk, 2012, 2019, 2022; Gottschalk & Glasø, 2013; Gottschalk & Gunnesdal, 2018; Gottschalk & Smith, 2015), this chapter has emphasized the Iranian context where the term "mafia" is frequently used.

Of course, when the term "mafia" appears, then many people think of Camorra or Cosa Nostra as well as the associated criminal families in Italian cities. However, the current state of Iran's courts – especially in the area of economy – points out that the mafia has shown its ugly and violent face. Although the official view has not shown much interest in addressing the issue of mafias, this neglect has certainly not led to the elimination of their crime. Mafia in Iran is known as organized crime.

Just like the term mafia has various definitions, so can the term organized crime have different meanings. Characteristics of organized crime in the Iranian context include preparation and commission of crime by a methodical organization that often "provides means of livelihood for its stewards" (Borricand et al., 1998, p. 316), benefits not only accruing to the stewards (the perpetrators of the material element of crime) but rather mainly go to coordinators as white-collar offenders where "perpetrators do not even know enough about them" (Salimi, 2003, p. 177), and existence is based on "creating fear and corruption" (Farani & Seydi, 2021, p. 60). Furthermore, organized crime is "the illegal and coordinated activities of a coherent group of people who, in collusion with each other and for the purpose of obtaining material benefits and power, engage in serious criminal activity and use any type of criminal means to achieve their goals" (Shams-Nateri, 2004, p. 111).

In the criminal law of the Islamic Republic of Iran, in the context of the concept of organized crime, Article 130 in the Islamic Penal Code has the following message: Anyone who is the leader of a criminal group shall be sentenced to the maximum punishment of the most severe crime committed by the members of that group in line with the goals of the same group (Najafi & Rahimi, 2018). This is different from Norwegian law, where a criminal can only be convicted of the crime the person has committed and not crimes that others have committed, even when the person was the leader of the group. However, in Norwegian law, an offender can receive a more severe punishment in terms of incarceration length if the offender committed the crime together with others with whom similar offenses were committed in the past.

The terminology is interesting. For example, moharebeh refers to waging war against God, which implies criminal acts against the government. Furthermore, mofsed-fel-arz means spreading corruption on earth, which can be applied to political crimes such as treason. Similar to Norwegian penal law, the Iranian penal code does not punish a criminal organization (Gyoki, 2022).

When there is discussion and debate about current issues and social problems, even in the state and quasi-state media in the Islamic Republic, it is rare that the word "mafia" is not mentioned. Today, "mafia" has become one of the most explanatory terms in the official literature of the Islamic Republic. If it is about football, the people involved talk about the football mafia to explain the situation and point to corruption. If it is about publishing problems, the people involved talk about the paper mafia. In the discussion of overdue loans, people talk about the loan mafia. In the case of high prices on meat, they turn to the meat import mafia. At some point, there were 35 meat importers. However, most of them were in the same families and networks, thereby reducing the number of independent importers drastically.

Some of these mafias are better known and are mentioned more frequently in public conversations and in the media (football, sugar, rice, and oil), while some are less known (paper, gold, drugs, land, medicine, meat, saffron, entrance examination schools, corn, cars, and antiques).

While scholars who have left Iran may express all kinds of opinions about the country, it is certainly more interesting to notice what scholars inside Iran identify as four issues related to mafias:

- **Centralized, Exclusive, and Anti-Competitive System:** When the sugar mafia is mentioned, it means that a significant part of the sugar imported into the country comes through this mafia; or when the car mafia is mentioned, it means those who control a high percentage of car imports.
- **Mass Interests Concentrated in These Groups:** In this sense, mafias are groups that take a significant part of the country's resources.
- **Government Rentier and Customer-Oriented System:** Those who use this expression indirectly want to say that there is a rent distribution system in the country that only selects certain people and groups as clients and asks them for support in return. The wheeling and dealing of managers cause preferential treatment of selected people.
- **The Secrecy and Non-Transparency of the People Who Benefit From the Rent System:** This is why fact-oriented media constantly want to reveal the names of people who are present in the mafia circles.

In our gender perspective, two mafia verdicts are of interest. The first verdict involved 30 people accused of disrupting the economic currency system of Iran. Among the defendants, there was one woman: Sodeh Shahraki. Therefore, the female fraction was 3.3%. The other verdict involved 45 defendants also accused of being economic disruptors in Iran. Among the defendants, there were two women: Fatemeh Shamani and Samaneh Haazrati Ashteyani. Therefore, the female fraction was 4.4%.

Fatemeh Shamani was convicted to five years of imprisonment. The organized crime was led by Mohammad Emami who, according to court records, exerted influence through Shamani on her husband who issued bank guarantees and facilities for the benefit of certain companies. Fatemeh Shamani was thus aiding in the disruption of the country's economic system.

Samaneh Haazrati Ashteyani was a former employee at Mellat bank who was convicted of betrayal of trust and acquisition of property through illegal means. She was convicted to endure six years of imprisonment and permanent exclusion from government services. Again, the verdict was a matter of disruption of the economic system of the country.

While court records could not be retrieved for Sodeh Shahraki, another female convict emerged. It was Pari Yadisar. Her case was heard in nine hearings, and the preliminary verdict was issued, but at the time of writing, it was in the Supreme Court for appeal, and the final verdict had not been issued. The case had 22 defendants led by a former manager at Capital Bank. All of them were prosecuted by Tehran's General and Revolutionary Prosecutor's Office, accused of participating in disrupting the country's economic system through disrupting the monetary and banking system. Pari Yadisar was accused of participating in nine counts of trust violation. She was also accused of ignoring others' trust violations. The relevant legislation was Article 37 of the Constitution of the Islamic Republic of Iran and Article 4 of the Criminal Procedure Law. She was one out of 22 defendants and thus represented 4.5%.

9.7 IRANIAN MAFIA CONVENIENCE THEMES

White-collar offenders' most common motivation for financial crime is greed at the individual level of possibilities (Bucy et al., 2008; Hamilton & Micklethwait, 2006). According to Goldstraw-White (2012), greed is defined as socially constructed needs and desires that can never be fully satisfied. Greed can be a strong desire to acquire more of something and a strong preference for wealth maximization. To pariahs, it might appear to be weird that rich individuals hold onto such areas of strength to turn out to be considerably more extravagant that they will overstep the law. However, as the definition suggests, greedy people are never content with what they have because they constantly yearn for more. Flourishing isn't a method, but an objective for eager people. When an organization fails to respond appropriately, greed can grow (Haynes et al., 2015). The following convenience proposition seems relevant for the Iranian mafia as indicated in Figure 9.1:

> As personal greed increases, financial crime will seem more convenient for a privileged individual in a trusted position.

An example is Reza Hamzelou, who was officially appointed as the CEO of Petrochemical Trading Company in March 2008. In the same year, he was also appointed as a member of the board of directors of Semga (Cultural Heritage and Tourism Investment of Iran). Among his other jobs, we can mention being a member of the board of directors of companies such as Fam Aluminum Manufacturing and Industrial Group Company, Tehran Silk Corridor Sustainable Development Company, Engineering Design and Supplying Parts and Chemicals Company for Petrochemical Industries, Petrochemical Transportation Company. Mr. Hosseini, representative of the prosecutor, said in court (Moj, 2019a, 2019b):

> The performance of the defendants as managers of petrochemical companies indicates that despite the correspondence of the officials and managers of the Ministry of Oil to prevent any interference and seizure of export products, they did not pay attention and tried to take it for their own benefit. In fact, the defendants did not import foreign currency from the sale of petrochemical products into the country, and by confiscating the foreign currency from exports, they deposited it into the accounts of their companies abroad, including Deniz, and their managers received commission or profit from this transfer.

Greed defined by Sajko et al. (2021, p. 961) as "an excessive materialistic desire to acquire personal wealth," is clearly seen in this case.

High goal commitment facilitates unethical behavior by increasing not only the motivation to achieve the goal but also the motivation to justify doing so by any means necessary (Locatelli et al., 2017). This is known as state moral disengagement, a process through which individuals justify unethical behavior (Moore, 2015) and disengage morally (Theoharakis et al., 2021). It is part of the dark side of ambitious goals. Therefore, the following hypothesis seems relevant for the Iranian mafia as indicated in Figure 9.1:

> As commitment to ambitious business goals increases, financial crime will seem more convenient for a privileged individual in a trusted position.

The main activity of the 13th tier defendant of the Hadi Talia Sani Petrochemical case was to identify needy and addicted people in order to obtain a full power of attorney from them regarding the identity of these people for company registration and other actions including banking affairs in line with the goals and interests of the Hassan Yavari network. The meat, sugar, steel, and tea mafia are among those who have a high social status and are in contact with the government's first-tier people, as they commit their crime through rent. In the petrochemical case, people bypassed the sanctions with the permission of the government, but instead

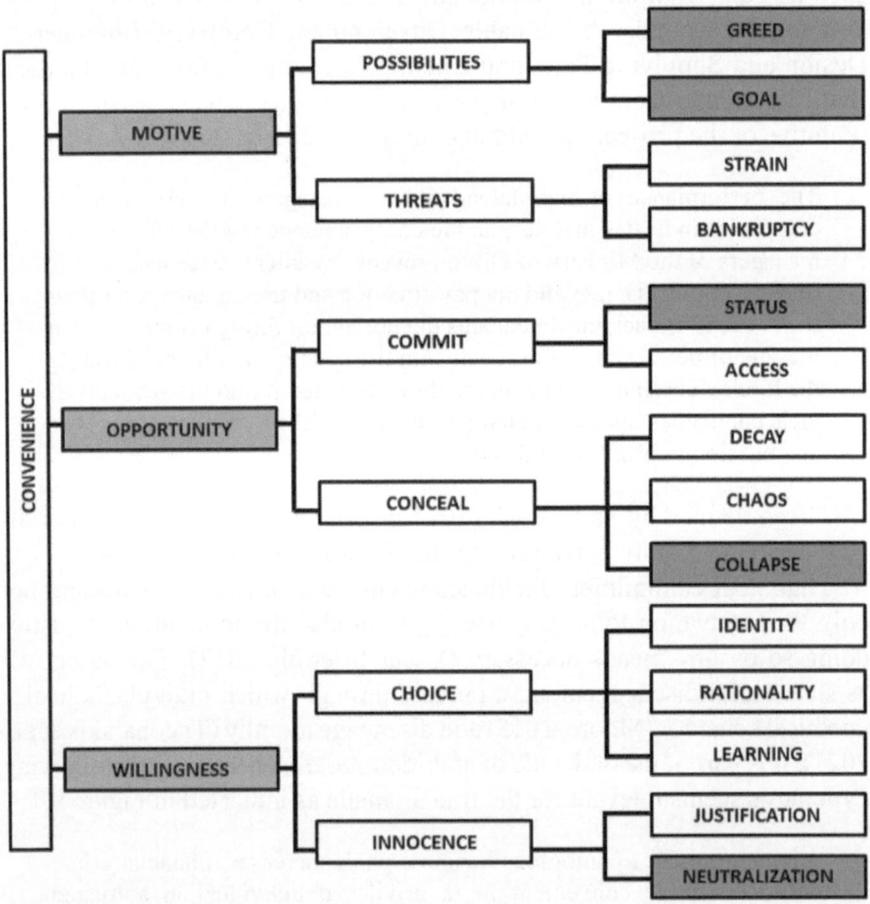

FIGURE 9.1 Convenience propositions for the Iranian mafia.

of depositing money for the benefit of the government, they took it for themselves based on greed.

The central column in Figure 9.1 illustrates the opportunity to commit and conceal wrongdoing (Gottschalk, 2022). Fukuyama argued that modern economic life requires trust in society (Zainabadi, 2008, p. 9). Trust is the acceptance of vulnerability to another's actions. Kim et al. (2009, p. 401) defined trust as "a psychological state comprising the intention to accept vulnerability based on positive expectations of the intentions or behavior of another." Spiekermann (2018, p. 291) found that all economic transactions depend on a certain degree of trust, without which transaction costs would simply be too high for economic activity:

> White-collar criminals abuse the good faith of various stakeholders, from customers to the general public, from shareholders to the authorities. Therefore, white-collar crime often coincides with the breach of trust.

This trust is sometimes in the individual and sometimes in the organization. In the research of Ghorchibeigi (2019) regarding white-collar offenders, many cases have been based on abuse of trust. In one case, a person established an investment company, displayed the company's letterhead and minutes, and performed fraudulent maneuvers to gain public trust. He had attracted people to invest. In another case, a person by creating a fake agency of one of the major domestic automobile companies, because he was a former employee of this company, was able to deliver the car below the official price of the factory and earlier than the scheduled time. In this way, he was able to defraud 33 billion tomans from about 9 people.

But in the case of the Iranian mafia, the core of the trust between the mafia and the government is that the government gave the mafia powers to circumvent international sanctions, but they abused these powers for their own benefit.

This means that the administrative system, due to the existence of defective laws and centralism in government institutions, allows statesmen, politicians, and other power holders to enter into financial corruption relations sometimes legally (rent) and sometimes illegally (Isna, 2018). Therefore, our studies are compatible with the following convenience proposition as illustrated in Figure 9.1:

> Higher social status for a privileged individual in a trusted position is associated with greater convenience in committing financial crime.

Participation in criminal networks can be attractive (Nielsen, 2003), especially if criminogenic market symptoms cause markets with crime forces to be the usual way of doing business (Chang et al., 2005). Therefore, Figure 9.1 indicates support for the following convenience proposition:

> Market collapse caused by rule complexity, cartels, crime networks, state reluctance to intervene, and other factors is associated with greater convenience in concealing financial crime for a privileged individual in a trusted position.

The opportunity to commit white-collar crime can be defined as follows: Individual and personality factors of the perpetrators and conditions, situations, or in criminological terms, opportunities that lead some people to deceive others or abuse the trust of other people or organizations for their own benefit under the title of internal and external causes in the occurrence of economic crimes in Iran have been explained. Economic criminals are very socially compatible with society, and in addition, the leaders of organized crime, the most dangerous state in terms of the four standard rankings in criminology, are known as the "dangerous state" (i.e., the worst state). Among the internal causes, we can mention the weakness of policy making and legislation, the weakness of executive policies, and the shaky actions of the executive branch, as well as the weak treatment of the judicial branch in the past years. Also, the most important external influencing factor is sanctions and restrictions on Iran's economy. This factor is important in our research because the public and private sectors are forced to turn the country's economy around by doing things like export and import in different ways, which are, of course, out of the ordinary. It seems that many cases of economic crime in recent years have been affected by the restrictions created through sanctions. The formation of secret companies and institutions in the name of individuals and even in the name of foreign partners has caused the loss of national capital and the transfer of the country's income to personal accounts. Among the most obvious examples, we can mention the 2 billion dollar oil embezzlement cases, the 124 million dollar oil rig, and the petrochemical case with more than six billion euros (Hatmi et al. 2018, p. 99).

> The market collapse, influenced by factors like rule complexity, cartels, crime networks, state reluctance to intervene, and others, is linked to the increased ease of concealing financial crimes for a privileged individual in a trusted position.

The central column in Figure 9.1 illustrates that willingness can be based on choice and innocence. Choice is a conscious decision to commit a crime, while innocence is a perception of lacking a role in wrongdoing (Gottschalk, 2022). The impression that surprisingly few white-collar criminals believe they have done anything wrong is the focus of personal willingness. When they are charged, tried, convicted, and sentenced, the majority of them feel like they are innocent and have been wronged. They deny responsibility, injury, and victim by employing neutralization strategies (Sykes & Matza, 1957). They denounce the perpetrators. They say they can get people to be more loyal and act normally. They argue that they are entitled and that the law was broken. They are okay with making their own mistakes. They assert that they were faced with a dilemma and had to make a reasonable tradeoff before committing the crime (Jordanoska, 2018; Kaptein & Helvoort, 2019). These claims make it easier for criminals to commit crimes because they do not see them as crimes and do not feel guilty about them (Cullen et al., 2021). Subsequently, Figure 9.1 demonstrates support for the accompanying accommodation suggestion:

> A conveniently positioned individual in a position of trust with a stronger ability to deny guilt is more willing to engage in financial crime.

The case of the oil mafia is one example related to the abuse of sanctions during the previous period of American sanctions. Unfortunately, during a time when top officials of the Iranian regime and the people of Iran were resisting the illegal sanctions imposed by the United States, certain individuals, including some bank managers, abused their powers and permissions. The government had granted some individuals and managers authority to find ways to bypass the sanctions, enabling them to sell oil and other goods, and deposit the proceeds from these sales into the government's account. These privileged individuals had a significant responsibility to address the sanctions and were required to find appropriate solutions for the sale and transfer of Iranian oil and other goods, as well as to transfer the funds from exports back to the country. They misused the assets and resources for personal gain or for others. Also, the defendants in this case claimed that their actions were aimed at solving the country's problems in order to evade the cruel sanctions, which have been encouraged by the country's security authorities. In the petrochemical case, Reza Hamzelou has repeatedly used the evasion of sanctions as a defense in the court hearings. They deny any crime by justifying that the money was temporarily kept in their company's account and then transferred to the government's account.

9.8 IRANIAN GENDER CONVENIENCE THEMES

Gottschalk (2022) has developed the theory of convenience to explain white-collar incidents. The theory suggests three dimensions of financial motive, organizational opportunity, and willingness for deviant behavior. There are fourteen convenience propositions as illustrated in Figure 9.2.

Prosecuted pink-collar offenders as defendants in court expressed various financial motives for their crimes. "How can you live with this low salary?" "I was under stress due to a dispute with the bank manager." "I had to save my reputation." "I started entrepreneurship, but the implementation problem and the obstacles created by the investor prevented me from doing the work." There was a "financial crisis." The need arises from the "low wages" of employees, so that as an employee, she has to commit financial occupational crimes, including embezzlement or accepting bribes to support daily life. This need can sometimes be due to financial pressures such as high treatment costs for a family member. It can also be caused by a person's lack of financial confidence. Ghorchibeigi (2019) found that economic motives were typically reactions to need rather than greed. Therefore, the strain perspective is marked in Figure 9.2.

Prosecuted pink-collar offenders as defendants in court expressed various organizational opportunities for their crime. "I had a creditor's check," one defendant said that the financial system of the bank is an integrated and large system, and what is important in this system is that nothing seems withdrawn or deducted from bank accounts. If money is taken out of the bank account for only a few hours or days and then returned to the bank account, there is no notice or loss to the bank. "Given that the mechanized and computerized system has been popular for several years, therefore, most of the employees of government agencies with these systems are not familiar." "I used to add salary lists of colleagues in the

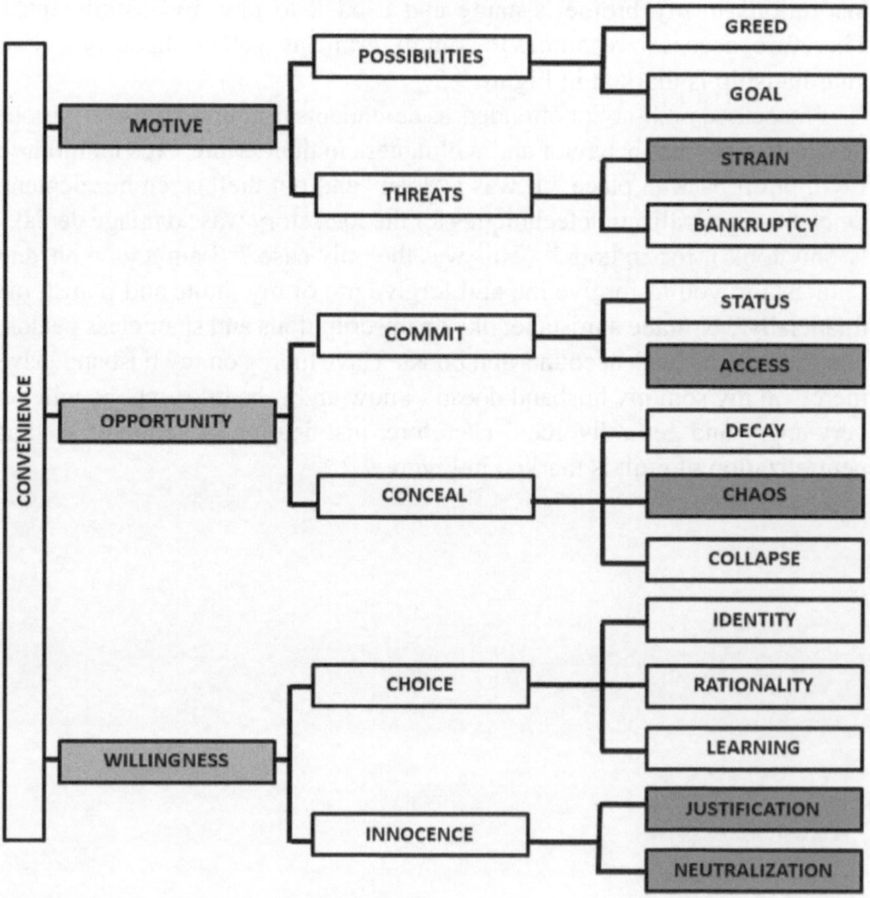

FIGURE 9.2 Convenience propositions for the Iranian pink-collar offenders.

computer and deposit the extra amounts to a personal account." "For the customers who paid their installments in cash, I would just sign the receipt and hand it over to the customer, then I would deposit the amount into my account, and in order to hide the date of payment of the installment, I used to make it before or after the due date." A person who was an employee of a government company entered the price of goods purchased for the organization higher than the actual amount by forging invoices and stamps, and after securing credit, took the extra money for own benefit. Another convict deposited embezzled money at another institution: "I deposited the education amount in an account with one of the financial and credit institutions in my brother's name and used it to pay my installments." Therefore, access to resources to commit crime as well as chaos by lack of guardianship is marked in Figure 9.2.

Prosecuted pink-collar offenders as defendants in court expressed various reasons for deviant behavior and willingness in their crime. "It's temporary; I will put it back in place." It was a "loan" and not theft or embezzlement. One of the neutralization techniques for the loan story was "damage denial." "I only took it for an hour." "This was the only case." "I am a woman, and I am asking you to forgive me and forgive me of my faults and punish me financially." "I made a mistake, like an unscrupulous and shameless person, I messed up the bank accounts and books. Have mercy on my husband, have mercy on my son; my husband doesn't know and if he finds out, he will get very angry and get a divorce." Therefore, justification of action as well as neutralization of guilt is marked in Figure 9.2.

CHAPTER 10

Female Cyber Offenders

There is no doubt that technology is connecting the world more and more, as more devices connect to the internet each day (Cisco, 2019). Accompanying this increase in technology is crime committed online. These new connections are creating opportunities for crimes such as hacking, online fraud, identity theft, spamming, and cyberbullying (Ngo & Jaishankar, 2017). However, a question remains as to whether this online crime or cybercrimes are also white-collar crimes.

This chapter establishes how white-collar crime and cybercrime can sometimes overlap. Specifically focusing on this book, we then consider how gender has been and continues to be important in cybercrime. Much like white-collar crime in general, cybercrime has a gendered history with an explicit tie to males. Finally, we consider the potential convenience dimensions that may be part of cybercrime and help explain some of the gender gap in cybercrime.

10.1 ONLINE CRIME DIVERSITY

Crime committed online, often referred to as cybercrime, can be classified in two ways. Crime which existed prior to the internet but the online space has provided a new medium (e.g., illegal drug trafficking) or new crime which was not possible before the internet (e.g., spreading malware) (Wall, 2010). Much like white-collar crime, there are a myriad of different cybercrimes with some not easily being distinguished as cybercrimes or not. One way to think about cybercrime is to consider the wide variety of crimes that it encompasses. Wall (2001) suggested several categories of cybercrime, including cyber-trespassing (e.g., hacking), cyber-deception/

The Gender Gap in White-Collar Crime: A Multi-Country Study of Women Offenders in Economic Crime.
Maryam Kamaei, Petter Gottschalk, and Thomas E. Dearden (Authors)

theft (e.g., stealing trade secrets), cyber pornography (e.g., obscenity violation), and cyber violence (e.g., online stalking or bullying). In many instances, researchers start by using the generic cybercrime term but focus their research on one specific crime (e.g., online bullying, hacking, identity theft). General definitions of cybercrime most often include crime which is facilitated by a computer (Ngo & Jaishankar, 2017).

White-collar crime definitions are not universal, and researchers must choose a specific definition when engaging in their research. Although debated, we largely focus on Sutherland's original definition of white-collar crime. He belongs to the elite in society where he enjoys legitimate access to resources. He commits financial crime in the course of his occupation. He is a person of respectability and high social status who commits crime in the course of professional activities (Craig & Piquero, 2017; Friedrichs et al., 2018; Logan et al., 2019; Schnatterly et al., 2018; Sutherland, 1939). In considering whether a cybercrime or criminal act is white-collar crime as well, we must consider when these definitions overlap.

Certainly, there are situations when cybercrime is not white-collar crime. As mentioned by Wall (2010), many crimes which were once offline have new elements online. Drug trafficking, even when done online now, is likely not a white-collar crime. The same can be said of traditional hacking, where an interested juvenile uses the family computer to access computers, servers, or other digital locations they are not supposed to have access to. In this case, we are missing both an organizational component and legitimate specialized access. However, in some instances, cybercrime is white-collar crime. The most prototypical examples include unhappy insiders, individuals who leverage their legitimate access to commit crime for personal benefit. The following is an example from Greitzer and Frincke (2010, pp. 1, 2):

> John, a company's long-time system administrator, is now a problem employee. Although the manager has received numerous complaints from coworkers about him consistently arriving late, he has never really caused any trouble in the past. As a result, the manager decides to write John a letter of warning for missing work last week. John talks to his manager after receiving the warning, loses his composure, and storms out of the office, calling to apologize later. The manager of John decides to blame his recent divorce. Additionally, the manager is aware that John may be harboring some resentment following his rejection for a promotion last month; John complained to Human Resources that the manager

> had been unfair to him, and the manager had to talk to him. During this time, John was stopped for driving under the influence a few weeks ago, according to the company's Security Office, which checks the local arrest records every day. After a few months have passed, John's divorce and DUI legal fees have left him struggling financially. He refused, citing his loyalty to the company, when a rival company approached him about a lucrative deal if he would obtain confidential company secrets for them. John now decides that he must entertain the idea because, in addition, he believes, "They owe me for not giving me that raise and promotion."

This crime would certainly fit both the definition of white-collar crime and cybercrime. The key component is the leverage of legitimate access. Individuals who work for organizations often have increased access to company information or money, especially as they move to higher positions of power. It is this access that allows them to commit white-collar crime. For example, it is the access that John had to trade secrets that allowed him to sell them, much like it is the access to money that allows someone to embezzle.

Although not every cybercrime is white-collar crime, there is enough overlap that it is worth considering the opportunity of cybercrime, especially as it relates to gender.

10.2 GENDERED COMPUTER USE

Historically, crime committed while using a computer has been stereotypically gendered, with young males being the perceived "hackers" (Alper, 2014; Thomas, 2002). Yet more recent evidence suggests that online crime is not only committed by males. However, the extent of female cybercrime is debated, with some studies finding males committing a higher proportion of cybercrime (e.g., Barlett & Coyne, 2014; Hinduja, 2007; Toupin, 2014) but others finding the opposite (Kowalski & Limber, 2007; Marcum et al., 2012).

Absent from much of the cybercrime work has been a consideration for gender as a moderator of theory. As mentioned earlier, the earliest media portrayals of hackers were almost exclusively male (Alper, 2014). Even today, the most famous hackers are all males. These include Kevin Mitnick, the hacker who inspired War Games, Kevin Poulsen, who hacked the Pentagon's ARPANET as a teenager, and Adrian Lamo who leaked sensitive US documents. Yet not all cybercrimes have been characteristically male-only.

One example of a crime that includes female cybercriminals is a romance or dating scam. These scams have emerged as the digital version of a paper-based scam, where criminals build an intimate relationship via the internet. They eventually request money claiming a dire situation such as unexpected hospital fees or travel expenses. In reality, the con artists simply steal the money, ending the relationship. While the victims are equally likely to be male and female (Whitty & Buchanan, 2012), in truth we don't know that offenders have a similar ratio. While the offender could have appeared as a female, their actual identity offline could have been male. Perhaps one reason for the underrepresentation is that females are also underrepresented in cybersecurity careers generally (Peacock & Irons, 2017). Estimates suggest that only between 10–15% of cybersecurity jobs are filled by females (LeClair et al., 2014; Reed et al., 2017). A number of different hypotheses have been presented for why this could be. These include the general "nerdiness" of the computer-based career (WSS, 2013), the socially constructed violent language around technology (e.g., data error) (Sanders, 2005) or a lack of familiar encouragement (Denner, 2011).

10.3 CONVENIENCE DIMENSIONS

To our knowledge, only one study has directly examined convenience and cybercrime. Braaten and Vaugh (2019) examined cryptocurrency crime litigation and convenience theory. Cryptocurrencies are a new form of digital currency that utilize blockchain technology to create a ledger of "coins" and transactions. These coins are often quite volatile (Karif, 2017) and are the preferred currency for many nefarious online transactions, including illegal drug sales.

Braaten and Vaugh (2019) argue that individuals who influence and artificially inflate the value of cryptocurrencies can be considered white-collar criminals as they utilize their power or positions of trust to defraud others. In essence, they are providing deliberately misleading information to potential investors. This is similar to other white-collar crimes such as penny-stock fraud and even Ponzi schemes. The crimes associated with such activities, as analyzed by the Braaten and Vaugh study, include operating unlicensed money transmitting businesses and/or money laundering, commodities fraud, securities fraud, creating bitcoin scams, bitcoin exchange fraud, and other crimes related to bitcoin, as well as owning, administering, or selling on the dark web.

Within the study, various convenience dimensions were considered. Naturally, these crimes are profit-driven and include a combination of opportunity and motivation. The opportunity is generally more available as anyone with a moderate degree of computer knowledge can create dark web websites and help market lesser-known or long-shot cryptocurrencies. The opportunity is increased by the concealment offered from layers of security. Both the websites on the dark web and the cryptocurrencies themselves are often difficult to trace or track. The authors conclude that "Defendants in various schemes were motivated by financial gain, either for the company or for personal use. Their roles and positions in the businesses allowed them to access resources that helped them perpetrate fraud against clients, investors, stockholders." (p. 17). Although much of the analysis is about law, they suggest that the framework of convenience is useful in understanding the motivation of cryptocurrency offenders.

Although only one study examines cybercrime and convenience theory directly, convenience theory is an integrated theory and includes components from other theories. There are numerous studies that examine the motivation of cyber offenders.

Likely the most studied theory in cybercrime is routine activities theory. Originally developed to address changing crime rates following World War II, this theory suggests that changes in structural routines create opportunities for crime. The intersection of a motivated or likely offender and a suitable target, combined with the absence of a capable guardian, leads to crime (Cohen & Felson, 1979). Cyber criminology literature necessitates a change to routine activities, where the intersection of offender and suitable target is expanded to include digital interaction (rather than physical location). Similarly, capable guardians now include digital tools such as firewalls and antivirus software (Holt & Bossler, 2009).

The theory of routine activities is rational. It includes a criminal with a particular need or motivation. They notice that a potential victim has what they want. They must also notice that no one is going to prevent or stop them. Convenience theory supports such notions, as an offender will rationally choose to commit a financially motivated crime. They leverage both their position and access, minimizing the chance that a capable guardian is either present or watching. For example, while audits may help detect fraudulent activity, the number of capable guardians able to prevent such activity is few. These would include other individuals who both have access to the defrauded accounts and can understand that certain transactions are fraudulent. In this way, the offender noticed a need they had, a financial motivation. They then found a suitable target, an account they had access to which had sufficient money. Finally, they could not detect a suitable guardian such as another employee or manager who would know they were defrauding the account.

The above example illustrates the potential for routine activities in white-collar crime generally, but today these accounts and transactions are nearly exclusively conducted on a computer. In this way, we see the overlap of white-collar and computer crime as most financial transactions are now taking place via computers.

Strain theory is also being used to explain cybercrime. For example, strain theory has been applied to acts of hacking, piracy, online scams, cyberstalking/harassment, and online hate speech (Chism & Steinmetz, 2018). This theory highlights the personal motivation aspect, asserting that an individual is struggling to achieve a specific goal (often financial) and sees that crime may be a viable solution to achieving the goal. Crimes themselves may be innovations that help solve a specific goal. For example, Larsson et al. (2012) suggest that digital piracy is an innovation where individuals found a way to share desirable copyrighted media and files. Strains fit well into convenience as they consider the motivation of the offender in committing a white-collar crime. While only one paper directly considers how cybercrime relates to convenience theory, there are good reasons to think that convenience is applicable to cybercrime. First, cybercrime and white-collar crime are increasingly overlapping as offenders, individuals, and businesses are increasingly relying on digital transactions and technology. This facilitates new opportunities for offenders, increases ease in committing white-collar crime, and potentially increases anonymity. Second, research into criminological theories and computer crime generally yield positive results for theories that overlap with convenience theory. In this chapter, we considered two theories, routine activities theory, and strain theory. Routine activities theory provides rational support for the decision-making of actors, while strain theory shows the motivation for offenders to commit the crime. Yet, consistent with this book's theme, it is important to consider how cybercrime could be differentiated by gender. Specifically, we ask why fewer females are committing cybercrime.

10.4 CONVENIENCE IN CYBERSPACE

The underrepresentation of females in cybersecurity jobs leads to one possible reason that there are fewer female white-collar cyber offenders. They are less likely to have organizational access to computer networks, servers, and other sensitive computer infrastructure. A main reason why cyber white-collar offenders are so dangerous is they already have legitimate access to business networks. If a hacker were to try and gain access from the outside, they would have additional steps needed to have as much access as an inside employee already has. This largely falls under the opportunity dimension of convenience theory. The combination of career choices and access tends to reduce the female's opportunity for white-collar cybercrime due to reduced legitimate access.

Beyond opportunity, even females who are in cybersecurity or other information-technology/computer-related positions may be less likely to abuse their access because of reduced personal willingness and financial motivation. As addressed in the other chapters, females are more likely to focus on social dimensions rather than materialism.

The combination of environmental factors (e.g., not being in cybersecurity or IT jobs as frequently) and psychological factors (e.g., being less compelled by financial motivation) may compound the difference in male and female cyber offenders. This leads to the current landscape, where we see far fewer female cyber offenders than males. Future research should further theoretically and empirically explore convenience themes in female cyber offending.

CHAPTER 11

Gendered Crime Convenience

This book is concerned with elite financial crime committed by women from the perspective of convenience theory. The majority of research has focused on the disadvantages that women face due to their gender in both legal and illegal activities. This book attempts a more balanced view of disadvantages and advantages for women in white-collar crime. After reviewing some of the gender literature in management research, this chapter specifically concentrates on convenience themes that represent advantages for women compared to men. There are several convenience themes advantageous to women when it comes to financial motives, organizational opportunities, and willingness for deviant behavior.

11.1 GENDER IN MANAGEMENT RESEARCH

Women as white-collar offenders are people of high social standing and respectability who engage in financial crime while carrying out their professional responsibilities (Craig & Piquero, 2017; Friedrichs et al., 2018; Logan et al., 2019; Schnatterly et al., 2018; Sutherland, 1939, 1983). In private businesses, public agencies, and other professional settings, criminals look for and take advantage of organizational opportunities for wrongdoing. They often have leadership and managerial roles. Therefore, the treatment of gender in management research is interesting in our context. Here we review the research literature on gender in leading management journals such as the Journal of Management, Academy of Management Journal, and Administrative Science Quarterly.

The Gender Gap in White-Collar Crime: A Multi-Country Study of Women Offenders in Economic Crime.
Maryam Kamaei, Petter Gottschalk, and Thomas E. Dearden (Authors)

Gupta and et al. (2020a: 560) assert that CEO firings vary depending on gender:

> We theorize and discover that female CEOs have a significantly higher probability of being fired than male CEOs. Maybe even more importantly, we discover a gender-based interaction between firm performance and CEO gender, with male CEOs being less likely to be fired when firm performance is low compared to high, whereas female CEOs are equally likely to be fired regardless of firm performance.

Assuming that female CEOs have at least the same desire as male CEOs to survive and succeed in their positions of challenging experiences (King et al., 2012), while experiencing greater termination vulnerability (Klein et al., 2019; Zhang & Qu, 2016), a potential gender-related motive for crime can exist in the different dismissal probabilities. Female CEOs have different influence tactics, where communal influence tactics seem most effective. According to Smith et al. (2013), sympathy, gentleness, and submissiveness are elements of communal behavior. Communal tactics embody involvement of others, interpersonal sensitivity, modesty, dependence, and submission. According to Kulik and Olekalns (2012), women apply an accommodating tactic, while men apply a negotiating tactic. Women have to be helpful, kind, sympathetic, understanding, and compassionate, while men have to be assertive, dominant, competitive, and achievement-oriented (Kossek et al., 2017).

Akinola et al. (2018) identified a specific shortcoming in female communal tactics. They discovered that women's negative associations with delegation are lessened when delegation is reframed as communal. As a result, female leaders were less likely than male leaders to take advantage of the benefits of delegation. When they delegated, they felt more guilty than men. When women did delegate, they had lower-quality interactions with subordinates. According to Triana et al. (2019), female CEOs and other elite women must compensate for being excluded from male-dominated networks, which is a form of gender discrimination, in part due to the low percentage of women (King et al., 2010). Differences in performance between men and women in a specific business setting were investigated by Brands and Mehra (2019). Women experienced threats rooted in negative stereotypes about women in that profession, which undermined their performance. Negative social evaluation of women harmed their professional task performance.

McClean et al. (2018) studied gender differences in the social consequences of speaking up. Men who spoke up assertively benefited the most in terms of status and leader emergence. Women received no benefit from speaking up assertively in terms of status or leader emergence.

Kanze and others (2018) asserted that men are expected to win startup funding while women are expected not to lose. They discovered that male entrepreneurs approach funding for their startups with a mindset to win, whereas female entrepreneurs approach funding for their startups with a mindset not to lose.

Dwivedi and others (2018) conducted a comparative study between 1989 and 2009 on all CEO successions involving female successors at the nation's largest corporations. According to their findings, women achieved success when gender-inclusive gatekeeping during succession was promoted by a combination of local firm-level factors and characteristics of predominantly male predecessors.

Brescoll (2011:622) concentrates on US legislators and their speaking conduct on the Senate floor.

> Results show major areas of strength for a connection between power and verbosity for male congresspersons, but a non-significant relationship for female legislators.

Gender was taken into account when Schaumberg and Flynn (2017) evaluated communality and leadership from a gender perspective. They discovered a female advantage in leadership evaluations when agency is expressed as self-reliance. The capacity to rely on one's own abilities to meet one's needs and goals is self-reliance. A self-reliant person is self-assured and does not rely on others to accomplish her goals. A personal trait known as self-reliance is characterized by a lack of excessive dependence on others, a sense of control over one's life, and initiative on one's part. Organization is concerned with the drive for achievement and the advancement of one's own interests, while collectivism is concerned with the drive for association and the advancement of others' interests. Briscoe and Joshi (2017) studied the persistent gender gap in earnings and rewards. They found that in the context of professional work, where the scope for organizational mechanisms to restrain the potential for bias is weak, the bias of gender gap in earnings and rewards is visible. They undertook a longitudinal analysis that highlights the influence of political beliefs on the gender gap in earnings. Political beliefs are an interrelated set of attitudes and values about the proper goals for society and how they should be achieved.

Han et al. (2017) focused on directional work-based respect in multiplex ties between business gatherings. They define deference as one actor's acknowledgment that the other is entitled to certain privileges. Lower-status actors support and provide higher-status actors with more trust and loyalty, even in times of deviance, than the latter are expected to return. The research empirically shows that interpersonal deference resulting from marriage affects business group market entries or exits, and in turn, each group's performance. Abraham (2017) investigated how manager discretion and gender influence gender wage disparity. The study applied the social identity perspective to shift the gender wage debate from inequality to potential equality depending on the gender of the executive determining wages for subordinates. The objective of the review was to decide if male and female directors vary in how they utilize the discretion managed by less formalized pay frameworks. Additionally, the study sought to determine the effects on pay of decision-makers' gender on employees at various levels of the organizational hierarchy.

Abraham (2020) presented a study on audience-based gender bias and gender role inconsistency three years later. She discovered that resource exchanges are influenced by gender inequality when third parties are involved. When deciding whether to connect a contact in a male-type occupation, decision-makers were most likely to favor male network contacts in third-party exchanges. Gender bias refers to a tendency toward or prejudice against a particular gender. Several management researchers have studied the gender wage gap. A slightly non-traditional perspective was chosen by Leslie et al. (2017) who found that some women experience a reverse wage gap. The study proposes a female premium for certain women. Organizations can perceive high-potential women – who have the abilities needed to reach the upper echelons of organizations, where women remain underrepresented – as more valuable for achieving organizational diversity goals than high-potential men. Therefore, such organizations reward exceptional women with higher pay. Also, Mun and Jung (2020) observed a reversal of the gender gap when they studied some companies that pushed gender diversity by favoring women for top positions. A third illustration of the inversion of the orientation hole is liberal sheets and boards who like to advance ladies as opposed to men to elite positions in organizations (Carnahan & Greenwood, 2018). A fourth example of potential reversal of the gender gap is the recognition of expertise, where Joshi (2014) suggests that the person conducting the evaluation can favor females' outcomes in problem-solving.

The gender wage gap is only one of several disadvantages for women that researchers have investigated. Another disadvantage is access to capital as an entrepreneur. Tonoyan et al. (2020) identified a gender gap in perceived start-up ease. They found that the gendering of labor market positions has the effect of reducing women's likelihood of acquiring entrepreneurship-relevant resources, experiencing entrepreneurial career previews, and being exposed to industry opportunity spaces for launching new firms. A third disadvantage is a reasonable work-family balance that women expect from themselves to a greater extent than men do (Padavic et al., 2020). Botelho and Abraham (2017) point to the double standards in recruitment procedures as a fourth drawback. They discovered that men and women are unfairly held to different standards. In multistage evaluations, applying the wrong standards results in different outcomes for men and women.

An outline of 50 years of observational orientation research was given by the editors of the Foundation of The Board Diary (Joshi et al., 2015). Between 1958 and 2015, the journal published 107 articles with gender as a focal construct. While none of the articles dealt with women in crime specifically, many of them touch on deviance and deviant behavior depending on gender. The content of research was typically barriers framing according to societal expectations to assign men more readily to managerial roles, while women in such roles faced bias and discrimination.

However, at the time of the overview article, there was indeed an article about women in crime in the journal. Cumming et al. (2015) talked about securities fraud and gender diversity. They gave three important insights and proposed a theory about how gender diversity on boards of directors affects all kinds of securities fraud. One of them is that fraud on boards with more women on them has a much lower impact on the stock market. To be a follower in crime might be a choice rather than a result of inequality by some women offenders. Even in self-managing teams where there are no gender differences initially, Lanaj and Hollenbeck (2015) found that typically male team members emerge as leaders.

11.2 GENDERED CRIME MOTIVES

Management researchers have found that female CEOs are significantly more likely to lose their jobs than male CEOs. Gupta and co. express that (2020a), female bosses have a similar level of dismissal likelihood regardless of firm performance. Female and male CEOs face the same risk of being fired when a company performs poorly; however, when a company performs well, only male CEOs see a significant decrease in this risk. The greater vulnerability in the central scenario for women could lead to strategic actions to reduce the likelihood of dismissal and to remain in top leadership positions (King et al., 2012). Joshi et al. state that female CEOs and other elite women must compensate for being excluded from networks dominated by men, which act as a type of gender barrier (Triana et al., 2019), in part due to the limited number of women (King et al., 2010). Female chiefs might support others to maintain power if they face job cuts.

Female presidents perceive and weakness more prominently (Klein et al., 2019; Zhang and Qu in 2016). Gupta and co. say that when women break through the glass ceiling, they end up on the glass cliff, where they face more risks, challenges, and dangers than men do. The dangers of falling from first-class positions are depicted in the glass bluff illustration. To avoid extra assessment and examination than men, money-related bad behavior might be a useful street to make due on the glass incline.

According to Brands and Mehra (2019), associations are social fields in which individuals form relationships with one another. The perseverance on the glass incline is dependent upon female effect techniques. According to Smith and others (2013), gender-specific communal strategies for women include collaboration, consultation, the indirect use of sexuality, personal appeals, exemplification, supplication, and ingratiation. Ingratiation is the process of gaining one's own acceptance or affection through subtle and persuasive flattery. According to Agnew (2014)'s perspective on social concern and crime, collaboration involves providing resources or personal assistance in exchange for compliance.

The social concern point of view is the main subject of comfort in Figure 2.1 regarding the rationale prospects of individual topics. Ill-conceived gain can help women in achieving goals that seem to mean a lot to them than to men. The offender must satisfy her desire to assist others as a social concern based on her accommodating style (Kulik & Olekalns, 2012). Agnew (2014) introduced the motive of social concern and crime, which is the desire to assist others, moving beyond the presumption of simple self-interest. Nevertheless, Paternoster et al. contend (2018) that good cause can be a self-serving, sane, and socially cognizant action. The feminine moral emphasizes social rather than material aspects, despite the rise of materialism in feminism (Sullivan, 2012). The paradigm of gendered focal concern asserts that women socialize into accepting nurturing role responsibilities that emphasize the significance of social relationships and communalistic orientations toward others. On the other hand, men are expected to be helpful, kind, sympathetic, understanding, and compassionate. This paradigm includes social concern. As a result of juggling these responsibilities, women develop identities as caregivers (Steffensmeier et al., 2013).

Klenowski and accomplices (2011, p. 58) conducted interviews with 20 condemned women and found that, as affirmed by a brief miscreant story in Part 2, "the most notable way that females framed their activities was to show that their ultimate goals were to provide ongoing support to those for whom they truly cared. Another factor that is gender-dependent is stress." According to Holtfreter's (2015) argument, gender-specific strain might exist. For example, there are indications that responses to specific strains and the strains experienced differ depending on gender. Brands and Mehra (2019) state that stress can lead to aggression and rage in men and depression and anxiety in women.

People who are under stress have fewer cognitive resources available to apply to the urgent task when they are anxious. When people are worried about their performance, they try to avoid thinking and feeling bad by taking actions that help them get out of stressful situations. Figure 2.1's motive-possibilities-corporate perspective for women suggests that for female executives, corporate goals, ambitions, objectives, and ends can become extremely important in order to alleviate the stress and anxiety brought on by the failure to achieve corporate goals. Even though female executives have broken through the glass ceiling (Dodge, 2009), Langton and Piquero (2017) claim that they will not succeed if tension, stress, and specifically uncertainty continue to exist.

One of the most well-known theoretical explanations for criminal motivation is the strain perspective (Agnew, 2005, 2012, 2013; Agnew and Froggio's 2007 work with Cleff et al., 2002, Hoffmann; 2007 by Langton and Piquero; Ngo & Paternoster, 2016). The strain perspective emphasizes the disappointment that results from failing to fulfill a responsibility, such as avoiding individual or corporate bankruptcy. Strains normally cause people to feel dreadful, which makes them feel obliged to take a healing action to close the gap between what they need and what truly happens. One potential response is to engage in criminal behavior. Individual and corporate risks described in Figure 2.1 can therefore evoke specific motivations among women due to gender differences in strains.

A possible female thought process is the gender gap in earnings. In many professional and managerial work settings, Briscoe and Joshi (2017) found that the gender pay gap persists (Abraham, 2020). A female in a subordinate role may therefore feel justified in theft. The value perspective explains how an individual may feel justified in the illegal redistribution of wealth if the current distribution is perceived as unfair (Burrai et al., 2015, p. 452):

> There is a desire, whether conscious or unconscious, to take corrective action to make the situation more equitable when equity is not perceived.

In convenience theory, the equity perspective may be a factor of motivation as well as a factor of willingness. As an inspirational component, the longing is available to get what every other person gets and in this way what the wrongdoer seems to be qualified for. The need is to get what one merits. On the other hand, the willingness is the justification for fair pay. The finding by Leslie et al. (2017) that a few exceptional women get exceptional salaries and bonuses does not necessarily trigger other women to try to become exceptional. Rather, the phenomenon of elite women is just as likely to trigger normal hard-working women to feel the betrayal and downgrading causing them to take remedial action to make the situation more equitable.

11.3 GENDERED CRIME OPPORTUNITIES

In terms of the opportunity-commit-status perspective, status is the first key theme in Figure 2.1. In this context, status refers to a person's social rank within a formal or informal hierarchy or their relative standing along a valued social dimension (Kakkar et al., 2020). Status is an individual's general position in a social order. When one individual recognizes that another is entitled to certain privileges, status differences lead to variations in opportunities (Han et al., 2017).

By utilizing female influence strategies (Smith et al., 2019), women's status can be influenced by their relationships with others in organizations as social arenas (Brands & Mehra, 2013). Female influence strategies are essential for both success and survival on the glass cliff. Smith et al. (2013, p. 1161) argue that collaboration, consultation, and the indirect use of sexuality, personal appeals, exemplification, supplication, and ingratiation are gender-specific strategies reserved for women.

The use of behaviors designed to make the target like you or appear friendly in order to get their support or compliance is known as ingratiation. Request is utilized when one inspires nurturance or commitment from an objective through self-devaluation or cases of vulnerability. Inspiring objective responsibility or wonder through activities like discipline or aiding is called representation. By appealing to their sense of friendship or loyalty, personal appeals are used to persuade a target to support or comply with one's own goals. The indirect use of sexuality as an influence tactic is the deliberate use of one's sexuality to gain favor with others. The act of seeking the participation or advice of others is known as consultation. Last but not least, collaboration entails providing support or resources in return for compliance.

A study by Kenny and Donnelly (2020) on how women, outnumbered and outranked, navigate work and careers In information technology, indirect use of sexuality has been found. Women exhibit femininity and are perceived as more moral than men. This perception of women makes it less likely that females are suspected of misconduct and crime.

Support from a successful predecessor who advocated for gender diversity and inclusion at the highest level may contribute to women's status. Dwivedi et al. (2018) suggest that a woman in CEO succession can benefit from the status and trust of the predecessor's post-succession board presence. They found that the type of ancestor support is novel to women. The connection between self-reliance and leadership evaluations is a third status advantage for women. Schaumberg and Flynn (2017, p. 1859) discovered that women's self-reliance is positively correlated with leadership evaluations, but not men's:

> According to our findings, independent female pioneers are deemed to be better than confident male pioneers. On the other hand, dominant leaders or leaders who are positively depicted but do not display any specific agentic characteristic show either a male benefit or no benefit at all. The female advantage in the relationship between self-reliance and

leadership evaluations is based on expectancy violation theory, which states that self-reliant female leaders are regarded as equally competent but more communal than self-reliant male leaders.

When it comes to pay structures, subordinates may perceive female leaders to be treated more favorably than male leaders, which is a fourth status advantage. Abraham (2017) found that employees who report to female managers had evidence of less gender pay disparity. In his study, manager gender had the implication that female managers pay male and female employees more equitably than male managers due to the discretion provided by less formalized pay systems. The value point of view here in this way makes sense of how an individual can communicate more trust and feel more faithful to a female chief than a male supervisor (Briscoe & Joshi, 2017).

The fact that women are better at listening to others than men is a fifth status advantage. Influential ladies take the floor not exactly influential men (Brescoll, 2011). Women demonstrate empathy and involvement by listening to colleagues and subordinates rather than yelling at them.

From an organizational opportunity perspective, the convenience of involving women to lessen reactions in the event of a crime is another enabler of crime in addition to status. For instance, Cumming et al. (2015) found that a gender-diverse board's securities fraud response is significantly less prominent in the stock market. Welcoming female investment can lessen the degree of judgment and outcomes later. Since women are held in lower regard than men, participation from women may also reduce detection risk.

Being a woman is advantageous when striving for elite membership with power and influence because there are some positions that are similar to those held by women and workplaces that are dominated by women. For instance, Tonoyan et al. (2020) suggest that in many economically developed Western nations, public administration is now dominated by women. Keep in mind that women hold the majority of public sector jobs in Norway. Only 19% of men and 48% of women are employed in the public sector. The open door structure in policy management is reliant upon institutional disintegration and absence of guardianship.

The struggle for gender diversity is another example, as it can make it easier for women than men to reach positions of power and influence where they can use resources to commit and cover up financial crimes.

> Mun and Jung (2018) tracked down those supervisors liable for corporate social responsibility (CSR) fundamentally pushed for orientation variety in the upper positions of their associations. A third model is liberal advancement panels and liberal board members who are likely to choose people for advancement into elite positions (Carnahan & Greenwood, 2018). The recognition of female expertise as more valuable, consistent, and accountable than male expertise is a fourth example of preferential treatment for women, resulting in an improvement in the opportunity structure for women (Joshi, 2014).

While a portion of the above comfort subjects in regards to hierarchical open door assist with carrying out crime, the female open door structure is less to find in the perpetrate viewpoint and more to find in the cover viewpoint. The obvious benefit for female offenders is basically that they don't face suspicions of wrongdoing to the extent that males do when something goes wrong. The straightforward analysis of corruption in Section 1 highlighted the difference in gender in suspicion. The study found support in an Australian survey, where women had less of a chance of engaging in corruption (Bowman & Gilligan, 2008). The lack of suspicion stems from a gender bias within the population in general and the criminal justice systems in particular. An inclination towards or prejudice against a certain gender falls under the realm of gender bias. Society and its criminal justice system focus on men as they are more likely to be perpetrators of crime. The laws governing society and the subsequent verdicts in courts take into account the cultural, moral, and ethical norms prevalent in that society. Ever since the female symbol of justice, the Greek Goddess Justitia, women have been considered more law-abiding than men.

When men have been involved in fraud in previous positions, these fraud-tainted male executives experience a loss of job opportunities and a dearth of alternative positions. According to Naumovska et al. (2020), this is not the case for fraud-tainted female executives. They argue that socio-economic pressures to redress the longstanding underrepresentation of women have generated a rising demand for female executives. A consequence of this increase in demand and perceived limited supply is a degree of reputational immunity granted to such sought-after executives when they are associated with corporate misconduct.

A major advantage for women in white-collar crime is thus the lack of suspicion when something goes wrong. Women avoid suspicion for two main reasons. One reason is that women pretend to be more morally robust and ethical in their behavior. For example, female board members talk most often about ethics (Dodge, 2007). The other reason is that women involved in conspiracies with others tend to play hidden minor or supporting roles rather than exposed leadership roles (Goncharov & Peter, 2019).

The lack of suspicion can derive from gender differences in trust when it comes to misconduct and crime. When it is less thinkable that women will do something wrong, then it is easier to trust them with certain tasks. Trust is an important contribution to the convenience of white-collar crime. According to Dearden (2016), the root cause of white-collar crime is a breach of trust. The acceptance of vulnerability based on positive expectations of another person's intentions and actions is implied by trust. Controlling a trusted person is often considered both unnecessary and a signal of mistrust. In many cultures, the opposite of showing trust is to monitor and question what a person is doing. For example, a board can tell management what to do, but they do not tell them how to do it. The board shows trust that management will do it in an acceptable manner. If the board would move from only controlling what management has done to how management did it, then it might be perceived as mistrust. Kim et al. (2009, p. 401) define trust as "a psychological state comprising the intention to accept vulnerability based on positive expectations of the intentions or behavior of another." The positive expectations can relate to what another does, how it is done, and when it is done. The positive expectations can relate to the reaction of another, where it is expected that the reaction will be understandable, acceptable, and favorable. Vulnerability means that trust can easily be violated without detection or correction of deviant behavior. Trust is associated with dependence and risk (Chan et al., 2020, p. 3):

> The trust depends on something or someone (the trustee or object of trust), and there is a possibility that expectations or hopes will not be satisfied, and that things will go wrong. Trust is not absolute, but conditional and contextual.

The notion of felt trust is also relational, just as the concept of trust is relational, necessitating a target by definition. Felt trust can impact an individual's inclination to wrongdoing, while genuine trust is essential for the open door structure for wrongdoing. According to Campagna et al., the gap between the two shows how well people comprehend how others perceive them (2020, p. 994).

A dyadic meta-perception—one person's belief about the thought, attitude, or perception held by another—is reflected in the concept of felt trust, as described in the more general literature on interpersonal perception.

In 2020, Uygur looked into charitable fraud in Wales and England. Numerous women work in the foundation sector. He examined 42 charities with and without fraud. According to his findings, a lack of trust in charitable organizations increases the likelihood of fraud. Additionally, Gottschalk (2017, p. 121) posed the following question regarding the detection and prevention of economic crime within religious organizations:

Is there an excessive amount of trust, freedom, individual authority, skepticism, loyalty, and control over the financial aspects of religious organizations?

When suspicions arise, women are less likely to be held accountable because they typically assume more ethical responsibilities than men. However, a study by Dalton and Ortegren (2011) shows that women's responses to ethical issues can be influenced by the social desirability response bias. Social desirability response bias significantly influences the relationship between gender and ethical decision-making, as women consistently report more ethical responses than men. A review of the empirical literature on ethical decision-making by O'Fallon and Butterfield (2005) indicates that there are often no differences between men and women. Adding to the comfort subject of communicating moral obligation, ladies can likewise extend their authoritative open door by communicating close to home force. A very steady finding in the feeling literature is that the two assumptions to ladies and conduct by ladies suggest greater personal power and deep expressiveness than men, and such differences hold for both good and negative emotions. Scott and Barnes (2011) suggest that the root of these differences may lie in role development, with women being socialized to be more emotionally expressive while men are socialized to be more emotionally restrained. For instance, when confronted with allegations of financial crime, females are more likely than males to respond by crying innocently. When a person who is crying tells a story, listeners are more likely to believe it. Misdirecting attribution of fault to others could follow (Eberly et al., 2011).

Women are less likely to be held accountable when suspicions arise because they tend to take on more ethical responsibilities than men do. However, a study by Dalton and Ortegren (2011) demonstrates that the social desirability response bias can influence women's responses to ethical issues. Females consistently report more ethical responses than males, indicating that the social desirability response bias is driving a significant portion of the relationship between gender and ethical decision-making. According to O'Fallon and Butterfield (2005), who conducted a review of the empirical ethical decision-making literature, there are frequently no differences found between men and women.

11.4 GENDERED CRIME WILLINGNESS

The disparity in earnings between men and women has the potential to both motivate and compel criminal activity. In the convenience theory, the equity perspective can serve as both a motivational and a willingness factor, as previously mentioned. The desire to obtain what the offender believes they are entitled to is present as a motivational factor. The requirement is to receive what one is due. On the other hand, the willingness is the justification for fair pay. Please keep in mind that Briscoe and Joshi (2017) discovered that the gender pay gap persists across many professional and managerial work settings. A female top part can in this way feel qualified for misappropriation. Burrai et al. claim that the value point of view makes sense of how an individual might accept they are qualified for unlawful abundance rearrangement. When financial compensation for the same job or work-life balance is not perceived as equitable (Padavic et al., 2020), then there is a reason to correct the situation to make it more equitable.

Female criminals may find it easier to play the follower role in crime than the leader role. According to the orientation job viewpoint, men are presumed to possess agentic qualities (such as assertiveness, confidence, and independence) and to engage in behaviors consistent with a leader's role as a result of orientation explicit cultural job and conduct assumptions (Lanaj & Hollenbeck, 2015, p. 1477):

> Women, on the other hand, are expected to act in ways that don't fit the role of a leader and to be helpful, nurturing, and kind to others.

This comfort topic doesn't involve imbalance as Lanaj and Hollenbeck (2015) concentrated on authority development in self-overseeing groups, where there at first are no orientation explicit jobs. Be that as it may, as such groups begin to work, guys will quite often take on positions of authority all the more regularly, while females take on devotee roles more frequently. Claim loyalty to the leader as the one who makes decisions to justify being a criminal follower (Glas & Einarsen, 2008).

Women's willingness to follow can also be rational, as they hope to avoid attention even if their criminal leaders are caught. Women have the ability to remain invisible (Gottschalk & Smith, 2015), making them easy to overlook or ignore (Smith et al., 2020). Ladies do not seem to fit the profile of a serious crook (Becker & McCorkel, 2011).

As continuous supporters in wrongdoing, as opposed to pioneers in wrongdoing, ladies have orientation-specific subjects in the readiness aspect of comfort theory as discussed here. For instance, ensuring reliability is a potential balance strategy for women as followers. According to Fehr et al. (2015), a follower has a belief in the morality of the leader's pressure, which can cause them to feel shame and guilt if they fail to support the leader. Glasø and Einarsen (2008) concentrated on feeling regulation in leader-follower relationships. They found that, instead of expressing or faking positive emotions like enthusiasm, interest, and calmness, leaders often suppress negative emotions like frustration, vulnerability, and discomfort. A leader may use language that followers may not necessarily understand. Followers continue to trust the messages of leaders, integrating them into the organization's culture (Holt & Cornelissen, 2014; Srivastava & Goldberg, 2017; Weick, 1995). The language used by leaders can lead followers to comply (Mawritz et al., 2017).

Some elite members engage in unethical behavior because they genuinely believe it is the right thing to do. Unethical, pro-organizational behavior involves engaging in corporate misconduct to benefit the perpetrator's organization. Strongly identifying with the organization's fate provides a basis for justifying actions that benefit the organization. Elite members are more likely to engage in unethical, pro-organizational behavior when they believe these actions are ethically justified, and these ethical beliefs are strongest among executives and other privileged individuals who strongly identify with the profession and the organization (Graham et al., 2020). Women may be more socially supportive of the organization and its members. When combined with follower loyalty, the gendered willingness to engage in misconduct implies a higher willingness among women compared to men.

Gendered crime willingness might result from differences in desistance among offenders. Desistance is a complex process by which individuals transform from offenders to non-offenders. Fredriksson and Gålnander

(2020, p. 614) studied how women transform from offenders into non-offenders: Terrifying parts of desistance processes originate from making a new, regulating way of life natural, while unrealistically getting to know a recognizable, freak way of life." Their findings highlight the mental and emotional struggles of a gradual, processual shift from one lifestyle and sense of self toward another.

CHAPTER 12

Future Gender Research

This chapter outlines research needs to begin testing the gendered crime and convenience theory. We begin by considering the myriads of definitional problems that plague white-collar crime, and by extension, female offenders. The section on modeling and testing white-collar offending pathways considers the need for testing the causal mechanisms. A general discussion of utilizing white-collar offending as a dependent measure is followed by a specific example. The following section, Validity in Main Effect Studies, addresses general concerns with internal, external, and ecological validity and how diverse methodological approaches and follow-up studies can address potential limitations. Advanced Pathways and Research conclude the chapter by discussing studies that incorporate multiple causal variables and utilize complex research designs.

Researchers examining white-collar crime quickly understand that a definition of white-collar crime is often elusive. White-collar offending varies by country and often includes a continuum of illegal behavior. For example, in the United States, white-collar offending can be a civil or a criminal violation. Although civil violations are not criminal, the back-end negotiations, including plea deals, deferred prosecution, and alternative dispute resolution, lead to many criminal violations either not being prosecuted or only containing civil remedies. For example, the use of alternative dispute resolution (ADR) has been increasing in recent years (Keilitz et al., 1988; Shavell, 1995) and can be used to avoid potential criminal or civil litigation. Many companies, for instance, insert arbitration agreements into their contracts or terms of service, which require the individual to utilize arbitration, a form of ADR, instead of civil court to settle disputes (Hall, 2012). A study conducted by the Consumer Financial Protection

The Gender Gap in White-Collar Crime: A Multi-Country Study of Women Offenders in Economic Crime.
Maryam Kamaei, Petter Gottschalk, and Thomas E. Dearden (Authors)

Bureau in which the ADR was mandated through arbitration clauses found a series of claims that could have been pursued through federal statutes, citing cases of fraud, state statute, and refutation of alleged debt claims. Specific statutory violations include the Fair Credit Billing Act, the Fair Debt Collection Practices Act, and the Truth in Lending Act (Consumer Financial Protection Bureau, 2013).

From its inception, white-collar crime, as defined by Edwin Sutherland, focused on the nature of the offender rather than the offense. His definition primarily focused on the offenses committed by those of high social status (Sutherland 1939). While there are historical reasons for his approach, such as a sociological push against criminologists focusing purely on street crime, his definition leads to questions about the nature of the offense. For example, would a high-paid banker buying cocaine or other street drugs constitute white-collar crime? Intuitively, people would likely say no. Focusing purely on the nature of the offender leads to an oversimplification of the intention of white-collar crime. As such, researchers need to carefully consider the definition of white-collar crime that they are using.

One early avenue of research is to empirically examine what various populations think white-collar crime is. Attitudinal surveys would allow researchers to determine the attitudes and values regarding white-collar offending, with initial attitudinal research seeking to describe and explain these differences.

To construct the attitudinal survey, an initial pilot study should be conducted that asks participants to find examples in each of the categories. This pilot study could survey business leaders and administrative agency personnel because of their particular expertise and involvement in white-collar offending decision making and regulation. The pilot study could then be used to create the survey by utilizing the scenarios produced by participants and re-administered to a sample of the same two populations, asking respondents to rank the scenarios on ethics and legality--creating the white-collar offending continuum. Consistent with the focus of our book, consideration should be examined by gender.

The survey would need to be tested for its reliability and validity. Split-half, a test designed to check that different parts (halves) of the test measure the same construct (e.g., white-collar offending), and alternate-form reliability tests, a test designed to ensure that minor variations in the test do not affect the overall consistency, should be performed (Litwin, 1995). In this situation, one would want to assess reliability to show consistency (split-half reliability) in the measurement and ensure that the white-collar continuum examples are being rated similarly (alternate-forms reliability) by participants. Although it is expected that different respondents may view the scenarios differently from each other (e.g., the participant may have different views of ethics and/or may not know the legality of a decision), reliability would be important to assess to ensure that the two groups of respondents (business leaders and administrative agency personnel) do not vary in their responses at different times of day or in different affective moods.

Validation efforts should include an assessment of multiple types of validity. The q-sort method could be used to ensure both face validity and construct validity. This validity test uses expert judgment to categorize each example into categories of white-collar offending, hopefully leading to a consensus within examples. Confirmatory factor analysis could be used to assess whether the scenarios and responses load onto their respective white-collar offenses.

After reliability and validity are demonstrated, the survey will be ready to administer to various populations. To adequately address differences between groups, surveys should focus on various key populations including business leaders (e.g., chief executive officers (CEOs), chief finance officers (CFOs), members of the board of directors, and other high-level management of major corporations), other business decision-makers (e.g., mid-level managers, sales associates), legislators (e.g., state and federal congressmen), and administrative agency personnel (e.g., Securities and Exchange Commission, Consumer Protection Bureau, and Federal Trade Commission). Other government enforcement agencies should also be surveyed if they are involved with white-collar offending in some capacity. For example, the Federal Bureau of Investigation often investigates and prosecutes cases stemming from other administrative agencies that do not have the capacity to prosecute or pursue legal action. Finally, the general public should be surveyed due to their role as economic participants and as individuals who are directly affected by white-collar offending.

Attitudinal surveys have the advantage of reaching large audiences and multiple populations. However, interpretation and generalizability within samples are often limited by the response rate. Before the survey is conducted, cluster samples could be utilized to target specific populations and individuals within the population. For example, in the business population one may use businesses or sectors as one cluster to ensure representation from a variety of businesses. Within each cluster one can then target specific demographic differences including gender and tenure. After the survey data has been collected, one way to determine if non-responders are different than responders is to compare late responders with early responders. Theoretical and empirical evidence suggests that late responders are often similar to non-responders (Lindner et al., 2001; Templeton et al., 1997). By examining the differences between early and late responders, researchers can have some degree of confidence in the generalizability of their sample. Finally, collecting demographic variables will allow weights to be computed and used to adjust the sample to be more representative of the population, provided the population demographics are known.

12.1 MODELING AND TESTING

Once initial attitudinal research on white-collar offending is complete, researchers should have a good understanding of the perceptions of white-collar crime. Utilizing white-collar offending as the dependent variable, one can test for explanatory factors discussed throughout this book and in other convenience theory articles as the independent variables. Methodologically, we are testing whether these factors (i.e., independent variables) lead to a change in white-collar crime (i.e., dependent variables).

White-collar crime research should also consider mediators and moderators. Mediators are when one factor is either fully or partially explained by another factor. The most classic criminal justice example is that crime and ice cream sales are related, but only explained through the mediator of temperature (Meyers et al., 2013). It is likely that some of the independent variables have both full and partial mediation in a full pathway model of white-collar crime. Moderators are variables that affect the direction and/or strength of another independent variable (Baron & Kenny, 1986). When introduced together, some factors may increase the likelihood of white-collar offending above and beyond the variable's individual influence in isolation. Likely, in many models, gender will be an important moderator. This is to say that gender changes the relationship between the independent variables and the dependent variables.

Although there are a number of different tests needed, we only highlight one example here. Moral awareness is when a problem or stimulus is identified as having a moral component to it (Rest, 1986). The first step to deciding a moral course of action is to identify that there is a moral component to the problem one is facing (Rest, 1986). Moral awareness is when a problem or stimulus is identified as having a moral component to it. For example, if someone takes products from their workplace for home use, they are committing an immoral activity, but may not consider it immoral if they first did not cognitively consider the action involving a moral dimension.

One potential component of white-collar crime could be how moral awareness leads to white-collar offending. A sample hypothesis could be:

> *H_1: Lack of moral awareness will lead to white-collar offending behavior if the offense is in the interest of the individual.*

Without recognition of morality (i.e., moral awareness), it is likely that individuals will consider what is in their best interest as there is no need to consider the consequences towards others. Just because one individual does not perceive an event as having a moral component, does not mean that they will commit the white-collar offense. It is logical to assume that they are likely to only take that course of action if the offense in some way benefits them or the organization in which they work. Lack of moral awareness reduces the inhibitions individuals feel when facing moral issues because the moral component is simply not identified.

In this research, the dependent variable would be the decision to commit a white-collar offense in any of the categories. The same scenarios from the attitudinal survey could be used as a measure of the dependent variable. In this survey, the individuals would be asked to place themselves into the decision-maker position of a hypothetical situation. Their decision to offend or not will be the measure of the dependent variable. To measure the independent variable, an additional measure of moral awareness would be included in the survey. Past validated measures of moral awareness are qualitative and ask decision-makers to identify important issues in making their decisions. Researchers then code for issues relating to morality, honesty, or integrity (Butterfield et al., 2000). Due to the qualitative nature and need for coding, inter-rater reliability would need to be assessed.

As with all experimental survey approaches, one issue is common-method variance. There are a few statistical solutions to both assess the influence of common method variance and help alleviate some of its influence (Podsakoff et al., 2012).

Follow-up studies could use experiments and ask participants to make particular decisions within the simulation. These scenarios would have multiple options, and each scenario would differ in the level of white-collar offending (e.g., one would have the opportunity to commit an illegal offense while another would have an opportunity to commit an immoral but not illegal offense). Consistent with experimental design procedures, individuals should be randomly assigned to the control group (group with options of moral-legal choice) and experimental test groups (groups with options of immoral-legal, moral-illegal, and immoral-illegal).

One concern with experimental approaches is low external validity and the potential for low ecological validity. Consistent with multi-method approaches, the survey should alleviate some concerns for external validity. An additional way to address external validity is to vary the population across experiments. Finally, if the experiment is designed carefully, the ecological validity can be high in experiments. For example, researchers could utilize an online financial trading simulation where participants buy and sell pretend stock. These online tools (e.g., http://www.marketwatch.com/game) are similar to how many real investors would trade at home. For added ecological validity, rewards could be given to participants based on their performance. This method allows for a high degree of realism while still allowing for the experiment to create manipulations (e.g., provide one group with insider information).

An important moderator to consider in these studies would be gender. If males and females have different moral awareness (currently this idea is contested in the literature with no consensus Lowry 2003), then this may be one difference in why there are fewer females than males committing white-collar crime.

12.2 MAIN EFFECT VALIDITY

Once the studies above have been conducted, research should be repeated across different populations. Often, experimental studies utilize students because of their ease of access in the university setting. Future research should also test other populations, either experimentally or through other methodological approaches. It may be that student populations behave differently, or their choices are affected by different psychological factors. For example, younger individuals (e.g., students) make more risky decisions than older populations (Gardner & Steinberg, 2005). Even across the populations surveyed in the attitudinal research, differences between groups have been found. For example, public employees (e.g., government legislators and administrative personnel) have been found to be more risk-averse than private employees (e.g., business managers and CEOs) (Bellante & Link, 1981; Butterfield et al., 2000). By utilizing different populations, external generalizability can be better established. Weisburd et al. (2001) offer a comprehensive descriptive study on the characteristics of white-collar offenders. Divisions can be made using their research. For example, one large group difference noted in the research is "one-shot" offenders versus repeat or life-course white-collar offenders. A second example is those who start their offending later in life as opposed to earlier (Romney et al., 1980; Weisburd et al., 1990; Weisburd et al., 2001).

The studies above should also vary by the type of white-collar offending researched. For example, research on white-collar crime finds that the characteristics of white-collar criminals vary by whether the offense was committed spur of the moment or whether it was planned (Baer, 2014). White-collar crime research gives researchers a starting point for delineating potentially important group differences in white-collar offending. First, different types of crime have historically been used to study white-collar crime. For example, one could compare the decision-making of insider traders with the decision-making of pump-and-dump-type stock fraud offenders. One could also vary the type of offense by industry. For example, one could compare the decision-making of financial offenders with the decision-making of medical worker offending. It is likely that by doing so, one will separate offenders by both industry and offense, for example, insider trading versus Medicaid/Medicare fraud. Establishing how white-collar offenders' decision-making changes based on the type of offense will increase the external validity of the studies, creating confidence in the generalizability of the results. A second difference researchers should assess is the difference in needed skill for the white-collar offense. Some offenses require considerable skill and/or being in a position of power or influence (e.g., financial market manipulations or antitrust). Other offenses require little skill and can be accomplished by nearly everyone (e.g., tax evasion or mail fraud).

There are multiple difficulties in reaching the populations that one would ideally like to use as participants. First, busy CEOs and businesses are unlikely to be amenable to taking a survey, or having their employees take surveys about their white-collar offending behaviors—even if the situations are hypothetical. In approaching organizations, one will explicitly need to state the benefits of the experiment or survey to sell this research. The benefits for the organization are immense. First, the research can help the organization understand how the employees and/or management view white-collar offending. For example, Arthur Anderson, an organization once known for complete uprightness and morality eventually fell into white-collar crime. As one insider suggested, it was as if their position of morality excused their unethical behavior because they were a moral organization (Toffler, 2003). In this situation, an understanding of the decision-making of the employees and managers may have provided insight on the offending that could have potentially been occurring. Second, white-collar offending is often costly to organizations. Research indicates that white-collar crime places additional financial burdens on organizations and they would be best served to prevent it (Schnatterly, 2003). Finally, organizations may benefit from the image that they are paying attention to white-collar offending issues. Managing one's organizational image is pivotal to the success and even survival of the organization (Elsbach, 2006). Publicly acknowledging an effort to study and understand a socially important issue (Holtfreter et al., 2008), such as white-collar offending, is likely to increase public approval and image.

Another hard-to-reach population includes prisoners. In the United States, Institutional Review Board policies, as governed by federal regulation 45 CFR 46, subpart C, define prisoners as a protected population, which raises procedural and methodological hurdles. Because the research is about criminal offending, the research is appropriate, but researchers would need to create additional safeguards to ensure that prisoners knew that their participation was completely voluntary and would have no negative reprisals if they did not participate.

While it may be easy to survey individuals on street corners, the general public is often difficult to survey utilizing a robust sampling method. Significant resources need to be in place to create random yet representative samples. One should have large sample frames that include multiple areas clustered by census demographic variables including average area income and population (i.e., multistage cluster sampling). Furthermore, demographic variables should be included to compute weights if random sampling does not yield representative samples. Polling centers or survey centers have already implemented these procedures. Fortunately, many universities have these centers in place that can assist professors in surveying the general public.

Many of the methods above were surveys or experiments. This was done largely because of the degree of control in experiments and the ability to obtain large amounts of information with minimal participant effort for surveys. Laboratory experiments and surveys are consistent with early psychological research methods. However, different methods should also be used to increase our understanding of how and when the independent variables work in real-world contexts. One way to do this is to utilize longitudinal methods, including longitudinal cross-sectional surveys, long-term simulations, and naturalistic experiments. These studies will help determine the effect of different independent variables when a myriad of pressures and influences are affecting the decision-making of the individual or offender. The multitude of influences and variables affecting individual decision-making is considered below.

12.2.1 PATHWAYS AND RESEARCH

In addition to independent and dependent variable designs, research must focus on the interactions between additional independent variables. Research designs that utilize numerous independent variables, mediators, and moderators can be created and analyzed using robust statistical analyses. This will create a body of literature that examines more completely the complexities and pathways associated with convenience theory.

Using an iterative process between theory and empirical research, researchers should seek to identify more complex pathways that stem from the significant pathways found in prior research. Although main-effect pathways are an appropriate first start in research, it is logical to assume that not all components of convenience theory will be present in every offender's case. First, some components are extremely unlikely, if not mutually exclusive from occurring during the same decision-making process. While each process could contribute to white-collar offending in different circumstances, not all will be present in the same offending decision. Second, some factors may fully mediate and take all of the other's variance, thus rendering its explanatory power null. For example, early research on sunk costs suggested that diffusion of responsibility could be the reason why sunk costs could occur (Arkes & Blumer, 1985). If this turns out to be true, measuring both sunk costs and deindividuation will lead to issues of multicollinearity and shared explanatory variance, requiring either theoretical (e.g., not including sunk costs because it is explained by deindividuation) or methodological fixes (e.g., standardization of variables or ridge regressions). In this situation, structural equation modeling (SEM) or Path Analysis models would provide a better understanding as mediators could be defined in the model. Finally, some factors may moderate the relationship between another factor and white-collar offending. For example, social learning is more likely to occur in situations of stress or uncertainty (Pabst, Schoofs, Pawlikowski, Brand, & Wolf, 2013; Starcke, Wolf, Markowitsch, & Brand, 2008). This will likely lead to a moderation between stress and social learning (i.e., in low stress social learning will be less important than in situations of high stress). Additionally, life-course offenders do not need to neutralize as much as first-time or one-time offenders (Romney et al., 1980; Weisburd et al., 1990; Weisburd et al., 2001).

Although still technically moderation effects, more powerful interactions between variables can create wide differences in the use of multiple independent variables. For example, psychopaths have low empathy and guilt (Blackburn, 1996; Skeem, Johansson, Andershed, Kerr, & Louden, 2007). The lack of empathy may drastically change how this type of individual chooses to offend. They may not need to utilize neutralization strategies because an individual without guilt would not need to justify their actions ethically. Psychopaths may also not need to have other social influences if they are behaving in hedonistic ways. In this situation, one independent variable, psychopathy, could drastically change the offending pathway.

To examine these complex relationships, large amounts of data will need to be collected. Cross-sectional surveys provide one mechanism for this collection. Multiple independent variables that were significant in earlier studies can be surveyed together and analyzed using multiple regression or SEM. Surveys could request information on various topics (e.g., economic, organizational, general, etc.) along with vignette measures of white-collar offending.

12.2.2 *ADVANCING THEORY AND RESEARCH*

More specific models will likely need to be utilized to increase explanatory power. The Path Analysis model may predict general white-collar offending, but models will likely be more useful if they are specific to known large population differences, offense types, or moderating variables. These clusters should be informed by the research on main effects and interactions. If large differences are found between types of offenders, the offense itself, other population differences, situational opportunity, or even other independent variables, then models should be dependent on these differences. Empirical differences may create the ability to cluster offenders, leading to differences in models between clusters.

For example, certain independent variables and situational factors may lead to the perception that quick action is required, thus leaving little time for lengthy consideration of the action itself. In these pathways, individuals will likely utilize fewer variables in their decision to offend. In our discussion of independent variables, the presence of two variables would likely lead to quicker decision pathways: stress and behavioral scripts. When individuals are under negative stress, they are likely to try to reduce that stress (Kassam, Koslov, & Mendes, 2009). Their decision-making is negatively affected, and they are less likely to search for alternatives before taking action (Pabst et al., 2013). Behavioral scripts are themselves an automatic patterned behavior. As one author mentions, following a script may cause the individual to not see their actions as a white-collar offense or one in need of further consideration (Gioia, 1992).

In fact, we have an example where one individual describes the brevity in his own decision-making when considering recalling the Ford Pinto. Although many of the factors may have occurred outside the individual's awareness (e.g., heuristics), this personal reflection article is still a good example of the influence of social scripts on decisions to offend. Dennis Gioia was the recall manager of Ford just prior to the Ford Pinto debacle. He remembers Pinto cases coming across his desk, only to ignore them. Gioia even went to see the burned wreckage of a Pinto but did not decide to recall the vehicle. In his analysis, Gioia attributes his lack of awareness of the Pinto problem to following the behavioral script of his job (Gioia, 1992). As the recall manager, he needed to process large amounts of information and cases quickly. Due to this, he developed an automated process that would help him determine quickly if a vehicle needed to be examined further. Yet in the case of the Pinto, the script did not allow him to see the problems. Just as Dennis Gioia failed to act, others following behavioral scripts may take actions that are white-collar offenses, such as overbilling the government for services or marketing financial tools that are known to be poor for clients simply because they are following their social scripts.

In this situation, it may be that two models are needed to accurately explain white-collar offending. One model could utilize offenders who make decisions quickly and thus may leave out longer deliberative reasoning, while another could consider the pathways offenders take when they have a longer time to consider the consequences of their decision. Below is an example of how two models could be created based on another variable: lack of moral awareness that refers to the ability to detect and appreciate the ethical aspects of a decision that must be taken by a decision-maker.

Finally, a combination of psychological and sociological factors exists that affect whether an individual commits a white-collar offense. Future theory and research can explore how psychological variables interact with sociological variables to create a more nuanced understanding of white-collar offending decisions.

Advanced statistical models exist to examine this type of data. Multilevel modeling, such as Hierarchical Linear Models, can handle data with different units of analysis. As the understanding of the psychological influences on white-collar offending progresses, sociological factors may be introduced into these advanced models using multilevel models.

CHAPTER 13

Convenience Perceptions

According to this book, gender influences the convenience of white-collar crime. The gender perspective implicitly depicts men as criminals and women as non-criminals. This chapter examines how potential offenders and non-offenders view convenience in white-collar crime. The dimensions, themes, and structural model of the integrated theory of convenience are once more presented in this chapter. Themes are the basis for convenience statements. According to the research, criminal activity will be more convenient for potential offenders than it will be for non-offenders. Based on their responses to a survey, 71 American sociology and criminology students were categorized as potential offenders or non-offenders. Understudies who comprehend that high-positioning leaders and others in favored positions perpetrate middle-class wrongdoing are viewed as reasonable guilty parties, while understudies who don't appreciate this peculiarity are viewed as possible non-guilty parties. The empirical tests show that, in comparison to assumed non-offenders, assumed offenders find greater motive, opportunity, and behavioral convenience by crime. Norwegian students studying business produced similar findings, expressing a greater comprehension of executive deviance.

The multi-level perspective makes testing the convenience theory difficult. Another test is admittance to wrongdoers and non-guilty parties for exact review. This chapter presents a simplified test that ranks criminology students as potential offenders or potential non-offenders based on how easily they perceive white-collar crimes. The unit of investigation is the possible wrongdoer and non-guilty party at the singular level, consequently staying away from authoritative and primary levels. The section tends to the accompanying examination question: What contrasts

The Gender Gap in White-Collar Crime: A Multi-Country Study of Women Offenders in Economic Crime.
Maryam Kamaei, Petter Gottschalk, and Thomas E. Dearden (Authors)

in the impression of accommodation in middle-class wrongdoing can be tracked down between possible guilty parties and non-wrongdoers? This exploration is significant because it tells the best way to make ideas work and makes it simpler to test an integrated criminological hypothesis for white-collar crime.

13.1 CRIMINOLOGY STUDENT SAMPLE

Students across two upper-level undergraduate criminology courses participated in the survey. Both courses were topics courses that were also electives, one being on white-collar crime and the other being on gender and crime. Although these classes are open to all majors, almost all students attending these courses were criminology and/or sociology majors. Overall, the courses were roughly equal in gender composition between males and females, and all students were traditional college-aged. Both classes had about 50 students. Because students were free to participate or not (see below) and there were likely some students in both classes who were instructed to only participate once, 71 total students participated in the survey.

The university is a large public institution in the eastern part of the United States. The survey was approved by the University Institutional Review Board. Consistent with privacy and ethical protections, no student was compelled to participate. A brief summary of the survey and informed consent was explained. Students then filled out the survey in Table 13.1. Informed consent and surveys were separated and turned in. To further protect student identity, no demographic information was obtained. Nevertheless, demographic factors like gender (Benson & Gottschalk, 2015; Steffensmeier et al., 2013) might be interesting, but they were avoided due to general regulations on personal information and data protection.

13.2 OFFENDERS AND NON-OFFENDERS

The degree to which respondents understand top leaders and other favored people mishandling their situations to perpetrate monetary wrongdoing is the classifying variable in this review. The variable has three items as recorded at the lower part of the poll in Table 13.1. On a scale from completely agreeing with (1) to completely disagreeing (5), each item

TABLE 13.1 Survey Questionnaire for Convenience Theory Research

How Much Do You Concur or Disagree with These Assertions?	Agree Disagree
CEOs and others in favored positions can profit from monetary wrongdoing at work to accomplish their own objectives	1 2 3 4 5 6
Monetary wrongdoing by top leaders and others in favored positions can assist associations with accomplishing their business objectives	1 2 3 4 5 6
CEOs and others in favored positions can profit from monetary wrongdoing at work to keep away from individual liquidation	1 2 3 4 5 6
Monetary wrongdoing by top chiefs and others in favored positions can assist associations with keeping away from Chapter 11	1 2 3 4 5 6
People in top positions have the potential chance to carry out monetary wrongdoing at work in view of their status	1 2 3 4 5 6
People in top positions have the valuable chance to perpetrate monetary wrongdoing at work on account of their admittance to assets	1 2 3 4 5 6
People in top positions have the chance to cover monetary wrongdoing at work where there is institutional decay	1 2 3 4 5 6
People in top positions have the chance to hide monetary wrongdoing at work where there is absence of oversight and control	1 2 3 4 5 6
People in top positions have the potential chance to hide monetary wrongdoing at work where the professional workplace has criminal market structures	1 2 3 4 5 6
Top leaders and others in advantaged positions may carry out monetary wrongdoing at work since they recognize too firmly with the business	1 2 3 4 5 6
Top chiefs and others in favored positions may perpetrate monetary wrongdoing at work since they make a sane evaluation	1 2 3 4 5 6
Top leaders and others in favored positions may carry out monetary wrongdoing at work when they gain culpability from others	1 2 3 4 5 6
Top leaders and others in advantaged positions may carry out monetary wrongdoing at work since they legitimize their activities	1 2 3 4 5 6
Top chiefs and others in special positions may perpetrate monetary wrongdoing at work since they dispose of culpability	1 2 3 4 5 6
It is reasonable that top bosses and other extraordinary individuals abuse their circumstances to execute financial bad behavior when they despise their singular bookkeeping records	1 2 3 4 5 6
It is justifiable that top bosses and other exceptional individuals abuse their circumstances to execute money related bad behavior when the business fights financially and faces the risk of indebtedness	1 2 3 4 5 6
It is reasonable that Chiefs and other extraordinary individuals abuse their circumstances to execute money related bad behavior by offering adjustments in degenerate countries to gain business contracts	1 2 3 4 5 6

was evaluated. With a Cronbach's alpha of 0.862, the three-item potential offending scale has an acceptable reliability score. The typical score on the potential culpable scale is 3.6761, which implies that respondents on average slightly differ with the explanations that culpable is reasonable. Respondents with scores below 3.6761 were considered potential offenders, while those with scores above 3.6761 were considered potential non-offenders. 33 of the 71 people who responded became potential criminals, while 38 became potential non-criminals.

The average score that respondents gave to each statement on the survey instrument is shown in Table 13.2. Table 13.2 shows assumed offenders with the label 1 and assumed non-offenders with the label 0. For most proclamations in accommodation hypothesis, potential wrongdoers concur more than potential non-guilty parties as delineated by lower scores among the 33 accepted guilty parties contrasted with the 38 expected non-wrongdoers. For instance, on a scale ranging from 1 to 5 on the motive-possibilities-individual scale, offenders have an average score of 2.2424, while non-offenders have an average score of 2.3947. Willingness-innocence-justification is the only exception, in which presumed offenders and non-offenders disagree more.

Although the research hypothesis that potential offenders will find white-collar crime to be more convenient than potential non-offenders will be supported by the differences between offenders and non-offenders, it is unclear whether all of these differences are statistically significant. For statistically distinct groups, a threshold of a p-value of 0.05 or less is ideal. However, the less demanding threshold of $p < 0.05$ is frequently regarded as quite acceptable.

There is just a single convenience explanation fulfilling the importance prerequisite in Table 13.3. Compared to potential non-offenders, potential offenders are significantly more in agreement with the statement regarding opportunity-conceal-collapse.

13.3 UNITED STATES – NORWAY COMPARISON

We'll compare our findings to those of a Norwegian study of a similar nature. In a business college in Oslo, students can pursue an elective seminar on "Initiative and Monetary Crime." The course focuses on two main areas. The primary subject is monetary crime in general and

TABLE 13.2 Mean Scores for Convenience for Assumed Offenders (1) Versus Non-Offenders (0)

Convenience Statements		N	Mean	Deviation
Motive-Possibilities-Individual	1	33	2,2424	1,62077
	0	38	2,3947	1,58608
Motive-Possibilities-Corporate	1	33	2,3939	1,63820
	0	38	2,5789	1,74962
Motive-Threats-Individual	1	33	1,9697	1,42489
	0	38	2,5526	1,60569
Motive-Threats-Corporate	1	33	2,4242	1,60137
	0	38	2,7368	1,62221
Opportunity-Commit-Status	1	33	1,6667	1,33853
	0	38	2,0000	1,59391
Opportunity-Commit-Access	1	33	1,4242	1,06155
	0	37	1,8108	1,41102
Opportunity-Conceal-Decay	1	33	1,9697	1,13150
	0	38	2,0789	1,34328
Opportunity-Conceal-Chaos	1	33	1,8485	1,20211
	0	38	2,0526	1,50580
Opportunity-Conceal-Collapse	1	33	1,8182	1,23629
	0	38	2,5263	1,63966
Willingness-Choice-Identity	1	33	2,6970	1,53062
	0	38	3,0000	1,43320
Willingness-Choice-Rationality	1	33	2,6970	1,55090
	0	38	3,2105	1,54496
Willingness-Choice-Learning	1	33	1,9697	1,26206
	0	38	2,3158	1,47236
Willingness-Innocence-Justification	1	32	2,4688	1,54470
	0	38	2,2895	1,55803
Willingness-Innocence-Neutralization	1	33	3,0909	1,62718
	0	38	3,5000	1,55529

white-collar crime specifically, where the theory of rationalization is introduced. The examination of fraud by private sector experts in financial crime, such as local law firms and global auditing firms, is the second topic. The course assessment is a research project where students evaluate a report of investigation by fraud examiners. At the beginning of the term,

TABLE 13.3 Importance of Convenience for Presumed Offenders in Comparison to Non-Offenders

	T-Statistic	Significance
Motive-Possibilities-Individual	–0.400	0.691
Motive-Possibilities-Corporate	–0.458	0.649
Motive-Threats-Individual	–10.607	0.113
Motive-Threats-Corporate	–0.815	0.418
Opportunity-Commit-Status	–0.946	0.347
Opportunity-Commit-Access	–10.283	0.204
Opportunity-Conceal-Decay	–0.367	0.714
Opportunity-Conceal-Chaos	–0.625	0.534
Opportunity-Conceal-Collapse	–20.029	0.046
Willingness-Choice-Identity	–0.861	0.392
Willingness-Choice-Rationality	–10.394	0.168
Willingness-Choice-Learning	–10.055	0.295
Willingness-Innocence-Justification	0.481	0.632
Willingness-Innocence-Neutralization	–10.082	0.283

students received the survey instrument during the final lecture in class. The questionnaire was completed by all present students. A total of 111 completed surveys were returned before students left the class.

With a Cronbach's alpha of 0.862, the three-item potential offending scale has an acceptable reliability score. The fact that respondents had an average score of 3.061 on the potential offending scale indicates that they only slightly agreed with the assertions that offending is understandable. Comparing this score to the score of 3.6761 is interesting. The only two possible explanations for the difference are sociology students versus business students and Norway versus the United States.

For all assertions in the comfort hypothesis, accepted wrongdoers in Norway (business students) agree more than expected non-guilty parties (business students) as indicated by lower scores among the 65 wrongdoers compared to the 46 non-guilty parties. Therefore, in terms of motive, opportunity, and willingness, offenders find crime to be more convenient than non-offenders. In contrast to the sample from the United States, where only one difference was found to be significant, the Norwegian sample had eight of the fourteen statements that were significant.

In conclusion, both Norwegian business students and sociology students in the United States were included in our study as potential offenders because they found it relatively understandable that high-ranking executives and others in privileged positions commit white-collar crime. Students who found it difficult to comprehend became potential non-offenders. When compared to non-offenders, the test of convenience theory demonstrates that offenders find greater behavioral, opportunity, and motive convenience from crime.

The current empirical research is exploratory and insufficient to support the convenience theory as an integrated explanation for the phenomenon of white-collar crime. In the future, it is hoped that more empirical evidence will be gathered to test the theory.

CHAPTER 14

Convenience Themes

Convenience theory is an integrated and deductive approach to explaining the white-collar crime phenomenon based on a number of perspectives from criminology, management, sociology, and psychology. There is convenience in the three dimensions of financial motive, organizational opportunity, and deviant behavior. Based on an empirical study of 268 convicted white-collar offenders in the state of Utah in the United States, this research identified the frequency of various convenience themes within the opportunity dimension. The most surprising result was the large number of victims who had trusted funds in the hands of offenders in an expectation to receive substantial returns from their investments. The principal-agent perspective, which suggests that both principals and agents have narrow self-interest, is applied to this result. Principals (victims) and agents (offenders) may have different risk aversions, knowledge asymmetry exists between the two parties, and the principal has incomplete information about the agent's contribution. Additionally, the interests of the principals and agents tend to diverge.

This chapter presents an empirical study of convicted white-collar offenders in Utah in the United States. This study uses data from Utah's White-collar Crime Offender Registry to examine common themes (Utah Attorney General's Office, 2020). The following research question is addressed in this chapter: What common topics prevail among sentenced middle-class wrongdoers? This research is important because the research literature suggests a number of themes, but few of them are tested or compared empirically.

The Gender Gap in White-Collar Crime: A Multi-Country Study of Women Offenders in Economic Crime.
Maryam Kamaei, Petter Gottschalk, and Thomas E. Dearden (Authors)

14.1 CONVENIENT OPPORTUNITY THEMES

Convenience theory's opportunity dimension focuses on the opportunities available to the offender to commit and conceal white-collar crime. Opportunity is any "potential course of action, made possible by a particular set of social conditions, which has been symbolically incorporated into an actor's repertoire of behavioral possibilities" (Coleman, 1987, p. 409). Convenience themes in the organizational dimension of convenience theory are illustrated in Figures 14.1 and 14.2.

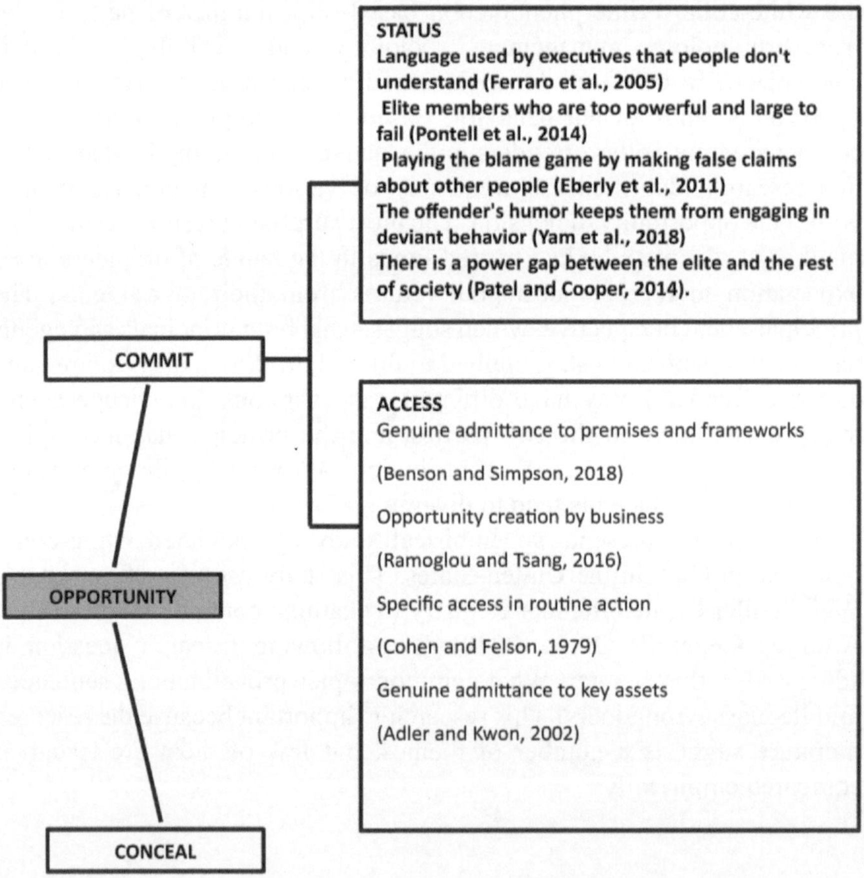

FIGURE 14.1 Convenience theory's structural model of opportunity (part 1:2).

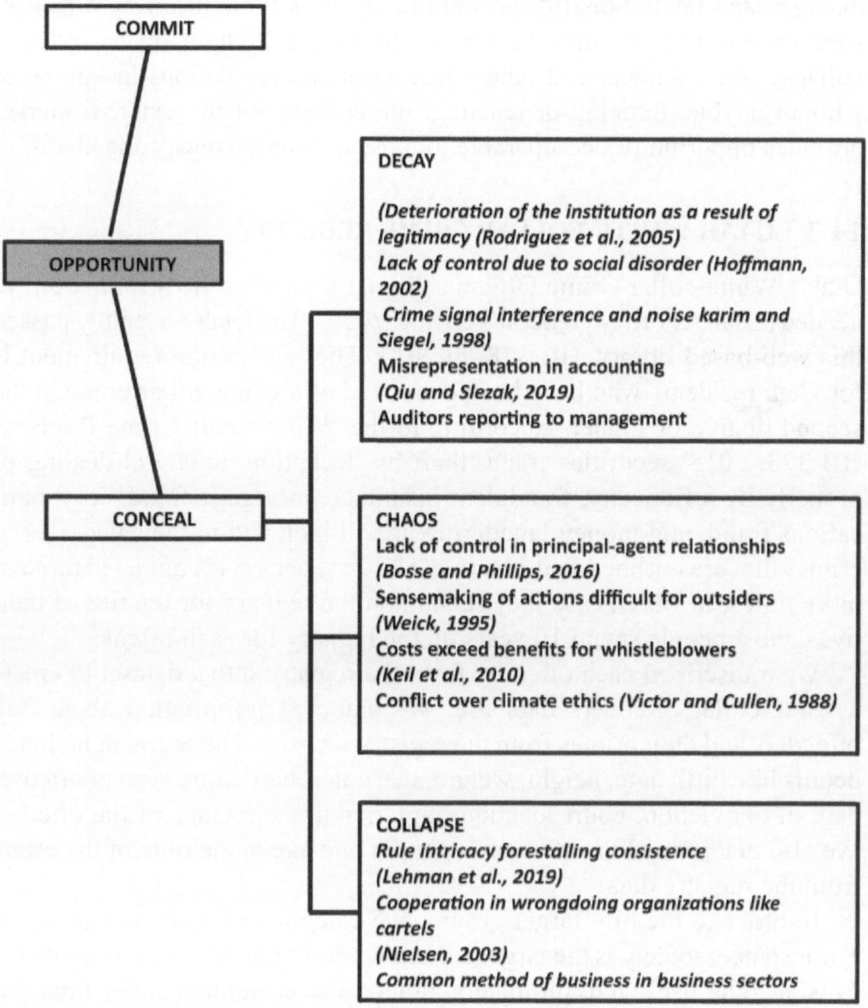

FIGURE 14.2 Structural model of opportunity in convenience theory (part 2:2).

Vadera and Aguilera (2008, p. 434) define a criminal opportunity as "the presence of a favorable combination of circumstances that renders a possible course of action relevant." A chance to fulfill one's desires, goals, and aspirations is appealing.

Due to the offender's status and legitimate access to resources, committing a financial crime may be convenient. Due to decay, chaos, and collapse, it may be convenient to conceal financial crime. Decay is brought on by disorganized institutional deterioration, chaos is brought on by a lack of supervision, and criminal market structures are brought on by external collapse. As offenders and others face laws and regulations in ignorance without anyone noticing or reacting, the collapse of the external market provides opportunities comparable to those of internal decay and chaos.

14.2 UTAH WHITE-COLLAR CRIME REGISTRY

Utah's White-collar Crime Offender Registry gave us the information we needed (Utah Attorney General's Office, 2020). The Utah Assembly passed this web-based library, HB 378, in 2015. The registration requirement is for Utah residents who have been convicted of a white-collar crime in the second degree or higher. According to the White-collar Crime Registry, HB 378, 2015, securities fraud, theft by deception, unlawful dealing of property by a fiduciary, fraudulent insurance, mortgage fraud, communications fraud, and money laundering are all included in the categories of crimes that are outlined in the statute. Unless a person is convicted three or more times, in which case they remain on the registry for the rest of their lives, most people spend 10 years on the registry for each offense.

We transcribed each offender from the registry into a dataset to create a white-collar offenders database. We gathered information about 268 offenders and their crimes from the registry website. The segment included details like birth date, height, weight, eye color, hair color, type of offense, date of conviction, court location, target, and a summary of the offense. We also determined the offender's gender and age at the time of the crime from the registry data.

In order to identify target groups, we categorized white-collar crime. For instance, society is the target when a white-collar criminal commits tax evasion. The bank and, ultimately, other bank customers suffer financial harm when a fraudster commits bank fraud.

When a middle-class offender commits misappropriation, then the business is the victim. When a wrongdoer receives a payoff, the briber's rivals become potential victims.

We could delve into the various targets and explain how males and females select targets, considering gender differences in crime. Bank fraud, for example, might have more severe consequences than embezzlement. According to Gotttschalk and Tcherni-Buzzeo (2017), employers might choose not to report a caught perpetrator to avoid public scrutiny, but financial institutions could take action. Therefore, one could argue that female offenders tend to lean towards embezzlement due to women's heightened concern for the consequences.

The predominant convenience themes among convicted white-collar offenders are the focus of this study. The opportunity dimension's convenience themes were identified using the offense summary. Text strings known as offense summaries can be as short as a few words or as long as this offense summary:

I persuaded my uncle to consent to the use of his commercial property as collateral for a loan that would be used as a down payment for a construction loan and held in escrow. The escrowed down payment was returned, and the construction loan was not funded. Instead of being used to pay off the loan on the uncle's property, the money that was returned was put to use for personal gain. The uncle was constantly misled about the loan's status and payments, and when the loan was not paid, he eventually lost his property to the lender who held collateral rights.

Using content analysis, we examined offense summaries for each of the 268 inmates in the Utah database. Any method or procedure that works to identify characteristics in texts and attempts to make valid inferences is known as content analysis (Duriau et al., 2007; Krippendorff, 1980; Patrucco et al., 2017). According to Bell, Bryman, and Harley (2018), content analysis makes the assumption that language reflects both how people comprehend their surroundings and their cognitive processes (Saunders et al., 2007). Cognizance alludes to what individuals think and how they think, and mental cycles influence the manner by which individuals interpret and understand what is around them. As a result, content analysis enables the identification and determination of pertinent text within a context (McClelland et al., 2010).

14.3 STATUS-ACCESS-DECAY-CHAOS-COLLAPSE

We classified each offense summary into one of the 21 themes illustrated in Figures 14.1 and 14.2, and listed here:

- **STATUS**
  1. Executive language that people do not understand (Ferraro et al., 2005)
  2. Elite members too big to fail and too powerful to jail (Pontell et al., 2014)

3. Blame game by misleading attribution to others (Eberly et al., 2011)
4. Offender humor distraction from deviant behavior (Yam et al., 2018)
5. Power inequality between elite members and others (Patel & Cooper, 2014)

- **ACCESS**
  6. Legal access to systems and premises (Benson & Simpson, 2018)
  7. Entrepreneurial opportunity creation (Ramoglou & Tsang, 2016)
  8. Access restricted to routine activities (Cohen & Felson, 1979)
  9. Access to strategic resources in a legal manner (Adler & Kwon, 2002)

- **DECAY**
  10. Institutional deterioration based on external legitimacy (Rodriguez et al., 2005)
  11. Inability to control because of social disorganization (Hoffmann, 2002)
  12. Interference and noise in crime signals (Karim & Siegel, 1998)
  13. Misrepresentation in accounting (Qiu & Slezak, 2019)
  14. Auditors reporting to management (Hurley et al., 2019)

- **CHAOS**
  15. In principal-agent relationships, lack of control (Bosse & Phillips, 2016)
  16. It is difficult for outsiders to make sense of actions (Weick, 1995)
  17. Whistleblowers face higher costs than rewards (Keil et al., 2010)
  18. Ethical climate conflict (Victor & Cullen, 1988)

- **COLLAPSE**
  19. Rule complexity preventing compliance (Lehman et al., 2019)
  20. Participation in crime networks such as cartels (Nielsen, 2003)
  21. Usual way of business in markets with crime forces (Chang et al., 2005)

Based on content analysis of each offense summary, we arrived at the following distribution of convenience themes in the organizational dimension for the Utah white-collar crime convicts as listed in Table 14.1.

TABLE 14.1 Convenience Themes in the Opportunity Dimension

Opportunity Convenience Themes	Sum
Status	
1. Executive language that people do not understand	3
2. Elite members too big to fail and too powerful to jail	2
3. Blame game by misleading attribution to others	0
4. Offender humor distraction from deviant behavior	0
5. Power inequality between elite members and others	13
Access	
6. Legitimate access to premises and systems	12
7. Opportunity creation by entrepreneurship	7
8. Specialized access in routine activity	19
9. Legitimate access to strategic resources	11
Decay	
10. Institutional deterioration based on external legitimacy	13
11. Inability to control because of social disorganization	28
12. Interference and noise in crime signals	18
13. Misrepresentation in accounting	7
14. Auditors reporting to management	0
Chaos	
15. Lack of control in principal-agent relationships	55
16. Sense-making of actions difficult for outsiders	13
17. Whistleblowers face higher costs than rewards.	0
18. Ethical climate conflict	0
Collapse	
19. Rule complexity preventing compliance	0
20. Participation in crime networks such as cartels	0
21. Usual way of business in markets with crime forces	67

The most frequent theme in Table 14.1 is the "usual way of business in markets with crime forces" with 67 out of 268 white-collar crime cases. However, this theme ended up as a collection of a variety of offenses where no special opportunities could be defined. Many of the cases were simple consumer fraud that does not match the white-collar crime concept very well. Therefore, theme 21 is of little interest to us and is excluded from further analysis.

The second most frequent theme is much more interesting and relevant to us, as it has to do with the problematic principal-agent relationship. 55 out of 268 cases were in this category. People had trusted their money in the hands of other people to make profits above normal levels. Here are some examples:

- Owns Kensington Holdings LLC, Full Moon Capital LLC, Lumen8 Equity Partners LLC, and Strebeck Synergy Group. Claimed the company invested in real estate and mining operations. Told investors they would receive interest annually; investments were secure and provided a promissory note in exchange for funds. Victims' funds were not invested, and victims did not receive funds after requesting their return.
- Fraudulently offered or sold investments in Capstone Equity Capital, LLC. Told investors their money would be used for hard money lending for a development project. Gave investors a document titled "Trust Deed Note," but did not grant an interest in the property. Used later investor money to pay earlier investors.
- Borrowed money on a short-term basis, promising to secure debt with deeds of trust on property, falsely claiming sufficient equity and net worth of millions of dollars. Executed deeds but never recorded them. Failed to pay back loans as scheduled or issued checks for payment on loans which were returned for insufficient funds. Used funds to pay previous investors, as well as business and personal expenses.
- Convinced a victim to invest in a new joint venture by misstating or omitting material facts. Investment money received was actually used for personal expenses.
- We apply to this outcome the head specialist viewpoint, which proposes tight personal responsibility among the two chiefs and specialists. The interests of chiefs (casualties) and specialists (wrongdoers) will generally separate, they might have different hazard avoidance, there is information deviation between the two gatherings, and the chief has defective information about the specialist's contribution. The agency perspective suggests that a chief is often unable to control a specialist who works for the head (Bosse & Phillips, 2016; Chrisman et al., 2007; Pillay & Kluvers, 2014; Williams, 2008).
- Table 14.2 sums up discoveries at the levels in Figure 14.2 that recognize situations with rot, tumult, and breakdown. Table 14.2 represents that most wrongdoers had no advantaged status or access. All things considered, most wrongdoers took advantage of circumstances described by rot, bedlam, and breakdown.

TABLE 14.2 Frequencies of Convenience Themes for Organizational Opportunity

Organizational Opportunity	Frequency	Fraction
Commit Crime Based On Status Too big to fail, blame game, offender humor	18	7%
Commit Crime Based On Access Legitimate access to resources, premises, and systems	49	18%
Conceal Crime Based On Decay Institutional deterioration, social disorganization	66	25%
Conceal Crime Based On Chaos Lack of control and guardianship, no whistleblowing	68	25%
Conceal Crime Based On Collapse Rule complexity, participate in cartels	67	25%
Total	268	100%

It is interesting to compare results from Utah with results from Norway, where the offender-based rather than the offense-based definition of white-collar crime was applied. Not surprisingly, in the comparison between Tables 14.2 and 14.3, the offender-based data have larger fractions for committing crime based on status and access to resources to commit crime.

In conclusion, empirical studies of white-collar crime are rare. Most studies rely on anecdotal evidence from case-based research. This article was based on a large dataset of 268 convicts in Utah that opened up for descriptive statistics of the opportunity structure for offenders. The dataset provides evidence that decay, chaos, and collapse enable many offenders to commit financial crime. Especially in the perspective of principal and agent, where the victim is a principal and the offender is an agent, the offender is able to defraud the victim because of knowledge asymmetry, risk diversion, and lack of transparency.

TABLE 14.3 Frequencies of Convenience Themes in Norway

Organizational opportunity	Frequency	Fraction
Status-Based Crime Committed Too big to fail, the blame game, and criminal humor	71	17%
Commit Crime Based On Access Access to systems, facilities, and resources in a legal manner	129	32%

TABLE 14.3 *(Continued)*

Organizational opportunity	Frequency	Fraction
Conceal Crime Based On Decay Institutional deterioration, social disorganization	76	19%
Discover Crime Inspired By Chaos No whistleblowing, no guardianship or control	98	24%
Conceal Crime Based On Collapse Rule intricacy, partake in cartels	34	8%
Total	408	100%

CHAPTER 15

Danish Offender Case

With the help of a Denmark case study, this chapter returns to the subject of gender. A female employee in Denmark's social security system was able to steal money from her employer for many years. Britta Nielsen is a hardworking employee who plays crucial roles in grant administration and is always available for additional work. Britta Nielsen, Dane's employer, wrote this in her 2016 recommendation for the Queen's Medal of Merit (p. 64). A silver medal was presented to Nielsen. The celebration marked 40 years of employment at the Danish Social Insurance Service. Since then, Nielsen has been accused of stealing approximately $20 million US dollars, or DKK 117 million. In 2018, police captured her in South Africa after she had been on the run for more than a month (Newth, 2018).

Britta Nielsen was accused of embezzlement the following year (NTB, 2019):

Socialstyrelsen has been accused of stealing DKK 117 million from the 65-year-old. At the point when she showed up in court on Thursday, she admitted to the charges against her, but not to the total amount charged by prosecutors. The following year, the BBC reported:

A woman who is accused of stealing 117 million Danish kroner (£13 million) is expected to be found guilty by a Danish court. Britta Nielsen spent 40 years distributing funds to the needy for the Danish Social Welfare Office.

PwC wrote in its report (2019, p. 3) In the 80-page report, BN is used 141 times to refer to Britta Nielsen, including:

There were 66 bank accounts in Denmark between 1993 and 2018, nine of which were credit cards.

In the period 1993–2018, a total of 66 bank accounts, nine were Danish financial institutions or credit cards.

The Gender Gap in White-Collar Crime: A Multi-Country Study of Women Offenders in Economic Crime.
Maryam Kamaei, Petter Gottschalk, and Thomas E. Dearden (Authors)

With an in-depth knowledge of social security processes and her central position in benefit administration, Britta Nielsen was able to cover up her fraud for a long time. She abused PAS from 2000 to 2007 and then used CAS to pay benefits. TAS (tilskudds administrations system/ benefits management system) did not distinguish between system users who registered information about potential beneficiaries and system users who initiated actual benefit payments. No one controlled Nielsen as she created fake beneficiaries with connected bank accounts and initiated payments to the same fake beneficiaries (Benson & Simpson, 2018; Cohen & Felson, 1979). Of course, there was a lack of control in the principal-agent relationship (Bosse & Phillips, 2016). She had to give money to the needy. Instead, she took some of the money herself. It may have had traces of sensational adventures (Craig & Puquero, 2017).

15.1 CONVENIENCE THEORY THEMES

By fabricating false welfare recipients, Britta Nielsen defrauded funds intended for disabled and vulnerable individuals. For defrauding the state of Denmark of DKK 117 million in social security funds, she received a sentence of six and a half years in prison (Ottermann, 2020).

Nielsen didn't simply make fictitious recipients. She additionally made fictitious undertakings – including one she called "Self-improvement" – that were qualified for funding. However, her personal bank accounts received the majority of the funds. In court, her attorney argued that there were no barriers to fraud and that every employee was aware of how simple it was to steal money (Ottermann, 2020).

According to reports, Nielsen told the court that adding your account number and flying to the Bahamas was a joke.

Goldstraw-White (2012) says that Nielsen was driven by avarice. Schoepfer and Piquero (2006) after she had purchased luxury properties in Denmark and South Africa for a long time. She gave three adult children a portion of the stolen money, and all three of them admitted to robbing for the money they received. According to reports, one of the girls bought a starter horse with money. As a result, the Nielsen scam scheme cost the Danish Treasury a lot of money (Ottermann, 2020).

During the trial in court, prosecutor Lisbeth Jorgensen stated, "She betrayed the trust she placed in him when she was hired by the National Welfare Board" (Ottermann, 2020). This could have been the result of a divergent professional identity (Obodaru, 2017) or a rational choice (Pratt & Cullen, 2005). Nielsen explained during the trial that she accidentally fell into a vicious cycle of wanting to improve the lifestyle of her children (Agnew, 2014). Nima Nabipour, her attorney, cited Nielsen's age and health as mitigating factors. When Nielsen became ill and needed to be taken to the hospital in an ambulance, the process was halted several times.

Figure 15.1 illustrates the suggested themes of expediency above. Her perceived innocence—lack of guilt—can be explained by the disappointing work environment that led to the law (Nichol, 2019), sliding down a slippery slope onto the wrong side of the law (Welsh et al., 2014), and a lack of self-control (Gottfredson & Hirschi, 1990).

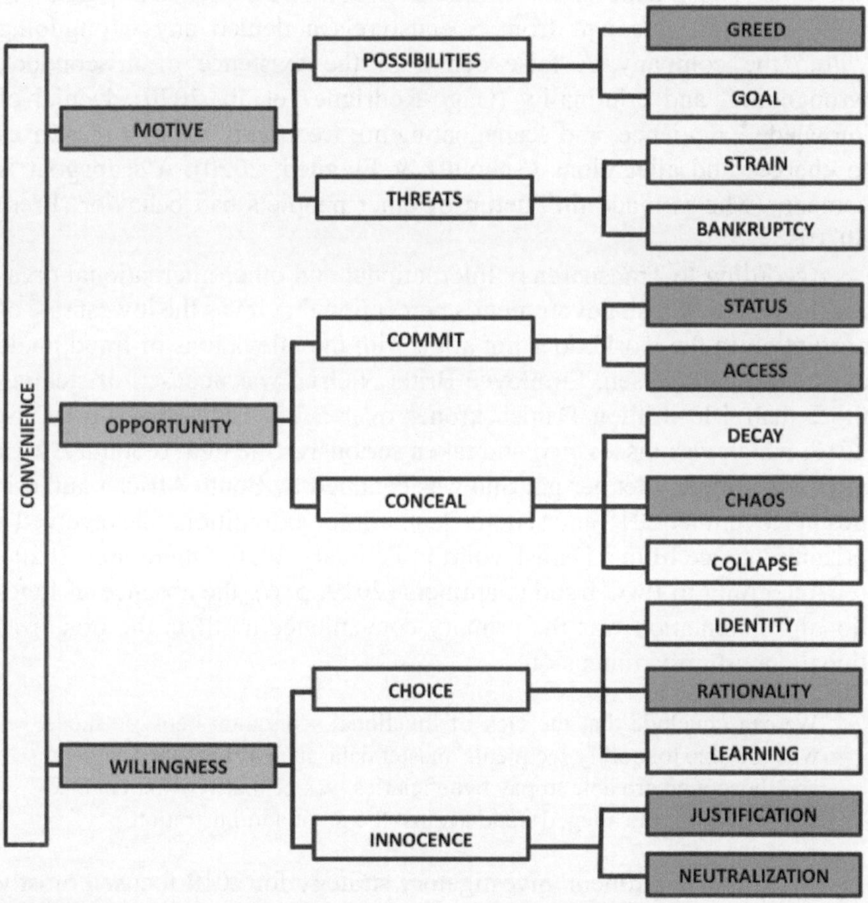

FIGURE 15.1 Convenience themes in the case of Britta Nielsen.

15.2 PwC FRAUD EXAMINATION OUTCOME

The National Board of Social Services in Denmark employed corporate investigators from the international auditing firm PwC (2019). The social services board (Socialstyrelsen) is housed in the Ministry of Social Affairs and Interior. The goal of Socialstyrelsen is to actively participate in social activities that benefit residents. Socialstyrelsen is in charge of a variety of social sector tasks and projects for a variety of groups, including children, young people, families, individuals with disabilities, AIDS and psycho-social initiatives, and adults with social issues. In addition to assisting vulnerable populations like the homeless and unemployed, Socialstyrelsen also offers social benefits to a sizeable portion of the Danish population.

The initial statement from Socialstyrelsen denied any wrongdoing within the company. A false denial of the existence of misconduct, wrongdoing, and criminality (Gago-Rodriguez et al., 2020). Denial of knowledge, deviance, and scapegoating are frequently the first responses to charges and allegations (Schoultz & Flyghed, 2020). A scapegoat is someone who is made the victim of other people's bad behavior (Eren, 2020).

According to Transparency International and other international organizations, the Danish government's perception that it has the lowest rate of corruption in the world does not align with the allegations of fraud made against Socialstirelsen. Employee Britta Nielsen was accused of stealing more than 100 million Danish kroner over a 25-year period in August 2018, which was discovered and taken seriously. She fled to South Africa after the company let her go. She was detained by South African authorities in November 2018 and sent to Denmark for extradition. She received a prison sentence from a Danish court in February 2020 (Ottermann, 2020).

According to PwC fraud examiners (2019, p. 6), the absence of functional segmentation was the primary convenience motif in the organizational opportunity dimension:

> We can conclude that the lack of functional separation between those who are able to modify recipients' master data, such as account numbers, and those who are able to pay beneficiaries was primarily what enabled BN to commit the alleged fraud against the grant administration.

PwC fraud examiners' investigatory strategy for 2019 focused mostly on reviewing financial statements and accounting. They tracked financial transactions from TAS payments to the business accounting system Navision Stat. They located 37 bank accounts that belonged to Nielsen after looking through accounting records from 1993 to 2018. However, not all of Nielsen's pertinent transactions could be recovered by the different banks.

The fraud investigators discovered that starting in 2016, when funds were allocated, email addresses of recipients were automatically notified. Administrative case handlers had the freedom to alter email addresses without any restrictions because email addresses are a component of the basic data. The eligible recipients of funding lost track of the grant administration's approval of their applications after their email addresses were changed.

Performance audits had been carried out at Socialstirelsen by the Danish Auditor General, but PwC fraud examiners were unable to access their findings. Consequently, they ignored information from other sources regarding the Auditor General's work. Instead, fraud investigators simply state that if they had examined the situation in Auditor General documents, their findings might have been different. But, fraud investigators stress that the Auditor General had already made suggestions that may have avoided Nielsen's level of convenience.

They guarantee to have made a few intriguing disclosures to the extent that they had the option to recover the items in Nielsen's email accounts. Based on their prior knowledge of the case, they used straightforward search terms and combinations. Sadly, the openly accessible version of the report makes these pages clear.

The Danish social security agency has 13 control flaws, according to the 2019 PwC report. According to Nielsen (2019), the main flaw was that an employee could create projects and pay grants at the same time. Moves were not exposed to the executives' endorsement or command over who approached monetary frameworks. The examination uncovered that various control capabilities had failed, which might have made sense of Nielsen's misrepresentation's submission.

PwC (2019) did not conduct interviews, or at least they did not mention interviews in their investigation report. This is amazing, as sources and witnesses ordinarily have noticed ways of behaving that can prompt new disclosures and more proof connected with exposures that have proactively happened. While the stolen sum confirmed is now huge, there is in similar cases often more money out there that proficient analysts could identify.

Most of the time, criminals admit to amounts that can be proven with hard evidence, but they are reluctant to talk about additional instances of fraud that investigators haven't found. In situations like these, other people might be able to point investigators in new directions for their inquiries. Colleagues and others are frequently willing to share their observations so long as interviewers treat interviewees fairly and honestly.

The command for PwC's (2019) examination was to recreate arrangements of occasions for maltreatment of social advantage installments and to make sense of how such monetary maltreatment could happen. Moreover, the order requested that specialists determine the magnitude of the misrepresentation for the period from 1977 to 2018. Finally, the order requested that examiners evaluate the control systems and control culture at Socialstirelsen. It appears that agents failed in completing their assessments according to the command.

Price Waterhouse Coopers (PwC) name their misrepresentation assessments as forensic examinations where they lay out facts and analyze issues. They use forensic accountants, lawyers, regulators who have retired, policing like police investigators, information technology experts, and corporate intelligence specialists. They suggest that fraud hides in the shadows, and fraudsters readily exploit the lack of awareness that creates perhaps fraudsters' most convenient opportunity.

15.3 KAMMERADVOKATEN EXAMINATION

Parallel to PwC (2019), which Socialstirelsen hired, the Danish government hired Paul Schmith (Kammeradvokaten, 2019) to determine whether executives' failure to manage controls allowed Britta Nielsen to commit fraud for such a long time (BBC, 2020; Newth, 2018; 2019 by Nielsen; NTB, 2019; 2020, Ottermann). Investigators were tasked with determining whether any official responsibility could be transferred to individuals. Relevant individuals held executive positions in the ministry, the Danish social security system, or another organization.

This mandate is intriguing because guilt attribution is a frequent issue in private economic crime policing. Attempts by suspects to falsely assign blame to others are the primary factor in determining the cause of a negative event, according to attribution theory (Keaveney, 2008) and the blame game hypothesis (Lee & Robinson, 2000) (Eberly et al., 2011). Self-blame is uncommon and rarely present. When something bad happens, no one will blame themselves. Attributing a negative event to one's behavior or disposition is self-blame. Some are too strong to even consider accusing. Pontell and others (2014) found that mismanagement in the financial sector was clearly to blame for the financial crisis, but that no one in the financial sector was particularly to blame. One typical illustration is the Lehmann Brothers collapse investigation. According to Slyke and Bales (2012), status-related factors like influential positions frequently prevent perceptions of blameworthiness.

In contrast to the PwC (2019) examination, Kammeradvokaten (2019) included a responsibility analysis and personal contact reflection with the social security agency. However, Kammeradvokaten is largely based on the work of PwC, and Søren Madsen was the whistleblower.

15.3.1 WHITE-COLLAR CONVENIENCE

It is expected of executives to manage their own organizations. In the event that they fail to execute guardianship against financial wrongdoing, such as misappropriation, they become responsible for offenses and misconduct. The themes of convenience that appear to be relevant to the management at Socialstirelsen are depicted in Figure 15.2.

Avoiding pain and stress in a stressful executive workday may be the motivation (Agnew, 2005, 2012; 2018 (Thaxton and Agnew). In terms of institutional decline, executives were to blame (Rodriguez et al., 2005), which resulted in an inability to exert control due to social disorder (Hoffmann, 2002). According to Lehman et al., in terms of rule complexity, collapse might be a third theme, which prevents compliance (2019).

Leader obliviousness can result from differential affiliation (Sutherland, 1983), where chiefs among themselves build up the conviction that they are in charge since higher class data determination frequently happens (Gamache & McNamara, 2019). They can say that they are innocent because they did not know about the crime (Cohen, 2001). Narcissism may be a problem for them (Zhu & Chen, 2015; Zvi & Elaad, 2018), in which they place a great deal of faith in their own capacity to lead the social security agency. Executives may assert that the crime went unnoticed by the company (Williams et al., 2019). By claiming that they were the victims of Britta Nielsen's crime, they could dispel any guilt, ignorance, or reluctance.

15.3.2 KAMMERADVOKATEN OUTCOME

Law office Kammeradvokaten (2019) arrived at the resolution that no previous or current chiefs at Socialstirelsen merited fault for such disappointments. In contrast, Nielsen's defense attorney argued in court that welfare safeguards were too lax and that management and her coworkers were aware of how easy it was to embezzle at work (Ottermann, 2020).

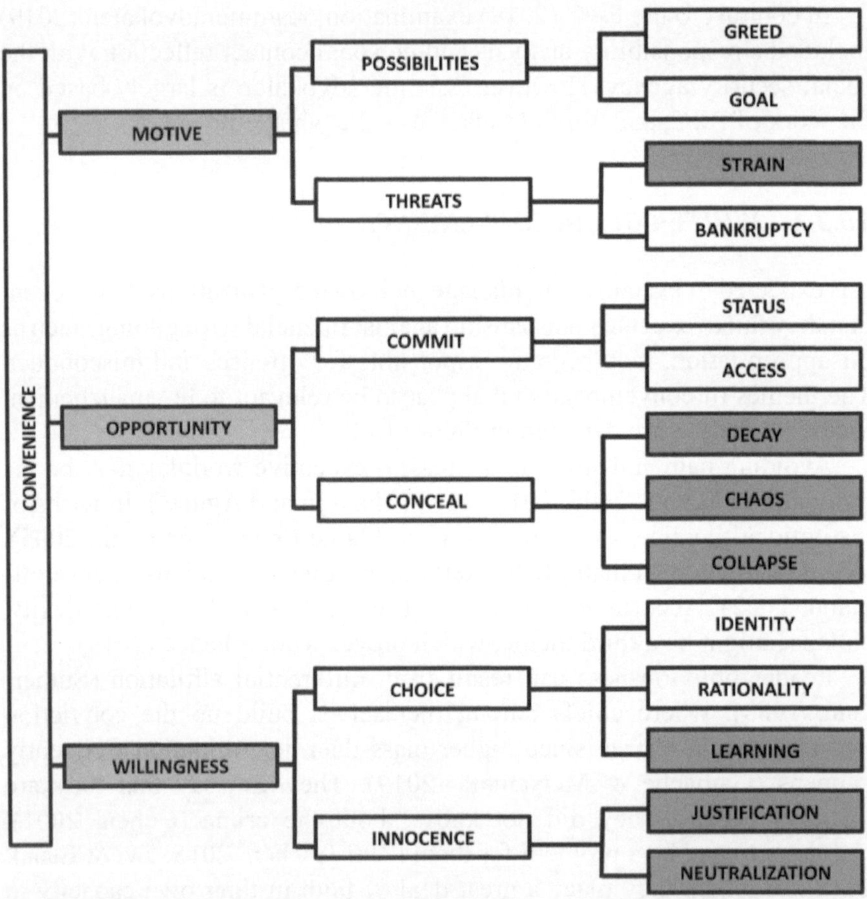

FIGURE 15.2 Convenience themes on account of leaders at Socialstirelsen.

The specialists saw that there were no signs of blackmail or relative irregularities in the help and various experts responsible for government retirement associate organizations. Based on this finding, they conclude that boards and others had no reason to react to an unknown event (Kammeradvokaten, 2019, p. 123):

We start by deciding, in light of the data that is accessible, that the administration's treatment of the comments made by the public authority review on records and reports was quickly deficient, considering that the issue was not completely resolved for at least three years. However, the alleged review shortcoming number 6 regarding records and reports that PwC identified cannot be directly linked to this analysis for not following up on the public review office's comments. The sixth alleged control flaw is Britta Nielsen's ability to disable the reminder function for these, and the auditor general did not mention that the accounting review has been sluggish. Although it must be considered obvious that the large case-file of accounts and reports has been instrumental in creating a control environment where it has been easier for Britta Nielsen to hide her fraud, the criticism raised here must be contrasted with the fact that there is not necessarily a correlation between Britta Nielsen's fraud and the absence of review of accounts and reports.

In this statement, attorneys from Kammeradvokaten (2019) express conflict with examiners from PwC (2019) and accordingly create disarray. The various probabilities of evidence may have contributed to their lack of comprehension of weaknesses. If lawyers apply the rule of beyond a reasonable doubt and auditors apply the rule of more likely than not, they may arrive at different conclusions regarding various pieces of evidence.

However, Kammeradvokaten (2019) keeps downplaying the lack of management attention that PwC (2019) identified in their report:

Likewise, it could promptly seem sketchy that the administration didn't appear to satisfactorily answer the public authority review's remarks in regards to control of payment and client access. On the other hand, we are unable to rule out the possibility that this was followed up on at the time.

According to the mandate, attorneys at Kammeradvokaten (2019) should identify individuals and institutions that might be responsible for a lack of controls; however, in their report, they instead contribute to the diffusion of responsibility.

The investigation was carried out by Kammeradvokaten partners Niels Banke and Lene Damkjær Christensen. The examiners came to the conclusion that neither the grant administration nor the national board of health and welfare bear any personal or functional responsibility, and as a result, they do not recommend any actions other than those that PwC had already emphasized. The only suggestion made by the examiners is that the national board of health and welfare could, if they so choose, enhance their own control mechanisms to make up for any deficiencies.

Conclusion

One of the key uncertainties regarding women in white-collar crime is the extent of gendered detection rate. As discussed in this book, there is indeed a significant difference between the magnitude of female offending and the magnitude of male offending if the detection rate is the same for both. However, as also extensively discussed in this book, there are many arguments suggesting that the probability of white-collar crime detection is lower when there is a female offender compared to a male offender. Simply stated, most people do not suspect women of wrongdoing to the extent they suspect men of wrongdoing. Gossett (2019: 1115) emphasizes the uncertainty when writing about women and white-collar crime in the encyclopedia of women and crime:

> As with any crime statistics, one must keep in mind that the numbers represent those convicted and not those who had never been caught.

While a sample of detected white-collar offenders in Norway suggests 6% women and 94% men, there are reasons to believe that the gender difference is not that substantial because of the gendered detection gap. It has been estimated in Norway that fewer than one out of ten white-collar offenders are caught and brought to justice. A gendered detection gap can cause substantial rethinking of women and men in white-collar crime. For example, if one out of ten men is detected, while one out of twenty women is detected, then the gender difference in crime is not that large after all. This is certainly an interesting avenue for future research.

As emphasized by an anonymous reviewer of this book manuscript, the book presents material that has been a relatively ignored topic in the extant criminology literature. The reviewer wrote in the feedback that the work

The Gender Gap in White-Collar Crime: A Multi-Country Study of Women Offenders in Economic Crime.
Maryam Kamaei, Petter Gottschalk, and Thomas E. Dearden (Authors)

"is an admirable undertaking on when, how, and why women commit" white-collar crime. However, reviewers have also made critical remarks. For example, they have questioned why there is a comparison between Utah and Norway, as those two parts of the world are different in many respects. Nevertheless, we decided to keep the comparison in the book, although it would be desirable to have samples that are more suited for comparison. Again, this is an encouragement for future research.

An important contribution of this book was the number of case studies of convicted women in Norway and one case study of a convicted woman in Denmark. It will be interesting to see more case studies from European countries such as France, Germany, and the United Kingdom.

Another important contribution of this book was the application of convenience theory to women in white-collar crime. The book has identified a number of gendered financial motives, organizational opportunities, and willingness enablers. Hopefully, future research may explore and exploit more issues that have gender differences in the perception of convenience when committing and concealing white-collar crime.

Bibliography

Abassi, A. (2021). Is sugar mafia winning against govt? *International the News*. Retrieved from: www.thenews.com.pk (accessed on 8 July 2024).

Abraham, M. (2017). Pay formalization revisited: Considering the effects of manager gender and discretion on closing the gender age gap. *Academy of Management Journal, 60*(1), 29–54.

Abraham, M. (2020). Gender-role incongruity and audience-based gender bias: An examination of networking among entrepreneurs. *Administrative Science Quarterly, 65*(1), 151–180.

Adler, P. S., & Kwon, S. W. (2002). Social capital. Prospects for a new concept. *Academy of Management Review, 27*(1), 17–40.

Afkar. (2012). Mashreqnews claims violations in steel business. *Afkar News*. Retrieved from: www.afkarnews.com (accessed on 8 July 2024).

Agnew, R. (1992). Foundation for a general strain theory of crime and delinquency. *Criminology, 30*(1), 47–87.

Agnew, R. (2005). *Pressured into Crime: An Overview of General Strain Theory*. Oxford University Press.

Agnew, R. (2012). Reflection on 'A revised strain theory of delinquency.' *Social Forces, 91*(1), 33–38.

Agnew, R. (2014). Social concern and crime: Moving beyond the assumption of simple self-interest. *Criminology, 52*(1), 1–32.

Aguilera, R. V., & Vadera, A. K. (2008). The dark side of authority: Antecedents, mechanisms, and outcomes of organizational corruption. *Journal of Business Ethics, 77*, 431–449.

Akers, R. L. (1989). A social behaviorist's perspective on integration of theories of crime and deviance. In S. F. Messner, M. D. Krohn, & A. E. Liska (Eds.), *Theoretical Integration in the Study of Deviance and Crime* (pp. 23–36). State University of New York Press.

Akhbar. (2012). Agricultural Bank skepticism. *Akhbar News*. Retrieved from: www.akhbarekhouzestan.blogfa.com (accessed on 8 July 2024).

Akinola, M., Martin, A. E., & Phillips, K. W. (2018). To delegate or not to delegate: Gender differences in affective associations and behavioral responses to delegation. *Academy of Management Journal, 61*(4), 1467–1491.

Almaqableh, L., Wallace, D., Pereira, V., Ramiah, V., Wood, G., Veron, J. F., Moosa, I., & Watson, A. (2022). Is it possible to establish the link between drug busts and the cryptocurrency market? *International Journal of Information Management, 71*, 102488. https://doi.org/10.1016/j.ijinfomgt.2022.102488.

Alper, M. (2014). "Can our kids hack it with computers?" Constructing youth hackers in family computing magazines (1983–1987). *International Journal of Communication, 8*(1), 673–698.

Anon. (2007). The sugar mafia. *Workers Liberty*. Retrieved from: www.workersliberty.org (accessed on 8 July 2024).

Arkes, H. R., & Blumer, C. (1985). The psychology of sunk cost. *Organizational Behavior and Human Decision Processes, 35*, 124–150.

Asker Bærum. (2012). Case 11-063509MED-AHER/1. *Asker and Bærum district court.*

Asting, C., & Gottschalk, P. (2022). Attorney fraud in the law firm: A case study of crime convenience theory and crime signal detection theory. *Deviant Behavior, 44*(4), 591–602. https://doi.org/10.1080/01639625.2022.2071657.

Baer, M. H. (2014). Confronting the two faces of corporate fraud. *Florida Law Review, 66*, 87–156.

Bai, M. (2020). Altså, hvorfor kunne de ikke bare smøre brødskiver, disse innvandrerkvinnene? (So, why could they not just grease slices of bread, these immigrant women?). *Nettavisen*. Retrieved from: www.nettavisen.no (accessed on 8 July 2024).

Baird, J. E., & Zelin, R. C. (2009). An examination of the impact of obedience pressure on perceptions of fraudulent acts and the likelihood of committing occupational fraud. *Journal of Forensic Studies in Accounting and Business, 1*(1), 1–14.

Bao, D., Kim, Y., Mian, G. M., & Su, L. (2019). Do managers disclose or withhold bad news? Evidence from short interest. *The Accounting Review, 94*(3), 1–26.

Barak, G. (2007). Doing news making criminology from within the academy. *Theoretical Criminology, 11*(2), 191–207.

Barlett, C., & Coyne, S. M. (2014). A meta-analysis of sex differences in cyber-bullying behavior: The moderating role of age. *Aggressive Behavior, 40*(5), 474–488.

Baron, R. M., & Kenny, D. A. (1986). The moderator–mediator variable distinction in social psychological research: Conceptual, strategic, and statistical considerations. *Journal of Personality and Social Psychology, 51*(6), 1173–1182.

Baron, S. W. (2004). General strain, street youth and crime: A test of Agnew's revised theory. *Criminology, 42*, 457–483.

Barton, H. (2004). Cultural reformation: A case for intervention within the police service. *International Journal of Human Resources Development and Management, 4*(2), 191–199.

Bazaar. (2022). The sugar mafia. *Bazaar News*. Retrieved from: www.bourseandbazaar.com.

BBC. (2020). Britta Nielsen: Danish social worker accused of stealing millions. *British Broadcasting Corporation*. Retrieved from: www.bbc.com (accessed on 8 July 2024).

Becker, S., & McCorkel, J. A. (2011). The gender of criminal opportunity: The impact of male co-offenders on women's crime. *Feminist Criminology, 6*(2), 79–110.

Belfort, J. (2008). *The Wolf of Wall Street: How Money Destroyed a Wall Street Superman.* London, UK: Hodder and Stoughton.

Bell, E., Bryman, A., & Harley, B. (2018). *Business Research Methods* (2nd ed.). Oxford, UK: Oxford University Press.

Bellante, D., & Link, A. N. (1981). Are public sector workers more risk averse than private sector workers? *Industrial and Labor Relations Review, 34*(3), 408–412.

Benartzi, S., Beshears, J., Milkman, K. L., Sunstein, C. R., Thaler, R. H., Shankar, M., Tucker-Ray, W., Congdon, W. J., & Galing, S. (2017). Should governments invest more in nudging? *Psychological Science, 28*(8), 1041–1055.

Benson, M. L. (2020). Theoretical and empirical advances in the study and control of white-collar offenders. *Justice Evaluation Journal, 4*(1), 1–20. https://doi.org/10.1080/24751979.2020.1808855.

Benson, M. L., & Chio, H. L. (2020). Who commits occupational crime? In M. L. Rorie (Ed.), *The Handbook of White-Collar Crime* (pp. 97–112). Hoboken, NJ: John Wiley and Sons.

Benson, M. L., & Gottschalk, P. (2015). Gender and white-collar crime in Norway: An empirical study of media reports. *International Journal of Law, Crime and Justice, 43*(4), 535–552.

Benson, M. L., & Harbinson, E. (2020). Gender and criminal thinking among individuals convicted of white-collar crime. *Criminal Justice Studies, 33*(1), 46–60. https://doi.org/10.1080/1478601X.2020.1709953.

Benson, M. L., & Simpson, S. S. (2015). *Understanding White-Collar Crime: An Opportunity Perspective*. New York, NY: Routledge.

Benson, M. L., & Simpson, S. S. (2018). *White-Collar Crime: An Opportunity Perspective* (3rd ed.). New York, NY: Routledge.

Benulic, B. (2018). *Inte Mitt Krig (Not my war)*. Cultura Aetatis Publishing, Sweden.

Berdahl, J. L. (2007). Harassment based on sex: Protecting social status in the context of gender hierarchy. *Academy of Management Review, 32*(2), 641–658.

Berge, I. (2010). Ny fengselsdom i den omfattende Tordenskjold-saken (New prison sentence in the comprehensive Tordenskjold case). Norwegian web-based newspaper *Nettavisen*. Retrieved from: www.nettavisen.no.

Bernat, I., & Whyte, D. (2020). State-corporate crime. In M. L. Rorie (Ed.), *The Handbook of White-Collar Crime* (pp. 191–208). Hoboken, NJ: Wiley and Sons.

Bjåen, B. K. (2020). Tek frå Født Fri–gjev til Bydelsmødre (Take away from Born Free–Give it to City Mothers). Daily Norwegian newspaper *Vårt Land*. Retrieved from: www.vl.no (accessed on 8 July 2024).

Bjerknes, O. T., & Fahsing, I. A. (2018). *Etterforskning–Prinsipper, metoder og praksis (Investigation–Principles, Methods, and Practice)*. Fagbokforlaget Publishing House, Bergen, Norway.

Bjørdal, S. (2020). Født Fri krever utbetaling for å svare på anklagene (Born Free requires payment to respond to the charges). Daily Norwegian newspaper *Vårt Land*. Retrieved from: www.vl.no (accessed on 8 July 2024).

Bjørkelo, B., Einarsen, S., Nielsen, M. B., & Matthiesen, S. B. (2011). Silence is golden? Characteristics and experiences of self-reported whistleblowers. *European Journal of Work and Organizational Psychology, 20*(2), 206–238.

Black, M., Yeung, J., & Yeung, D. (2022). *Insider Threat and White-Collar Crime in Non-Government Organisations and Industries–A Literature Review*. Rand Corporation Australia. Retrieved from: www.rand.org (accessed on 8 July 2024).

Blackburn, R. (1996). Replicated personality disorder clusters among mentally disordered offenders and their relation to dimensions of personality. *Journal of Personality Disorders, 10*(1), 68–81.

Blickle, G., & Schütte, N. (2017). Trait psychopathy, task performance, and counterproductive work behavior directed toward the organization. *Personality and Individual Differences, 109*, 225–231.

Blickle, G., Schlegel, A., Fassbender, P., & Klein, U. (2006). Some personality correlates of business white-collar crime. *Applied Psychology: An International Review, 55*(2), 220–233.

Bogen, T. (2008). *Hvor var du, historien om mitt liv (Where were you, the story of my life)*. Schibsted Publishing, Oslo, Norway.

Borricand, J., Abrandabadi, N., & Hossein, A. (1998). Organized crime in French criminal law. *Legal Research Quarterly, 1*(21–22), 313–334.

Bosse, D. A., & Phillips, R. A. (2016). Agency theory and bounded self-interest. *Academy of Management Review, 41*(2), 276–297.

Bossler, A. M., & Burrus, G. W. (2011). The general theory of crime and computer hacking: Low self-control hackers? In T. J. Holt & B. H. Schell (Eds.), *Corporate Hacking and Technology-Driven Crime: Social Dynamics and Implications* (pp. 38–67). Hershey, PA: IGI Global.

Bossler, A., & Holt, T. (2009). On-line activities, guardianship, and malware infection: An examination of routine activities theory. *International Journal of Cyber Criminology, 3*(1), 400. Retrieved from: https://www.questia.com/library/journal/1P3-1988429601/on-line-activities-guardianship-and-malware-infection (accessed on 8 July 2024).

Botelho, T. L., & Abraham, M. (2017). Pursuing quality: How search costs and uncertainty magnify gender-based double standards in a multistage evaluation process. *Administrative Science Quarterly, 62*(4), 698–730.

Bourgoin, A., Bencherki, N., & Faraj, S. (2020). "And who are you?": A performance perspective on authority in organizations. *Academy of Management Journal, 63*(4), 1134–1165.

Bourse and Bazaar. (2019). Iranians forced to forgo meat staples as prices soar. *Bourse & Bazaar Foundation*. Retrieved from: www.bourseandbazaar.com (accessed on 8 July 2024).

Bowles, H. R., & Flynn, F. (2010). Gender and persistence in negotiation: A dyadic perspective. *Academy of Management Journal, 53*(4), 769–787.

Bowman, D., & Gilligan, G. (2008). Public awareness of corruption in Australia. *Journal of Financial Crime, 14*(4), 438–452.

Braaten, C. N., & Vaughn, M. S. (2019). Convenience theory of cryptocurrency crime: A content analysis of U.S. federal court decisions. *Deviant Behavior, 42*(8), 958–978. https://doi.org/10.1080/01639625.2019.1706706.

Bradshaw, E. A. (2015). "Obviously, we're all oil industry": The criminogenic structure of the offshore oil industry. *Theoretical Criminology, 19*(3), 376–395.

Brands, R. A., & Mehra, A. (2019). Gender, brokerage, and performance: A construal approach. *Academy of Management Journal, 62*(1), 196–219.

Brandvold, Å. (2020). Fra frihetskamp til intern strid (From freedom fight to internal conflict). Daily Norwegian newspaper *Klassekampen*, 1, 10, 13.

Brenner, P. S. (2016). Cross-national trends in religious service attendance. *Public Opinion Quarterly, 80*(2), 563–583.

Brescoll, V. L. (2011). Who takes the floor and why: Gender, power, and volubility in organizations. *Administrative Science Quarterly, 56*(4), 622–641.

Brickey, K. F. (2006). In Enron's wake: Corporate executives on trial. *Journal of Criminal Law and Criminology, 96*, 397–433.

Briscoe, F., & Joshi, A. (2017). Bringing the boss's politics in: Supervisor political ideology and the gender gap in earnings. *Academy of Management Journal, 60*(4), 1415–1441.

Britton, D. M. (2000). Feminism in criminology: Engendering the outlaw. *Annals of the American Academy of Political and Social Science, 571*, 57–76.

Bucy, P. H., Formby, E. P., Raspanti, M. S., & Rooney, K. E. (2008). Why do they do it? The motives, mores, and character of white-collar criminals. *St. John's Law Review, 82*, 401–571.

Buggeland, S. A., Hassan, A., Johnsen, N., & Kristiansen, T. (2020). Varslet mot Rehman-stiftelse: Mener penger ble brukt feil (Warned against Rehman foundation: Believes money was spent incorrectly). Daily Norwegian newspaper *VG*. Retrieved from: www.vg.no (accessed on 8 July 2024).

Burns, R. G., & Orrick, L. (2002). Assessing newspaper coverage of corporate violence: The dance hall fire in Gotenburg. *Critical Criminology, 11*, 137–150.

Burrai, E., Font, X., & Cochraine, J. (2015). Destination stakeholders' perceptions of volunteer tourism: An equity theory approach. *International Journal of Tourism Research, 17*, 451–459.

Bussmann, K. D., Niemeczek, A., & Vockrodt, M. (2018). Company culture and prevention of corruption in Germany, China and Russia. *European Journal of Criminology, 15*(3), 255–277.

Butterfield, K. D., Treviño, L. K., & Weaver, G. R. (2000). Moral awareness in business organizations: Influences of issue-related and social context factors. *Human Relations, 53*(7), 981–1018.

Calvete, E., Orue, I., Estévez, A., Villardón, L., & Padilla, P. (2010). Cyberbullying in adolescents: Modalities and aggressors' profile. *Computers in Human Behavior, 26*(5), 1128–1135.

Campagna, R. L., Dirks, K. T., Knight, A. P., Crossley, C., & Robinson, S. L. (2020). On the relation between felt trust and actual trust: Examining pathways to and implications of leader trust meta-accuracy. *Journal of Applied Psychology, 105*(9), 994–1012.

Campbell, A., Muncer, S., & Bibel, D. (2001). Women and crime: An evolutionary approach. *Aggression and Violent Behavior, 6*(5), 481–497.

Campbell, D. T., & Fiske, D. W. (1959). Convergent and discriminant validation by the multitrait-multimethod matrix. *Psychological Bulletin, 56*(2), 81–105.

Cardao-Pito, T. (2021). An embezzler test for norms, standards and regulations. *Journal of Financial Crime, 29*(3). https://doi.org/10.1108/JFC-06-2021-0140.

Carnahan, S., & Greenwood, B. N. (2018). Managers' political beliefs and gender inequality among subordinates: Does his ideology matter more than hers? *Administrative Science Quarterly, 63*(2), 287–322.

Carroll, J., & Weaver, F. M. (2017). Shoplifters' perceptions of crime opportunities: A process-tracing study. In D. B. Cornish & R. V. Clarke (Eds.), *The Reasoning Criminal: Rational Choice Perspectives on Offending* (pp. 19–38). Routledge.

Cauffman, E. (2008). Understanding the female offender. *The Future of Children, 18*(2), 119–142.

Ceccato, V., & Benson, M. L. (2016). Tax evasion in Sweden 2002–2013: Interpreting changes in the rot/rut deduction system and predicting future trends. *Crime, Law and Social Change, 66*, 217–232.

Chan, F., & Gibbs, C. (2020). Integrated theories of white-collar and corporate crime. In M. L. Rorie (Ed.), *The Handbook of White-Collar Crime* (pp. 191–208). John Wiley & Sons.

Chan, F., & Gibbs, C. (2022). When guardians become offenders: Understanding guardian capability through the lens of corporate crime. *Criminology, 60*(2), 321–341. https://doi.org/10.1111/1745-9125.12300.

Chan, H. C., Myers, W. C., & Heide, K. M. (2010). An empirical analysis of 30 years of US juvenile and adult sexual homicide offender data: Race and age differences in the victim–Offender relationship. *Journal of Forensic Sciences, 55*(5), 1282–1290.

Chang, J. J., Lu, H. C., & Chen, M. S. (2005). Organized crime or individual crime? Endogenous size of a criminal organization and the optimal law enforcement. *Economic Inquiry, 43*(3), 661–675.

Chatterjee, A., & Pollock, T. G. (2017). Master of puppets: How narcissistic CEOs construct their professional worlds. *Academy of Management Review, 42*(4), 703–725.

Chattopadhyay, P., Glick, W. H., & Huber, G. P. (2001). Organizational actions in response to threats and opportunities. *Academy of Management Journal, 44*(5), 937–955.

Chen, Y., & Moosmayer, D. C. (2020). When guilt is not enough: Interdependent self-construal as moderator of the relationship between guilt and ethical consumption in a Confucian context. *Journal of Business Ethics, 161*, 551–572.

Chen, Y., & Sun, Y. (2003). Age differences in financial decision-making: Using simple heuristics. *Educational Gerontology, 29*(7), 627–635.

Chism, K. A., & Steinmetz, K. F. (2018). Technocrime and strain theory. In K. F. Steinmetz & M. R. Nobles (Eds.), *Technocrime and Criminological Theory* (pp. 88–107). Routledge.

Chrisman, J. J., Chua, J. H., Kellermanns, F. W., & Chang, E. P. C. (2007). Are family managers agents or stewards? An exploratory study in privately held family firms. *Journal of Business Research, 60*(10), 1030–1038.

Cialdini, R. B., Reno, R. R., & Kallgren, C. A. (1990). A focus theory of normative conduct: Recycling the concept of norms to reduce littering in public places. *Journal of Personality and Social Psychology, 58*(6), 1015–1026.

Cianci, A. M., Clor-Proell, S. M., & Kaplan, S. E. (2019). How do investors respond to restatements? Reputation and the announcement of corrective actions. *Journal of Business Ethics, 158*, 297–312.

Cisco. (2019). Cisco Visual Networking Index: Forecast and trends, 2017–2022 White Paper. https://www.cisco.com/c/en/us/solutions/collateral/service-provider/visual-networking-index-vni/white-paper-c11-741490.html#_Toc532256789 (accessed on 8 July 2024).

Clark, L. A., Foote, D. A., Clark, W. R., & Lewis, J. L. (2010). Equity sensitivity: A triadic measure and outcome/input perspectives. *Journal of Managerial Issues, 22*(3), 286–305.

Clarkson, R., & Darjee, R. (2022). White-collar crime: A neglected area in forensic psychiatry? *Psychiatry, Psychology and Law, 29*(6), 926–952. https://doi.org/10.1080/13218719.2021.1995522.

Cleff, T., Naderer, G., & Volkert, J. (2013). Motives behind white-collar crime: Results of a quantitative study in Germany. *Society and Business Review, 8*(2), 145–159.

Cohen, L. E., & Felson, M. (1979). Social change and crime rate trends: A routine activity approach. *American Sociological Review, 44*, 588–608.

Cohen, S. (2001). *States of Denial: Knowing About Atrocities and Suffering*. Polity Press.

Coleman, J. (1987). Toward an integrated theory of white-collar crime. *American Journal of Sociology, 93*(2), 406–439.

Comey, J. B. (2009). Go directly to prison: White-collar sentencing after the Sarbanes-Oxley Act. *Harvard Law Review, 122*, 1728–1749.

Consumer Financial Protection Bureau. (2013). Arbitration study preliminary results: Section 1028(a) Study results to date. Retrieved from: http://files.consumerfinance.gov/f/201312_cfpb_arbitration-study-preliminary-results.pdf (accessed on 8 July 2024).

Corston, B. (2007). *A Review of Women with Particular Vulnerabilities in The Criminal Justice System*. Home Office.

Craig, J. M., & Piquero, N. L. (2016). The effects of low self-control and desire-for-control on white-collar offending: A replication. *Deviant Behavior, 37*(11), 1308–1324.

Craig, J. M., & Piquero, N. L. (2017). Sensational offending: An application of sensation seeking to white-collar and conventional crime. *Crime and Delinquency, 63*(11), 1363–1382.

Croall, H. (2003). 'Men's businesses? Some gender questions about white collar crime. *Crime and Justice Studies*, The Centre for Crime and Justice Studies, 53, 26–27.

Crosina, E., & Pratt, M. G. (2019). Toward a model of organizational mourning: The case of former Lehman Brothers bankers. *Academy of Management Journal, 62*(1), 66–98.

Cullen, F. T., & Wilcox, P. (2010). *Encyclopedia of Criminological Theory*. Sage Publications.

Cullen, F. T., Graham, A., Jonson, C. L., Pickett, J. T., Sloan, M. M., & Haner, M. (2021). The denier in chief: Faith in Trump and techniques of neutralization in a pandemic. *Deviant Behavior, 43*(7), 892–851. https://doi.org/10.1080/01639625.2021.1918035

Cumming, D., Leung, T. Y., & Rui, O. (2015). Gender diversity and securities fraud. *Academy of Management Journal, 58*(5), 1572–1593.

Dalton, D., & Ortegren, M. (2011). Gender differences in ethics research: The importance of controlling for the social desirability response bias. *Journal of Business Research, 103*, 73–93.

Daly, K. (1989a). Gender and varieties of white-collar crime. *Criminology, 27*(4), 769–794.

Daly, K. (1989b). Rethinking judicial paternalism: Gender, work-family relations, and sentencing. *Gender and Society, 3*(1), 9–36.

Damghanian, H., & Ghaleroudkhani, F. G. (2022). Discretionary workplace behaviors: The effect of communication satisfaction on workplace deviance and OCB with the mediation role of justice sensitivity. *Iranian Journal of Management Studies, 15*(1), 155–168.

Dearden, T. E. (2016). Trust: The unwritten cost of white-collar crime. *Journal of Financial Crime, 23*(1), 87–101.

Dearden, T. E. (2017). An assessment of adults' views on white-collar crime. *Journal of Financial Crime, 24*(2), 309–321.

Dearden, T. E. (2019). How modern psychology can help us understand white-collar criminals. *Journal of Financial Crime, 26*(1), 61–73.

Dearden, T., & Gottschalk, P. (2021). Gender and white-collar crime: Convenience in target selection. *Deviant Behavior, 42*(11), 1485–1493.

Deloitte. (2017). *Gransking, Byggesaksavdelingen, Drammen kommune* (Investigation, Building regulations department, Municipality of Drammen). Oslo, Norway.

Denner, J. (2011). What predicts middle school girls' interest in computing? *International Journal of Gender, Science and Technology, 3*(1), 53–69.

Desmond, S. A., Rorie, M., & Sohoni, T. (2022). Working for God: Religion and occupational crime and deviance. *Deviant Behavior, 44*(2), 159–174. https://doi.org/10.1080/01639625.2021.2022968.

Dhall, R., & Selimovic, T. (2020). *Vedtak om tilbakehold av tilskudd* (Decision on withholding of grants) [Letter to chairperson at Born Free, Jan Sverre Asker]. IMDi (Integration and Diversity Directorate).

Dilmaç, B. (2009). Psychological needs as a predictor of cyber bullying: A preliminary report on college students. *Kuram ve Uygulamada Egitim Bilimleri, 9*(3), 1307–1325.

DN. (2020). DN mener: Shabana skuffer, men her er det også mer som skurrer (DN means: Shabana disappoints, but here there is more going on). *Dagens Næringsliv*, p. 2.

Dodge, M. (2007). Women who commit white-collar crime. In H. N. Pontell & G. Geis (Eds.), *International Handbook of White-Collar and Corporate Crime* (pp. 379–405). Springer Science + Business Media.

Dodge, M. (2009). *Women and White-Collar Crime*. Prentice Hall.

Dodge, M. (2020). Who commits corporate crime? In M. L. Rorie (Ed.), *The Handbook of White-Collar Crime* (pp. 113–126). John Wiley and Sons.

Dollar, D., Fisman, R., & Gatti, R. (2001). Are women really the "fairer sex"? Corruption and women in government. *Journal of Behavior, Economic and Organization, 46*(4), 423–429.

Donk, D. P. van, & Molloy, E. (2008). From organizing as projects, to projects as organizations. *International Journal of Project Management, 26*, 129–137.

Donner, C. M., Marcum, C. D., Jennings, W. G., Higgins, G. E., & Banfield, J. (2014). Low self-control and cybercrime: Exploring the utility of the general theory of crime beyond digital piracy. *Computers in Human Behavior, 34*, 165–172.

Downing, S., Kang, J. S., & Markman, G. D. (2019). What you don't see can hurt you: Awareness cues to profile indirect competitors. *Academy of Management Journal, 62*(6), 1872–1900.

Dugstad, L. (2011a). Innrømmer bedrageriet (Admits the fraud). *Dagens Næringsliv*, pp. 6–7.

Dugstad, L. (2011b). Fikk 380.000 for svindel (Got 380,000 for fraud). *Dagens Næringsliv*, p. 11.

Duriau, V. J., Reger, R. K., & Pfarrer, M. D. (2007). A content analysis of the content analysis literature in organization studies: Research themes, data sources, and methodological refinements. *Organizational Research Methods, 10*(1), 5–34.

Dwivedi, P., Joshi, A., & Misangyi, V. F. (2018). Gender-inclusive gatekeeping: How (mostly male) predecessors influence the success of female CEOs. *Academy of Management Journal, 61*(2), 379–404.

Eberly, M. B., Holley, E. C., Johnson, M. D., & Mitchell, T. R. (2011). Beyond internal and external: A dyadic theory of relational attributions. *Academy of Management Review, 36*(4), 731–753.

Eghtesad. (2013). Tahmasab Mazaheri and the tea mafia. *Eghtesad Online*. http://www.eghtesadonline.com (accessed on 8 July 2024).

Eisenberg, N., & Miller, P. A. (1987). The relation of empathy to prosocial and related behaviors. *Psychological Bulletin, 101*(1), 91–119.

Elsbach, K. D. (2006). *Organizational Perception Management*. Lawrence Erlbaum Associates.

Engdahl, O. (2015). White-collar crime and first-time adult-onset offending: Explorations in the concept of negative life events as turning points. *International Journal of Law, Crime and Justice, 43*(1), 1–16.

Eren, C. P. (2020). Cops, firefighters, and scapegoats: Anti-money laundering (AML) professionals in an era of regulatory bulimia. *Journal of White-Collar and Corporate Crime, 2*(1), 1–12. https://doi.org/10.1177/2631309X20922153

Ernst & Young. (2013). *Gransking–NRVS* (Investigation–NRVS). Ernst & Young, Oslo, Norway.

Ernst & Young. (2019). *Rapport Stiftelsen Bergensklinikkene* (Report Foundation Bergen Clinics). Ernst & Young, Oslo, Norway.

Ernst & Young. (2020). *Notat vedrørende undersøkelser utført for IMDi* (Report concerning investigation conducted for IMDi). Ernst & Young, Oslo, Norway.

Eryilmaz, A. (2018). Comparison of offender and non-offender young men to setting goals for life and attributing meaning to life. *Journal of Religion and Health, 57*(4), 1350–1362.

Esfahani, M. N., Sharifi, S., Gheitani, A., & Esfahani, M. N. (2022). Analysis and modeling of absenteeism management in Iran Revenue Tax Agency using mixed method. *Iranian Journal of Management Studies, 15*(3), 595–611.

Estrada, F., Bäckman, O., & Nilsson, A. (2016). The darker side of equality? The declining gender gap in crime: Historical trends and an enhanced analysis of staggered birth cohorts. *British Journal of Criminology, 56*(6), 1272–1290.

Estrada, F., Nilsson, A., & Pettersson, T. (2019). The female offender: A century of registered crime and daily press reporting on women's crime. *Nordic Journal of Criminology, 20*(2), 138–156.

Etemad. (2011). The sugar mafia. Etemad News. www.etemadnews (accessed on 8 July 2024).

Farani, E.G., & Seydi, S. (2021). Fight against organized crimes in the light of protection of witnesses' security in Iranian, American and international criminal law. *Journal of Legal Research, 20*(46), 55–70.

Farquhar, J.D., & Rowley, J. (2009). Convenience: A services perspective. *Marketing Theory, 9*(4), 425–438.

Fehr, R., Yam, K.C., & Dang, C. (2015). Moralized leadership: The construction and consequences of ethical leader perceptions. *Academy of Management Review, 40*(2), 182–209.

Ferraro, F., Pfeffer, J., & Sutton, R.I. (2005). Economics language and assumptions: How theories can become self-fulfilling. *Academy of Management Review, 30*(1), 8–24.

Født Fri. (2020). Tilsvar til Integrerings- og mangfoldsdirektoratet (IMDi) fra stiftelsen Født Fri (Response to the Directorate for Integration and Diversity (IMDi)). Foundation Born Free, Oslo, Norway, 13 pages.

Fosse, G., & Magnusson, G. (2004). *Mayday Mayday! Kapteinene først i livbåtene* (Mayday Mayday! The captains first in the lifeboats). Oslo, Norway: Kolofon Publishing.

Fredriksson, T., & Gålnander, R. (2020). Fearful futures and haunting histories in women's desistance from crime: A longitudinal study of desistance as an uncanny process. *Criminology, 58*, 599–618.

Fremmerlid, T. (2013). Ønsker ytterligere gransking (Wants Further Investigation). Local Norwegian newspaper *Romerikes Blad.* www.rb.no (accessed on 8 July 2024).

Fremmerlid, T. (2014a). Har levert politianmeldelse (Has Delivered Police Report). Local Norwegian newspaper *Romerikes Blad.* www.rb.no (accessed on 8 July 2024).

Fremmerlid, T. (2014b). BI-professor lite imponert over granskingen av Moskva-skolen–burde gått dypere (BI professor little impressed by the investigation of the Moscow school–Should have gone deeper). Local Norwegian newspaper *Romerikes Blad.* www.rb.no (accessed on 8 July 2024).

Fried, Y., & Slowik, L.H. (2004). Enriching goal-setting theory with time: An integrated approach. *Academy of Management Review, 29*(3), 404–422.

Friedrichs, D.O. (2009). *Trusted Criminals: White-Collar Crime in Contemporary Society.* Belmont, CA: Wadsworth.

Friedrichs, D.O. (2010). Integrated theories of white-collar crime. In *Encyclopedia of Criminological Theory*, pp. 479–486. Edited by Francis T. Cullen and Pamela Wilcox. Los Angeles, CA: Sage Publications.

Friedrichs, D.O. (2020). White-collar crime: Definitional debates and the case for a typological approach. In *The Handbook of White-Collar Crime*, pp. 16–31. Edited by Melissa L. Rorie. Hoboken, NJ: John Wiley and Sons, chapter 2.

Friedrichs, D.O., Schoultz, I., & Jordanoska, A. (2018). Edwin H. Sutherland. In *Routledge Key Thinkers in Criminology*. London, UK: Routledge.

Froggio, G., & Agnew, R. (2007). The relationship between crime and 'objective' versus 'subjective' strains. *Journal of Criminal Justice, 35*, 81–87.

Füss, R., & Hecker, A. (2008). Profiling white-collar crime. Evidence from German-speaking countries. *Corporate Ownership & Control, 5*(4), 149–161.

Gago-Rodriguez, S., Marquez-Illescas, G., & Nunez-Nickel, M. (2020). Denial of corruption: Voluntary disclosure of bribery information. *Journal of Business Ethics, 162*, 609–626.

Galvin, B.M., Lange, D., & Ashforth, B.E. (2015). Narcissistic organizational identification: Seeing oneself as central to the organization's identity. *Academy of Management Review, 40*(2), 163–181.

Galvin, M.A. (2020). Gender and white-collar crime–Theoretical issues. *Criminal Justice Studies, 33*(1), 61–69. Published online. doi.org/10.1080/1478601X.2020.1709954.

Galvin, M.A., Loughran, T.A., Simpson, S.S., & Cohen, M.A. (2018). Victim compensation policy and white-collar crime: Public preferences in a national willingness-to-pay survey. *Criminology and Public Policy, 17*, 553–594.

Gamache, D.L., & McNamara, G. (2019). Responding to bad press: How CEO temporal focus influences the sensitivity to negative media coverage of acquisitions. *Academy of Management Journal, 62*(3), 918–943.

Garcia-Rosell, J.C. (2019). A discursive perspective on corporate social responsibility education: A story co-creation exercise. *Journal of Business Ethics, 154*, 1019–1032.

Gardner, M., & Steinberg, L. (2005). Peer influence on risk taking, risk preference, and risky decision making in adolescence and adulthood: An experimental study. *Developmental Psychology, 41*(4), 625–635.

Garrett, S. (1987). *Gender*. London, UK: Tavistock Institute.

Gaulin, S. (2020). Jeg ble lovet full anonymitet for å si noe negativt om Shabana Rehman (I was promised full anonymity for saying something negative about Shabana Rehman). Web-based discussion forum *Subjekt*. www.subjekt.no (accessed on 8 July 2024).

Geest, V.R., Weisburd, D., & Blokland, A.A.J. (2017). Developmental trajectories of offenders convicted of fraud: A follow-up to age 50 in a Dutch conviction cohort. *European Journal of Criminology, 14*(5), 543–565.

Ghaffari, M., Svystunova, L., & Jarvis, L. (2022). Cracking the box or stretching its walls? Exploiting institutional plasticity in Iranian creative advertising. *Human Relations, 75*(9), 1707–1740.

Ghazi-Tehrani, A.K., & Pontell, H.N. (2022). Comparative criminology and white-collar crime. In Ghazi-Tehrani, A.K. & Pontell, H.N. (Eds.), *Wayward Dragon* (pp. 33–49). Springer Series on Asian Criminology and Criminal Justice Research.

Ghorchibeigi, M. (2019). Qualitative analysis of white-collar delinquency: Understanding the contexts and motives. *Journal of Social Problems in Iran, 10*(1), 217–238.

Gigerenzer, G., & Gaissmaier, W. (2010). Heuristic decision making. *Annual Review of Psychology, 62*(1), 451–482.

Gioia, D.A. (1992). Pinto fires and personal ethics: A script analysis of missed opportunities. *Journal of Business Ethics, 11*(5–6), 379–389.

Glasø, L., & Einarsen, S. (2008). Emotion regulation in leader-follower relationships. *European Journal of Work and Organizational Psychology, 17*(4), 482–500.

Goldstraw-White, J. (2012). *White-Collar Crime: Accounts of Offending Behavior*. London, UK: Palgrave Macmillan.

Goncharov, I., & Peter, C. D. (2019). Does reporting transparency affect industry coordination? Evidence from the duration of international cartels. *The Accounting Review, 94*(3), 149–175.

Goossen, M., Seva, I. J., & Larsson, D. (2016). Basic human values and white-collar crime: Findings from Europe. *European Journal of Criminology, 13*(4), 434–452.

Gossett, J. (2019). Women and white-collar crime. In F. P. Bernat & K. Frailing (Eds.), *The Encyclopedia of Women and Crime* (pp. 1114–1117). New York, NY: John Wiley and Sons.

Gottfredson, M. R., & Hirschi, T. (1990). *A General Theory of Crime*. Palo Alto, CA: Stanford University Press.

Gottfredson, R. K., Wright, S. L., & Heaphy, E. D. (2020). A critique of the leader-member exchange construct: Back to square one. *The Leadership Quarterly, 31*, 101385. doi: 10.1016/j.leaqua.2020.101385.

Gottschalk, P. (2012). Gender and white-collar crime: Only four percent female criminals. *Journal of Money Laundering Control, 15*(3), 362–373.

Gottschalk, P. (2017). Convenience in white-collar crime: Introducing a core concept. *Deviant Behavior, 38*(5), 605–619.

Gottschalk, P. (2017). White-collar crime: Detection and neutralization in religious organizations. *International Journal of Police Science & Management, 19*(2), 120–126.

Gottschalk, P. (2019). Stage model for female criminals: Business school students' perceptions of white-collar offenders. *Journal of Gender Studies, 28*(6), 720–729.

Gottschalk, P. (2022). Trusted chief executives in convenient white-collar crime. *Crime & Delinquency*. doi: 10.1177/00111287221104737.

Gottschalk, P., & Glasø, L. (2013). Gender in white-collar crime: An empirical study of pink-collar criminals. *International Letters of Social and Humanistic Sciences, 04*, 22–34.

Gottschalk, P., & Gunnesdal, L. (2018). *White-Collar Crime in the Shadow Economy: Lack of Detection, Investigation, and Conviction Compared to Social Security Fraud.* London, UK: Palgrave Macmillan, Springer Publishing.

Gottschalk, P., & Smith, R. (2015). Gender and white-collar crime: Examining representations of women in media. *Journal of Gender Studies, 24*(3), 310–325.

Gottschalk, P., & Tcherni-Buzzeo, M. (2017). Reasons for gaps in crime reporting: The case of white-collar criminals investigated by private fraud examiners in Norway. *Deviant Behavior, 38*(3), 267–281.

Goulette, N. (2020). What are the gender differences in risk and needs of males and females sentenced for white-collar crime? *Criminal Justice Studies, 33*(6), 1–15. doi:10.1080/1478601X.2020.1709951.

Graf-Vlachy, L., Oliver, A. G., Banfield, R., König, A., & Bundy, J. (2020). Media coverage of firms: Background, integration, and directions for research. *Journal of Management, 46*(1), 36–69.

Graham, K. A., Resick, C. J., Margolis, J. A., Shao, P., Hargis, M. B., & Kiker, J. (2020). Egoistic norms, organizational identification, and the perceived ethicality of unethical pro-organizational behavior: A moral maturation perspective. *Human Relations, 73*(9), 1249–1277.

Greitzer, F. L., & Frincke, D. A. (2010). Combining traditional cyber security audit data with psychosocial data: Towards predictive modeling for insider threat mitigation. In F. L. Greitzer & D. A. Frincke (Eds.), *Insider Threats in Cyber Security* (pp. 85–113). Boston, MA: Springer.

Griffin, D., & Tversky, A. (2002). The weighting of evidence and the determinants of confidence. In T. Gilovich, D. Griffin, & D. Kahneman (Eds.), *Heuristics and Biases: The Psychology of Intuitive Judgment* (pp. 230–249). New York, NY: Cambridge University Press.

Grindaker, M. H. (2011). Tiltalt for barnehagebedrageri (Indicted for kindergarten fraud). *Dagens Næringsliv*, p. 13.

Grønningsæter, F. (2022). Russlands svarte økonomi (Russia's black economy). *Kapital, 5*, 16–23.

Guldberg, M. (2020). Født Fri har brukt pengene rett (Born Free has used the money right). *Aftenposten*, p. 24.

Gupta, C. M., & Gottschalk, P. (2022). To what extent is white-collar crime understandable? An empirical study of determinants based on the theory of convenience. *Crime & Delinquency*. doi:10.1177/00111287221131492.

Gupta, V. K., Mortal, S. C., Silveri, S., Sun, M., & Turban, D. B. (2020a). You're fired! Gender disparities in CEO dismissal. *Journal of Management, 46*(4), 560–582.

Gupta, V. K., Mortal, S., Chakrabarty, B., Guo, X., & Turban, D. B. (2020b). CFO gender and financial statement irregularities. *Academy of Management Journal, 63*(3), 802–831.

GWW. (2009). Tea smuggling. *The Green World Weekly*, 59.

Gyoki, M. R. (2022). Does everything in the country really have a "mafia"? *Alef News*. Retrieved from: www.alef.ir (accessed on 8 July 2024).

Haantz, S. (2002). Women and White-collar Crime. National White-collar Crime Center. Retrieved from: www.nw3c.org (accessed on 8 July 2024).

Haines, F. (2014). Corporate fraud as misplaced confidence? Exploring ambiguity in the accuracy of accounts and the materiality of money. *Theoretical Criminology, 18*(1), 20–37.

Hall, G. (2012). Arbitration agreements: Read the fine print. *NBC*. Retrieved from: http://www.nbc12.com/story/20157528/arbitration-agreements-read-the-fine-print (accessed on 8 July 2024).

Halse, A., & Selimovic, T. (2020). Krav om utbetaling av innvilget statsstøtte–Varsel om utvidelse av grunnlag for tilbakehold (Request for payment of granted state funding–Notice of extension of basis for withdrawal). Letter from IMDi directorate, 2 pages.

Hambrick, D. C., & Lovelace, J. B. (2018). The role of executive symbolism in advancing new strategic themes in organization: A social influence perspective. *Academy of Management Review, 43*(1), 110–131.

Hamilton, S., & Micklethwait, A. (2006). *Greed and Corporate Failure: The Lessons from Recent Disasters*. Basingstoke, UK: Palgrave Macmillan.

Hammond, J. M. (2018). Pink-collar crime: Women and crime committed at work. *Review of Social Studies, 5*(2), 39–59.

Han, J., Shipilov, A. V., & Greve, H. R. (2017). Unequal bedfellows: Gender role-based deference in multiplex ties between Korean business groups. *Academy of Management Journal, 60*(4), 1531–1553.

Hansen, F., Klungtveit, H. S., Fretland, R. A., Meldalen, S. G., Egeberg, K., Thoresen, K., Jappee, G., & Monsen, Ø. N. (2009). Drept etter bittert oppgjør (Killed after bitter settlement). *Dagbladet*. Retrieved from: www.dagbladet.no (accessed on 8 July 2024).

Hansen, L. L. (2009). Corporate financial crime: Social diagnosis and treatment. *Journal of Financial Crime, 16*(1), 28–40.

Hansen, L. L. (2020). Review of the book "Convenience Triangle in White-Collar Crime: Case Studies of Fraud Examinations." *ChoiceConnect, 57*(5). Middletown, CT: Association of College and Research Libraries.

Harbinson, E. (2020). Investigating women and men convicted of white-collar offenses on federal community supervision: Sample and methods. *Criminal Justice Studies, 33*(1), 4–12. doi:10.1080/1478601X.2020.1709949.

Hareide, K. E. (2006). Kristian Gerhard Jebsen Skipsrederi vant frem i Bergen tingrett, og er tilkjent rund 60 millioner kroner i erstatning [Kristian Gerhard Jebsen Shipping won in Bergen district court, and is awarded around NOK 60 million in compensation]. *Nettavisen*. Retrieved from: www.nettavisen.no (accessed on 8 July 2024).

Hatami, I., Pakzad, B., Farahbakhsh, M., & Khosravi, H. (2019). Analysing the causes of economic crimes in Iran in light of economic criminology theories. *Naja Strategic Studies Journal, 4*(11), 91–114.

Hausman, R., Tyson, L. D., & Zahidi, S. (2008). *Global Gender Gap Report 2008*. Geneva, Switzerland: World Economic Forum.

Hawdon, J., Bernatzky, C., & Costello, M. (2019). Cyber-routines, political attitudes, and exposure to violence-advocating online extremism. *Social Forces, 98*(1), 329–354.

Hay, C. (2003). Family strain, gender, and delinquency. *Sociological Perspectives, 46*, 107–135.

Hay, C., & Ray, K. (2020). General strain theory and cybercrime. In T. J. Holt & A. M. Bossler (Eds.), *The Palgrave Handbook of International Cybercrime and Cyberdeviance* (pp. 583–600).

Haynes, K. T., Josefy, M., & Hitt, M. A. (2015). Tipping point: Managers' self-interest, greed, and altruism. *Journal of Leadership & Organizational Studies, 22*, 265–279.

Helsingeng, A. (2020). Gjennomgang av EYs undersøkelse av stiftelsen Født Fri på oppdrag av IMDi av 18. september 2020 [Review of EY's investigation of the foundation Born Free on behalf of IMDi of September 18, 2020]. Oslo, Norway: Bull & Co.

Hendricks, J. M. (2022). An evaluation of the perceived punishment of corporations for criminal misconduct: A multiple case study (Doctoral dissertation, Northcentral University).

Heyman, J., & Sailors, J. (2016). A respondent-friendly method of ranking long lists. *International Journal of Market Research, 58*(5), 693–710.

Higgins, E. T. (1997). Beyond pleasure and pain. *American Psychologist, 52*, 1280–1300.

Hill, G. D., & Harris, A. R. (1981). Changes in the gender patterning of crime 1953–77: Opportunity vs. identity. *Social Science Quarterly, 62*(4), 658–671.

Hinduja, S. (2007). Neutralization theory and online software piracy: An empirical analysis. *Ethics and Information Technology, 9*(3), 187–204.

Hoffman, M. L. (2001). *Empathy and Moral Development: Implications for Caring and Justice*. Cambridge, UK: Cambridge University Press.

Hoffmann, J. P. (2002). A contextual analysis of differential association, social control, and strain theories of delinquency. *Social Forces, 81*(3), 753–785.

Holt, R., & Cornelissen, J. (2014). Sensemaking revisited. *Management Learning, 45*(5), 525–539.

Holt, T. J., & Bossler, A. M. (2009). Examining the applicability of lifestyle-routine activities theory for cybercrime victimization. *Deviant Behavior, 30*(1), 1–25.

Holt, T. J., & Morris, R. G. (2009). An exploration of the relationship between MP3 player ownership and digital piracy. *Criminal Justice Studies, 22*(4), 381–392.

Holt, T. J., Burruss, G. W., & Bossler, A. M. (2010). Social learning and cyber-deviance: Examining the importance of a full social learning model in the virtual world. *Journal of Crime and Justice, 33*(2), 31–61.

Holtfreter, K. (2005). Is occupational fraud 'typical' white-collar crime? A comparison of individual and organizational characteristics. *Journal of Criminal Justice, 33*, 353–365.

Holtfreter, K. (2015). General theory, gender-specific theory, and white-collar crime. *Journal of Financial Crime, 22*(4), 422–431.

Holtfreter, K., Beaver, K. M., Reisig, M. D., & Pratt, T. C. (2010). Low self-control and fraud offending. *Journal of Financial Crime, 17*(3), 295–307.

Holtfreter, K., Van Slyke, S., Bratton, J., & Gertz, M. (2008). Public perceptions of white-collar crime and punishment. *Journal of Criminal Justice, 36*(1), 50–60.

Hoodfar, H., & Sadr, S. (2010). Islamic politics and women's quest for gender equality in Iran. *Third World Quarterly, 31*(6), 885–903.

Høydal, H. F. (2020). Født stri [Born difficult]. *VG Helgemagasin (Weekend magazine)*, pp. 40–50.

Huang, J., Diehl, M. R., & Paterlini, S. (2020). The influence of corporate elites on women on supervisory boards: Female directors' inclusion in Germany. *Journal of Business Ethics, 165*, 347–364.

Huang, L., & Knight, A. P. (2017). Resources and relationships in entrepreneurship: An exchange theory of the development and effects of the entrepreneur-investor relationship. *Academy of Management Review, 42*(1), 80–102.

Huffman, M. L., Cohen, P. N., & Pearlman, J. (2010). Engendering change: Organizational dynamics and workplace gender desegregation. *Administrative Science Quarterly, 55*, 255–277.

Huisman, W. (2020). Blurred lines: Collusions between legitimate and illegitimate organizations. In M. L. Rorie (Ed.), *The Handbook of White-Collar Crime* (pp. 139–158). Hoboken, NJ: Wiley & Sons.

Huisman, W., & Erp, J. (2013). Opportunities for environmental crime. *British Journal of Criminology, 53*, 1178–1200.

Hurley, P. J., Mayhew, B. W., & Obermire, K. M. (2019). Realigning auditors' accountability: Experimental evidence. *The Accounting Review, 94*(3), 233–250.

Hussain, M., & Sultan, S. (2020). Shabana Rehman mister statsstøtten: Behandlingen av Født Fri vekker bekymring [Shabana Rehman loses state aid: The treatment of Born Free raises concerns]. *Dagbladet*. Retrieved from: www.dagbladet.no (accessed on 8 July 2024).

Isenberg, D. J. (1986). Group polarization: A critical review and meta-analysis. *Journal of Personality and Social Psychology, 50*(6), 1141–1151.

Isna. (2018). Is there a "mafia" in Iran? *Iranian Students News Agency*. Retrieved from: www.isna.ir (accessed on 8 July 2024).

Jalilvand, M. R., Vosta, S. N., & Yasini, A. (2017). Motivational antecedents of whistle-blowing in Iranian public service organizations. *Iranian Journal of Management Studies, 10*(2), 385–408.

Johnsen, N. (2014). Frank Aarebrot om First House: Vi vet ikke hvem de representerer [Frank Aarebrot about First House: We do not know who they represent]. *VG*. Retrieved from: www.vg.no (accessed on 8 July 2024).

Johnsen, N. (2020a). Shabana Rehman til VG: -Dette er jo ikke sant [Shabana Rehman to VG: -This is simply not true]. *VG*. Retrieved from: www.vg.no (accessed on 8 July 2024).

Johnsen, N. (2020b). Brukte 1,45 millioner på å granske Rehman-stiftelse [Spent 1.45 million to investigate Rehman foundation]. *VG*. Retrieved from: www.vg.no (accessed on 8 July 2024).

Johnsen, N., & Mikalsen, H. (2020). Sitter i styret i Født Fri: -Jeg advarte Shabana [Sitting on the board of Born Free: -I warned Shabana]. *VG*. Retrieved from: www.vg.no (accessed on 8 July 2024).

Johnsen, N., Hassan, A., & Hansen, F. (2020). Førte regnskap for Rehman-stiftelse: Avviser alle anklager [Kept accounts for Rehman foundation: Denies all charges]. *VG*. Retrieved from: www.vg.no (accessed on 8 July 2024).

Jones, T. M. (1991). Ethical decision making by individuals in organizations: An issue-contingent model. *Academy of Management Review, 16*(2), 366–395.

Jonnergård, K., Stafsudd, A., & Elg, U. (2010). Performance evaluations as gender barriers in professional organizations: A study of auditing firms. *Gender, Work and Organization, 17*(6), 721–747.

Jordanoska, A., & Schoultz, I. (2020). The discovery of white-collar crime: The legacy of Edwin Sutherland. In M. L. Rorie (Ed.), *The Handbook of White-Collar Crime* (pp. 3–15). Hoboken, NJ: John Wiley & Sons.

Joshi, A. (2014). By whom and when is women's expertise recognized? The interactive effects of gender and education in science and engineering teams. *Administrative Science Quarterly, 59*(2), 202–239.

Joshi, A., Neely, B., Emrich, C., Griffiths, D., & George, G. (2015). Gender research in AMJ: An overview of five decades of empirical research and calls to action. *Academy of Management Journal, 58*(5), 1459–1475.

Kakkar, H., Sivanathan, N., & Gobel, M. S. (2020). Fall from grace: The role of dominance and prestige in the punishment of high-status actors. *Academy of Management Journal, 63*(2), 530–553.

Kamaei, M., & Abolhasani, S. (2020). An analysis of the article of criminal offense: Women and crimes committed in the workplace. *Legal Research, 42*, 429–442.

Kammeradvokaten. (2019). Ansvarsvurdering vedrørende Sagen om Svindel med Tilskuddsmidler–Offentlig Rapport [Responsibility Assessment Regarding the Case of Fraud with Benefits Funds–Public Report]. Copenhagen, Denmark: Poul Schmith.

Kang, E., & Thosuwanchot, N. (2017). An application of Durkheim's four categories of suicide to organizational crime. *Deviant Behavior, 38*(5), 493–513.

Kanze, D., Huang, L., Conley, M. A., & Higgins, E. T. (2018). We ask men to win and women not to lose: Closing the gender gap in startup funding. *Academy of Management Journal, 61*(2), 586–614.

Kapital. (2010a). Block Watne-millionær ble svindlet [Block Watne millionaire was swindled]. *Kapital, 14*, 35–36.

Kapital. (2010b). Rammet av et mystisk virus? [Harmed by a mysterious virus?]. *Kapital, 19*, 35.

Kaptein, M., & Helvoort, M. (2019). A model of neutralization techniques. *Deviant Behavior, 40*(10), 1260–1285.

Karim, K. E., & Siegel, P. H. (1998). A signal detection theory approach to analyzing the efficiency and effectiveness of auditing to detect management fraud. *Managerial Auditing Journal, 13*(6), 367–375.

Kassam, K. S., Koslov, K., & Mendes, W. B. (2009). Decisions under distress stress profiles influence anchoring and adjustment. *Psychological Science, 20*(11), 1394–1399.

Kawasaki, T. (2020). Review of comparative studies on white-collar and corporate crime. In M. L. Rorie (Ed.), *The Handbook of White-Collar Crime* (pp. 437–447). Hoboken, NJ: Wiley and Sons.

Keaveney, S. M. (2008). The blame game: An attribution theory approach to marketer-engineer conflict in high-technology companies. *Industrial Marketing Management, 37*, 653–663.

Keil, M., Tiwana, A., Sainsbury, R., & Sneha, S. (2010). Toward a theory of whistleblowing intentions: A benefit-cost differential perspective. *Decision Sciences, 41*(4), 787–12.

Keilitz, S., Gallas, G., & Hanson, R. (1988). State adoption of alternative dispute resolution: Where is it today? *State Court Journal, 12*, 4–11.

Kennedy, J. P. (2020). Organizational and macro-level corporate crime theories. In M. L. Rorie (Ed.), *The Handbook of White-Collar Crime* (pp. 175–190). Hoboken, NJ: Wiley and Sons.

Kenny, E. J., & Donnelly, R. (2020). Navigating the gender structure in information technology: How does this affect the experiences and behaviors of women? *Human Relations, 73*(3), 326–350.

Kerik, B. B. (2015). *From Jailer to Jailed: My Journey from Correction and Police Commissioner to Inmate #84888-054*. NY: Threshold Editions.

Kharif, O. (2017). All you need to know about bitcoin's rise, from $0.01 to $15,000. *Bloomberg Businessweek*. Retrieved from: https://www.bloomberg.com/news/articles/2017-12-01/understanding-bitcoin-s-rise-0-01-to-11-000-quicktake-q-a (accessed on 8 July 2024).

Kim, P. H., Dirks, K. T., & Cooper, C. D. (2009). The repair of trust: A dynamic bilateral perspective and multilevel conceptualization. *Academy of Management Review, 34*(3), 401–422.

King, E. B., Botsford, W., Hebl, M. R., Kazama, S., Dawson, J. F., & Perkins, A. (2012). Benevolent sexism at work: Gender differences in the distribution of challenging developmental experiences. *Journal of Management, 38*(6), 1835–1866.

King, E. B., Hebl, M. R., George, J. M., & Matusik, S. F. (2010). Understanding tokenism: Antecedents and consequences of a psychological climate of gender inequity. *Journal of Management, 36*(2), 482–510.

Kjørholt, D. (2020). Stopper pengestøtten til Født Fri [Stops the money support for Born Free]. *Klassekampen*, p. 7.

Klein, F. B., Chaigneau, P., & Devers, C. E. (2019). CEO gender-based termination concerns: Evidence from initial severance agreements. *Journal of Management, 47*(3), 1–26. doi: 10.1177/0149206319887421.

Kleinewiese, J. (2020). Situational action theory and the particular case of settings including a group. *European Journal of Criminology, 19*(5), 1–17. doi: 10.1177/1477370820953088.

Klenowski, P. M., Copes, H., & Mullins, C. W. (2011). Gender, identity, and accounts: How white-collar offenders do gender when making sense of their crime. *Justice Quarterly, 28*(1), 46–69.

Kleppe, M. K. (2011). Banktopp dømt til tre års fengsel [Bank top convicted to three years prison]. *Finansavisen*, pp. 30–31.

Kleppe, M. K. (2012a). Too easy to abuse public funds. *Finansavisen*, pp. 6–7.

Kleppe, M. K. (2012b). Økokrim: -En advarsel mot fløteskumming [Økokrim: -A warning against foaming the cream]. *Finansavisen*. Retrieved from www.finansavisen.no (accessed on 8 July 2024).

Knotterus, J. D., Ulsperger, J. S., Cummins, S., & Osteen, E. (2006). Exposing Enron: Media representations of ritualized deviance in corporate culture. *Crime Media Culture, 2*(2), 177–195. doi:10.1177/1741659006065532.

Kolade, O. J., & Kehinde, O. (2013). Glass ceiling and women career advancement: Evidence from Nigerian construction industry. *Iranian Journal of Management Studies, 6*(1), 77–97.

Kolsrud, K. (2020). Tingretten nekter Shabana Rehman bevissikring av EY-lydopptak [The district court denies Shabana Rehman evidence by EY sound recording]. *Rett24*. Retrieved from www.rett24.no (accessed on 8 July 2024).

König, A., Graf-Vlachy, L., Bundy, J., & Little, L. M. (2020). A blessing and a curse: How CEOs' trait empathy affects their management of organizational crises. *Academy of Management Review, 45*(1), 130–153. doi:10.5465/amr.2017.0207

Kossek, E. E., Su, R., & Wu, L. (2017). "Opting out" or "pushed out"? Integrating perspectives on women's career equality for gender inclusion and interventions. *Journal of Management, 43*(1), 228–254. doi:10.1177/0149206316671606.

Kostova, T., Roth, K., & Dacin, M. T. (2008). Institutional theory in the study of multinational corporations: A critique and new directions. *Academy of Management Review, 33*(4), 994–1006.

Kowalski, R. M., & Limber, S. P. (2007). Electronic bullying among middle school students. *Journal of Adolescent Health, 41*(6), S22–S30.

Kowalski, R. M., Giumetti, G. W., Schroeder, A. N., & Reese, H. H. (2012). Cyber bullying among college students: Evidence from multiple domains of college life. *Cutting-Edge Technologies in Higher Education, 5*, 293–321.

Krippendorff, K. (1980). *Content Analysis: An Introduction to its Methodology*. Sage publications.

Krohn, M. D., & Eassey, J. M. (2014). Integrated theories of crime. In J. Mitchell Miller (Ed.), *The Encyclopedia of Theoretical Criminology* (pp. 458–463). Chichester, UK: John Wiley and Sons.

Krokfjord, T. P. (2017). Dømt for millionbedrageri, har brukt fire identiteter: Slik er John Andrew Tollefsens nye barnehageplan [Convicted of millions fraud, has used four identities: Such is John Andrew Tollefsen's new daycare plan]. *Dagbladet*. Retrieved from www.dagbladet.no (accessed on 8 July 2024).

Kroneberg, C., & Schulz, S. (2018). Revisiting the role of self-control in situational action theory. *European Journal of Criminology, 15*(1), 56–76. doi:10.1177/1477370817738782.

Kulik, C. T., & Olekalns, M. (2012). Negotiating the gender divide: Lessons from the negotiation and organizational behavior literatures. *Journal of Management, 38*(4), 1387–1415. doi:10.1177/0149206311432450.

Lahig. (2010). Tea smuggling. *Lahig News*. Retrieved from www.lahig.ir (accessed on 8 July 2024).

Lanaj, K., & Hollenbeck, J. R. (2015). Leadership over-emergence in self-managing teams: The role of gender and countervailing biases. *Academy of Management Journal, 58*(5), 1476–1494. doi:10.5465/amj.2013.0652.

Langberg, Ø. K. (2011). Banksjef dømt for utroskap [Bank manager convicted of infidelity]. *Bergens Tidende*. Retrieved from www.bt.no (accessed on 8 July 2024).

Lange, D. (2008). A multidimensional conceptualization of organizational corruption control. *Academy of Management Review, 33*(3), 710–729.

Langton, L., & Piquero, N. L. (2007). Can General Strain Theory Explain White-Collar Crime? A Preliminary Investigation of the Relationship between Strain and Select White-Collar Offenses. *Journal of Criminal Justice, 35*(1), 1–15. doi: 10.1016/j.jcrimjus.2006.11.006.

Larsson, S., Svensson, M., & Kaminski, M. (2012). Online piracy, anonymity, and social change. *Convergence: An International Journal of Research into New Media Technologies, 19*(1), 95–114. doi:10.1177/1354856512469572.

LeClair, J., Shih, L., & Abraham, S. (2014, February). Women in STEM and cyber security fields. In *Proceedings of the 2014 Conference for Industry and Education Collaboration* (pp. 5–7).

Lee, F., & Robinson, R. J. (2000). An attributional analysis of social accounts: Implications of playing the blame game. *Journal of Applied Social Psychology, 30*(9), 1853–1879.

Lehman, D. W., Cooil, B., & Ramanujam, R. (2019). The effects of rule complexity on organizational noncompliance and remediation: Evidence from restaurant health inspections. *Journal of Management, 46*(8), 0 14920631984226. doi:10.1177/0149206319842262.

Leonard, W. N., & Weber, M. G. (1970). Automakers and dealers: A study of criminogenic market forces. *Law and Society Review, 4*(3), 407–424.

Leslie, L. M., Manchester, C. F., & Dahm, P. C. (2017). Why and when does the gender gap reverse? Diversity goals and the pay premium for high potential women. *Academy of Management Journal, 60*(2), 402–432. doi:10.5465/amj.2014.0361.

Lindgren, S. Å., & Theandersson, C. (2000). Från storsvindel til småfiffel: Teman i internationell ekobrottsforskning [From great fraud to small offenses: Topics in international financial crime research]. *BRÅ-rapport 2000: 23, Brottsförebyggande rådet*. Retrieved from: www.bra.se (accessed on 8 July 2024).

Lindner, J. R., Murphy, T. H., & Briers, G. E. (2001). Handling nonresponse in social science research. *Journal of Agricultural Education, 42*(4), 43–53.

Lindvåg, A. W. H. (2020a). IMDi med endelig konklusjon: Født Fri får ikke statsstøtte [IMDi with final conclusion: Born Free does not get state funding]. *Vårt Land*. Retrieved from www.vl.no (accessed on 8 July 2024).

Lindvåg, A. W. H. (2020b). IMDi stopper støtten til Født Fri [IMDi stops the support for Born Free]. *Vårt Land*, p. 8.

Liska, A. E., Krohn, M. D., & Messner, S. F. (1989). Strategies and requisites for theoretical integration in the study of crime and deviance. In S. F. Messner, M. D. Krohn, & A. E. Liska (Eds.), *Theoretical Integration in the Study of Deviance and Crime* (pp. 1–20). Albany, NY: State University of New York Press.

Litwin, M. S. (1995). *How to Measure Survey Reliability and Validity*. Thousand Oaks, CA: Sage.

Locatelli, G., Mariani, G., Sainati, T., & Greco, M. (2017). Corruption in public projects and megaprojects: There is an elephant in the room! *International Journal of Project Management, 35*(3), 252–268. doi: 10.1016/j.ijproman.2016.12.004

Logan, M. W., Morgan, M. A., Benson, M. L., & Cullen, F. T. (2019). Coping with imprisonment: Testing the special sensitivity hypothesis for white-collar offenders. *Justice Quarterly, 36*(2), 225–254. doi:10.1080/07418825.2018.1474260.

Löschper, G. (2000). Crime and Social Control as Fields of Qualitative Research in the Social Sciences. *Forum Qualitative Social Research, 1*(1), Article 9. Retrieved from: www.qualitative-research.net (accessed on 8 July 2024).

Lowry, D. (2003). An investigation of student moral awareness and associated factors in two cohorts of an undergraduate business degree in a British university: Implications for business ethics curriculum design. *Journal of Business Ethics, 48*(1), 7–19. doi:10.1023/A:1023640902944.

Lutz, J. R. (2019). Pink-collar crime. In F. P. Bernat & K. Frailing (Eds.), *The Encyclopedia of Women and Crime* (pp. 791–796). New York, NY: John Wiley and Sons.

Mæland, K. B. (2020). Regnskapsfører om granskingsavhør: Det er en drittpakke. De var ute etter å ta Shabana Rehman [The keeper of accounts about investigation interrogation: It is a shit package. They were looking to catch Shabana Rehman]. *Nettavisen*. Retrieved from www.nettavisen.no (accessed on 8 July 2024).

Mæland, K. B., & Vege, H. H. (2020). En av granskerne av Født Fri har tidligere fått kraftig kritikk etter påvist justismord. Det stilles spørsmål ved etterforskningsmetodene også fra professor [One of the investigators of Born Free has previously received strong criticism after murder injustice. A professor also questions the investigation methods]. *Nettavisen*. Retrieved from www.nettavisen.no (accessed on 8 July 2024).

Mai, H. T. X., & Olsen, S. O. (2016). Consumer participation in self-production: The role of control mechanisms, convenience orientation, and moral obligation. *Journal of Marketing Theory and Practice, 24*(2), 209–223.

Marcum, C. D., Higgins, G. E., Freiburger, T. L., & Ricketts, M. L. (2012). Battle of the sexes: An examination of male and female cyber bullying. *International Journal of Cyber Criminology, 6*(1), 904–911.

Maslow, A. H. (1943). A theory of human motivation. *Psychological Review, 50*(4), 370–396.

Mawritz, M. B., Greenbaum, R. L., Butts, M. M., & Graham, K. A. (2017). I just can't control myself: A self-regulation perspective on the abuse of deviant employees. *Academy of Management Journal, 60*(4), 1482–1503.

McClanahan, B., & South, N. (2020). 'All knowledge begins with the senses': Towards a sensory criminology. *British Journal of Criminology, 60*, 3–23.

McClean, E. J., Martin, S. R., Emich, K. J., & Woodruff, T. (2018). The social consequences of voice: An examination of voice type and gender status and subsequent leader emergence. *Academy of Management Journal, 61*(5), 1869–1891.

McClelland, P. L., Liang, X., & Barker, V. L. (2010). CEO commitment to the status quo: Replication and extension using content analysis. *Journal of Management, 36*(5), 1251–1277.

McKenndal, M. A., & Wagner, J. A. (1997). Motive, opportunity, choice, and corporate illegality. *Organization Science, 8*, 624–647.

Merton, R. K. (1938). Social structure and anomie. *American Sociological Review, 3*, 672–682.

Mesmer-Magnus, J. R., & Viswesvaran, C. (2005). Whistleblowing in an organization: An examination of correlates of whistleblowing intentions, actions, and retaliation. *Journal of Business Ethics, 62*(3), 266–297.

Messerschmidt, J. M. (1997). *Crime as Structured Action: Gender, Race, Class, and Crime in the Making*. Thousand Oaks, CA: Sage Publications.

Messerschmidt, J. W. (2013). *Crime as Structured Action: Doing Masculinities, Race, Class, Sexuality, and Crime* (2nd ed.). London, UK: Rowman & Littlefield Publishers.

Meyers, L. S., Gamst, G., & Guarino, A. J. (2013). *Applied Multivariate Research: Design and Interpretation* (2nd ed.). United States: Sage.

Michel, P. (2008). Financial crime: The constant challenge of seeking effective prevention solutions. *Journal of Financial Crime, 15*(4), 383–397.

Middelhoff, T. (2017). *Der Sturz: Die Autobiografie von Thomas Middelhoff* [The Fall: The autobiography of Thomas Middelhoff]. Stuttgart, Germany: LangenMuller in der F.A. Herbig Verlagsbuchhandlung.

Mirkhalili, S. M., & Khodadoost, B. (2017). Change from white-collar criminals to red-collar criminals. *Quarterly Journal of Legal Studies, 1*(3), 129–156.

Modaressi Alam, Z., Davoudi, A., & Elahe Vardizadeh, S. (2017). Analyzing women's participation in Iran. *Economic Journal – Bimonthly Review of Economic Issues and Policies, 17*(9 and 10), 111–138.

Moj. (2019). The sugar mafia. *Moj News*. Retrieved from: www.mojnews.com (accessed on 8 July 2024).

Moj. (2019a). The accused in the first row. *Moj News*. Retrieved from: www.mojnews.com (accessed on 8 July 2024).

Monazamitabar, J. (2009). Investigation of the consequences of white-collar crimes on national security. *NAJA Strategic Studies Quarterly, 11*(Spring), 141–167.

Montella, E. C. (2016). *Full Circle: A Memoir of Learning in Too Far and the Journey Back*. Sanibel, FL: Triple M Press.

Moore, C. (2015). Moral disengagement. *Current Opinion in Psychology, 6*, 199–204.

Morino, V. (2021). *Situating the Social in Fraud Management Practices: A Case-Based Approach* (Doctoral dissertation, University of Leicester).

Mpho, B. (2017). Whistleblowing: What do contemporary ethical theories say? *Studies in Business and Economics, 12*(1), 19–28.

Mun, E., & Jung, J. (2020). Change above the glass ceiling: Corporate social responsibility and gender diversity in Japanese firms. *Administrative Science Quarterly, 63*(2), 409–440.

Najafi, M., & Rahimi, A. (2018). Comparative study of organized crimes in the criminal justice system of France and Iran. *Supervision & Inspection, 1397*(45), 95–118.

Nasiri, M. (2014). Mechanisms for controlling white collar crimes: Criminal and non-criminal patterns. *Detective Scientific Quarterly, 28*, 7–24.

Naumovska, I., Wernicke, G., & Zajac, E. J. (2020). Last to come and last to go? The complex role of gender and ethnicity in the reputational penalties for directors linked to corporate fraud. *Academy of Management Journal, 63*(3), 881–902.

Naylor, R. T. (2003). Towards a general theory of profit-driven crime. *British Journal of Criminology, 43*, 81–101.

Ndrecka, M. (2020). Gender and white-collar crime–Implications for corrections research and practice. *Criminal Justice Studies, 33*(1), 70–78. https://doi.org/10.1080/1478601X.2020.1709955.

Newman, D. J. (1958). White collar crime. *Law and Contemporary Problems, 23*(4), 735–753.

Newth, M. (2018). Britta Nielsen (64) mistenkt for å ha stjålet 140 millioner [Britta Nielsen (64) suspected of having stolen 140 million]. *VG*. Retrieved from www.vg.no (accessed on 8 July 2024).

Ngo, F. T., & Paternoster, R. (2016). Toward an understanding of the emotional and behavioral reactions to stalking: A partial test of general strain theory. *Crime and Delinquency, 62*(6), 703–727.

Ngo, F., & Jaishankar, K. (2017). Commemorating a decade in existence of the international journal of cyber criminology: A research agenda to advance the scholarship on cybercrime. *International Journal of Cyber Criminology, 11*(1), 1–9.

Nichol, J. E. (2019). The effects of contract framing on misconduct and entitlement. *The Accounting Review, 94*(3), 329–344.

Nielsen, M. K. (2019). New report concludes: How Britta Nielsen could swindle for DKK 120 million for 25 years. *Danish public broadcasting Danmarks Radio*. Retrieved from: www.dr.no (accessed on 8 July 2024).

Nielsen, R. P. (2003). Corruption networks and implications for ethical corruption reform. *Journal of Business Ethics, 42*(2), 125–149.

Nikru News. (2022). Interview with Afshin Sadr Dadres, CEO of the Central Light Livestock Union. *Nikru News*. Retrieved from: www.nikru.ir/news/ (accessed on 8 July 2024).

Noor, S., Isa, F. M., & Nor, L. M. (2021). Women empowerment through women entrepreneurship: A comparison between women entrepreneurs and fulltime housewife in Pakistan. *Iranian Journal of Management Studies, 14*(2), 347–363.

NTB. (2011). Funnet skyldig i korrupsjon [Found guilty of corruption]. *Aftenposten, Business section*, June 9, p. 2.

NTB. (2012). Ektepar dømt for grov utroskap [Married couple convicted of gross infidelity]. *Aftenposten*, March 1, p. 10.

NTB. (2019). Dansk kvinne for retten i storstilt svindelsak [Danish women prosecuted in court in a big fraud case]. *ABC nyheter*. Retrieved from www.abcnyheter.no (accessed on 8 July 2024).

O'Fallon, M. J., & Butterfield, K. D. (2005). A review of the empirical ethical decision-making literature: 1996–2003. *Journal of Business Ethics, 59*, 375–413.

Oakley, A. (1974). *The Sociology of Housework*. New York, NY: Pantheon Books.

Obodaru, O. (2017). Forgone, but not forgotten: Toward a theory of forgone professional identities. *Academy of Management Journal, 60*(2), 523–553.

Oka, R. (2021). Introducing an anthropology of convenience. *Economic Anthropology, 8*(2), 188–207.

Olafsen, A. H. (2017). The implications of need-satisfying work climates on state mindfulness in a longitudinal analysis of work outcomes. *Motivation and Emotion, 41*(1), 22–37.

Olafsen, A. H., Niemiec, C. P., Halvari, H., Deci, E. L., & Williams, G. C. (2017). On the dark side of work: A longitudinal analysis using self-determination theory. *European Journal of Work and Organizational Psychology, 26*(2), 275–285.

Onna, J. H. R. (2020). From the avalanche to the game: White-collar offenders on crime, bonds, and morality. *Crime, Law and Social Change, 74*, 405–431. https://doi.org/10.1007/s10611-020-09899-x.

Østrem, V. (2020a). Født Fri-kritikken: Offentlige midler skal brukes med ydmykhet. *Vårt Land*. Retrieved from: http://www.vl.no (accessed on 8 July 2024).

Østrem, V. (2020b). Vi kjenner denne saken godt [Email from news editor Veslemøy Østrem]. *Vårt Land*. Retrieved from: veslemoy.ostrem@vl.no.

Østrem, V. (2020c). Saks-id:6863 Shabana Rehman mot Vårt Land–tilsvar fra Vårt Land [Case id. 6863 Shabana Rehman against Vårt Land–response from Vårt Land]. *Pressens faglige utvalg*. Retrieved from: http://www.presse.no/pfu/ (accessed on 8 July 2024).

Østrem, V. (2020d). Kafka-kritikk fra Rolness. *Aftenposten*. Retrieved from: http://www.aftenposten.no/meninger (accessed on 8 July 2024).

Othman, R., & Ameer. (2022). In employees we trust: Employee fraud in small businesses. *Journal of Management Control, 33*, 189–213. https://doi.org/10.1007/s00187-022-00335-w.

Ottermann, P. (2020). Danish social worker jailed for stealing £13m of government funds. *The Guardian*. Retrieved from: www.theguardian.com (accessed on 8 July 2024).

Pabst, S., Schoofs, D., Pawlikowski, M., Brand, M., & Wolf, O. T. (2013). Paradoxical effects of stress and an executive task on decisions under risk. *Behavioral Neuroscience, 127*(3), 369–379.

Padavic, I., Ely, R. J., & Reid, E. M. (2020). Explaining the persistence of gender inequality: The work-family narrative as a social defense against the 24/7 work culture. *Administrative Science Quarterly, 65*(1), 61–111.

Patchin, J. W., & Hinduja, S. (2011). Traditional and nontraditional bullying among youth: A test of general strain theory. *Youth and Society, 43*(2), 727–751.

Patel, P. C., & Cooper, D. (2014). Structural power equality between family and nonfamily TMT members and the performance of family firms. *Academy of Management Journal, 57*(6), 1624–1649.

Paternoster, R., Jaynes, C. M., & Wilson, T. (2018). Rational choice theory and interest in the "fortune of others." *Journal of Research in Crime and Delinquency, 54*(6), 847–868.

Patrucco, A. S., Luzzini, D., & Ronchi, S. (2017). Research perspectives on public procurement: Content analysis of 14 years of publications in the Journal of Public Procurement. *Journal of Public Procurement, 16*(2), 229–269.

Paxton, K. (2012). Pink collar criminality. Retrieved from: www.pinkcollarcrime.com (accessed on 8 July 2024).

Peacock, D., & Irons, A. (2017). Gender inequalities in cybersecurity: Exploring the gender gap in opportunities and progression. *International Journal of Gender, Science and Technology, 9*(1), 25–44.

Petrocelli, M., Piquero, A. R., & Smith, M. R. (2003). Conflict theory and racial profiling: An empirical analysis of police traffic stop data. *Journal of Criminal Justice, 31*(1), 1–11.

Pew Research Center (2014). Adults in Utah. *Pew Research Center Religion and Public Life*. Retrieved from: www.pewforum.org (accessed on 8 July 2024).

Pickett, K. H. S., & Pickett, J. M. (2002). *Financial Crime Investigation and Control*. New York, NY: John Wiley and Sons.

Piening, E. P., Salge, T. O., Antons, D., & Kreiner, G. E. (2020). Standing together or falling apart? Understanding employees' responses to organizational identity threats. *Academy of Management Review, 45*(2), 325–351.

Pillay, S., & Kluvers, R. (2014). An institutional theory perspective on corruption: The case of a developing democracy. *Financial Accountability and Management, 30*(1), 95–119.

Pinto, J., Leana, C. R., & Pil, F. K. (2008). Corrupt organizations or organizations of corrupt individuals? Two types of organization-level corruption. *Academy of Management Review, 33*(3), 685–709.

Piquero, N. L. (2012). The only thing we have to fear is fear itself: Investigating the relationship between fear of falling and white-collar crime. *Crime and Delinquency, 58*(3), 362–379.

Piquero, N. L. (2018). White-collar crime is crime: Victims hurt just the same. *Criminology and Public Policy, 17*(3), 595–600.

Piquero, N. L., & Schoepfer, A. (2010). Theories of white-collar crime and public policy. In H. D. Barlow & S. H. Decker (Eds.), *Criminology and Public Policy: Putting Theory to Work*. Temple University Press.

Piquero, N. L., Tibbetts, S. G., & Blankenship, M. B. (2005). Examining the role of differential association and techniques of neutralization in explaining corporate crime. *Deviant Behavior, 26*(2), 159–188.

Podsakoff, P. M., MacKenzie, S. B., & Podsakoff, N. P. (2012). Sources of method bias in social science research and recommendations on how to control it. *Annual Review of Psychology, 63*, 10.11–10.31.

Podsakoff, P. M., MacKenzie, S. B., Lee, J. Y., & Podsakoff, N. P. (2003). Common method biases in behavioral research: A critical review of the literature and recommended remedies. *Journal of Applied Psychology, 88*(5), 879–903.

Pollock, O. (1950). *The Criminality of Women*. New York, NY: Barnes & Co.

Pontell, H. N., & Geis, G. (2007). *International Handbook of White-Collar and Corporate Crime*. New York, NY: Springer.

Pontell, H. N., Black, W. K., & Geis, G. (2014). Too big to fail, too powerful to jail? On the absence of criminal prosecutions after the 2008 financial meltdown. *Crime, Law and Social Change, 61*(1), 1–13.

Prabhakar, K., & Chawla, A. (2022). Behind a white-collar crime. *Journal of Forensic Sciences and Criminal Investigation, 15*(4), 1–3.

Pratt, M. G., Kaplan, S., & Whittington, R. (2019). Editorial essay: The tumult over transparency: Decoupling transparency from replication in establishing trustworthy qualitative research. *Administrative Science Quarterly, 65*(1). https://doi.org/10.1177/0001839219887663.

Pratt, T. C., & Cullen, F. T. (2005). Assessing macro-level predictors and theories of crime: A meta-analysis. *Crime and Justice, 32*, 373–450.

PwC. (2019). *Ekstern Undersøgelse af Tilskudsadministrationen 1977–2018* [External Examination of the Benefits Administration 1977–2018], February. Oslo, Norway: auditing firm PwC.

Qiu, B., & Slezak, S. L. (2019). The equilibrium relationships between performance-based pay, performance, and the commission and detection of fraudulent misreporting. *The Accounting Review, 94*(2), 325–356.

Qu, J. (2021). The challenge against economic regulation ethics under the Covid-19 epidemic: An analysis of unethical behavior of convenience. *Converter Magazine, 2021*(5), 74–79.

Quds. (2012). Ghazipour asked the Ministry of Commerce. *Quds Online*. Retrieved from: www.qudsonline.ir (accessed on 8 July 2024).

Rachlew, A. (2009). Justisfeil ved politiets etterforsking–noen eksempler og forskningsbaserte mottiltak [Misjudgement of the police investigation–Some examples and research-based countermeasures]. Doctoral dissertation, University of Oslo, Department of Law.

Rachlew, A. (2020a). Født Fri-gransking full av feil [Born Free investigation full of errors]. **Vårt Land,** (pp. 10–11).

Rachlew, A. (2020b). IMDi har valgt å ikke anmelde Født Fri [IMDi has chosen not to report Born Free]. Vårt Land. Retrieved from: www.vl.no (accessed on 8 July 2024).

Ramoglou, S., & McMullen, J. S. (2022). "What is opportunity?" From theoretical mystification to everyday understanding. *Academy of Management Review*. Retrieved from: www.journals.aom.org (accessed on 8 July 2024).

Ramoglou, S., & Tsang, E. W. K. (2016). A realist perspective of entrepreneurship: Opportunities as propensities. *Academy of Management Review, 41*, 410–434.

Reed, J., Zhong, Y., Terwoerds, L., & Brocaglia, J. (2017). The 2017 Global Information Security Workforce Study: Women in Cybersecurity [Online]. Retrieved from: https://iamcybersafe.org/wp-content/uploads/2017/03/WomensReport.pdf (accessed on 8 July 2024).

Reed, S. M., & Rorie, M. L. (2022). More than "male" and "female": The role of gender identity in white-collar offending intentions. *Crime, Law and Social Change, 80*, 79–103. https://doi.org/10.1007/s10611-023-10074-1.

Reese, B., & Constantin, K. (2021). Gender, status, & tax offences over time. *Deviant Behavior, 42*(7), 903–918.

Reese, B., & McDougal, M. K. (2018). Gender, status, and tax offenses. *Deviant Behavior, 39*(12), 1647–1657.

Rehg, M. T., Miceli, M. P., Near, J. P., & Scotter, J. R. V. (2009). Antecedents and outcomes of retaliation against whistleblowers: Gender differences and power relationships. *Organization Science, 19*(2), 221–240.

Reimann, A. (2012). Norway's gender quota: A laboratory for the advancement of women. *Der Spiegel*. Retrieved from: www.spiegel.de (accessed on 8 July 2024).

Rest, J. R. (1986). *Moral Development: Advances in Research and Theory*. New York: Praeger.

Reymert, P. Å. (2020a). Født Fri-gransking full av feil [-Born Free investigation full of errors]. *Vårt Land*, pp. 10–11.

Reymert, P. Å. (2020b). IMDi har valgt å ikke anmelde Født Fri [IMDi has chosen not to report Born Free]. *Vårt Land*. Retrieved from: www.vl.no (accessed on 8 July 2024).

Reyns, B. W. (2013). Online routines and identity theft victimization: Further expanding routine activity theory beyond direct-contact offenses. *Journal of Research in Crime and Delinquency, 50*(2), 216–238.

Reyns, B. W., Fisher, B. S., Bossler, A. M., & Holt, T. J. (2019). Opportunity and self-control: Do they predict multiple forms of online victimization? *American Journal of Criminal Justice, 44*(1), 63–82.

Rieber-Mohn, L. (2020). Libe Rieber-Mohn svarer Nettavisen og Erik Stephansen [Libe Rieber-Mohn answers Nettavisen and Erik Stephansen]. *Nettavisen*. Retrieved from: www.nettavisen.no (accessed on 8 July 2024).

Robb, G. (2006). Women and white-collar crime. *British Journal of Criminology, 46*, 1058–1072.

Rodriguez, P., Uhlenbruck, K., & Eden, L. (2005). Government corruption and the entry strategies of multinationals. *Academy of Management Review, 30*(2), 383–396.

Röglinger, M., Pöppelbuss, J., & Becker, J. (2012). Maturity model in business process management. *Business Process Management Journal, 18*(2), 328–346.

Rohall, P. J. (2019). Investigating Pink Collar Crime with Kelly Paxton. *Fraudbeat*. Retrieved from: www.fraudbeat.com (accessed on 8 July 2024).

Rolness, K. (2020). Kafka-prosess mot Shabana Rehman [Kafka process against Shabana Rehman]. *Aftenposten*. Retrieved from: www.aftenposten.no (accessed on 8 July 2024).

Romney, M. B., Albrecht, W. S., & Cherrington, D. J. (1980). Red-flagging the white-collar criminal. *Management Accounting, 61*(9), 51–57.

Rooziato. (2020). The Mafia Sultans. *Rooziato News*. Retrieved from: www.rooziato.com (accessed on 8 July 2024).

Rorie, M. L. (2015). An integrated theory of corporate environmental compliance and overcompliance. *Crime, Law and Social Change, 64*(2–3), 65–101.

Rorie, M. L. (Ed.). (2020). *The Handbook of White-Collar Crime*. Hoboken, NJ: Wiley and Sons.

Rosoff, S. M. (2009). The role of the mass media in the Enron fraud. In H. N. Pontell & G. Geis (Eds.), *International Handbook of White-Collar and Corporate Crime*. New York, NY: Springer.

Rothe, D. L., & Medley, C. (2020). Beyond state and state-corporate crime typologies: The symbiotic nature, harm, and victimization of crime of the powerful and their continuation. In M. L. Rorie (Ed.), *The Handbook of White-Collar Crime* (pp. 81–94). Hoboken, NJ: John Wiley and Sons.

Ruhland, E. L., & Selzer, N. (2020). Gender differences in white-collar offending and supervision. *Criminal Justice Studies, 33*(1), 13–30.

Ruud, S. (2020). Stiftelse fikk støtte før den var etablert [Foundation received funding before it was established]. *Aftenposten*, p. 8.

Ryan, P. C. (2021). Correlation Study of Embezzlement and Economic Conditions in New England [Doctoral dissertation, Liberty University]. School of Business.

Sajko, M., Boone, C., & Buyl, T. (2021). CEO greed, corporate social responsibility, and organizational resilience to systemic shocks. *Journal of Management, 47*(4), 957–992.

Salimi, S. (2003). Transnational organized crime, Palermo convention's effects. *International Law Review, 20*(29), 169–212.

Salimi, S. (2009). White-collar criminals and criminal justice of Iran. *Private Law Studies, 38*(4), 239–245.

Salten. (2004). Case 03-1130M, Salten district court, sentence dated August 6.

Sanders, J. (2005). *Gender and technology in education: A research review*. http://www.josanders.com/pdf/gendertech0705.pdf (accessed on 8 July 2024).

Sandø, T. (2020). Den såkalte granskingen av Født Fri følger samme mønster som vi opplevde [The so-called investigation of Born Free follows the same pattern as we experienced]. *Nettavisen*. www.nettavisen.no (accessed on 8 July 2024).

Saunders, M., Lewis, P., & Thornhill, A. (2007). *Research Methods for Business Students* (5th ed.). Pearson Education.

Schanzenbach, M., & Yaeger, M. L. (2006). Prison time, fines, and federal white-collar criminals: The anatomy of a racial disparity. *Journal of Criminal Law and Criminology, 96*(2), 757–794.

Schaumberg, R. L., & Flynn, F. J. (2017). Self-reliance: A gender perspective on its relationship to communality and leadership evaluations. *Academy of Management Journal, 60*(5), 1859–1881.

Schnatterly, K. (2003). Increasing firm value through detection and prevention of white-collar crime. *Strategic Management Journal, 24*(7), 587–614.

Schnatterly, K., Gangloff, K. A., & Tuschke, A. (2018). CEO wrongdoing: A review of pressure, opportunity, and rationalization. *Journal of Management, 44*(6), 2405–2432.

Schoepfer, A., & Piquero, N. L. (2006). Exploring white-collar crime and the American dream: A partial test of institutional anomie theory. *Journal of Criminal Justice, 34*(3), 227–235.

Schoultz, I., & Flyghed, J. (2016). Doing business for a "higher loyalty"? How Swedish transnational corporations neutralize allegations of crime. *Crime, Law and Social Change, 66*(2), 183–198.

Schoultz, I., & Flyghed, J. (2019). From "we didn't do it" to "we've learned our lesson": Development of a typology of neutralizations of corporate crime. *Critical Criminology, 28,* 739–757. https://doi.org/10.1007/s10612-019-09483-3.

Schoultz, I., & Flyghed, J. (2020a). Denials and confessions: An analysis of the temporalization of neutralizations of corporate crime. *International Journal of Law, Crime and Justice, 62,* 100389. https://doi.org/10.1016/j.ijlcj.2020.100389.

Schoultz, I., & Flyghed, J. (2020b). "We have been thrown under the bus": Corporate versus individual defense mechanisms against transnational corporate bribery charges. *Journal of White Collar and Corporate Crime, 2*(1). https://doi.org/10.1177/2631309X20911883.

Scott, B. A., & Barnes, C. M. (2011). A multilevel field investigation of emotional labor, affect, work withdrawal, and gender. *Academy of Management Journal, 54*(1), 116–136.

Shams-Nateri, M. E. (2004). Organized crimes. *Journal of Jurisprudence and Law, 1,* 109–130.

Sharp, D. J., & Salter, S. B. (2005). Project escalation and sunk costs: A test of the international generalizability of agency and prospect theories. *Journal of International Business Studies, 28*(1), 101–121.

Shavell, S. (1995). Alternative dispute resolution: An economic analysis. *Journal of Legal Studies, 24*, 1–28.

Shepherd, D. W. J., & Button, M. (2019). Organizational inhibitions to addressing occupational fraud: A theory of differential rationalization. *Deviant Behavior, 40*(8), 971–991.

Silvola, N. M. (2020a). Shabana Rehman tar oppgjør med mediene–Har klaget Vårt Land til PFU: -Jeg har stått helt sjanseløs [Shabana Rehman attacks the media–Has submitted complaint regarding newspaper Vårt Land: -I have been completely without a chance]. *Journalisten.* www.journalisten.no (accessed on 8 July 2024).

Silvola, N. M. (2020b). Vårt Land i PFU-tilsvar: -Har pågått en aktiv jakt etter hvem som er våre kilder [Newspaper Vårt Land in PFU response: -There has been an active search for our sources]. *Journalisten.* www.journalisten.no (accessed on 8 July 2024).

Silvola, N. M. (2020c). Firmaet bak Født Fri-rapport klager Nettavisen inn for PFU [The firm behind Born Free report complains about Nettavisen to PFU]. *Journalisten.* www.journalisten.no (accessed on 8 July 2024).

Simpson, S. S., Galvin, M. A., Loughran, T. A., & Cohen, M. A. (2022). Perceptions of white-collar crime seriousness: Unpacking and translating attitudes into policy preferences. *Journal of Research in Crime and Delinquency, 60*(5), 002242782210920.

Skeem, J., Johansson, P., Andershed, H., Kerr, M., & Louden, J. E. (2007). Two subtypes of psychopathic violent offenders that parallel primary and secondary variants. *Journal of Abnormal Psychology, 116*(2), 395.

Skomakerstuen, B. (2020). Melby ikke involvert i Født Fri-avgjørelsen [Melby not involved in the Born Free decision]. *Nettavisen.* www.nettavisen.no (accessed on 8 July 2024).

Slettholm, A. (2020a). Rehmans pengebruk er Abid Rajas problem [Rehman's money spending is Abid Raja's problem]. *Aftenposten*, p. 8.

Slettholm, A. (2020b). Argumentene for å strupe Født Fri-støtten er overbevisende [The arguments for throttling Born Free support are compelling]. *Aftenposten*, p. 34.

Slyke, S. R. V., & Bales, W. D. (2013). Gender dynamics in the sentencing of white-collar offenders. *Criminal Justice Studies, 26*(2), 168–196.

Smith, A. N., Watkins, M. B., Burke, M. J., Christian, M. S., Smith, C. E., Hall, A., & Simms, S. (2013). Gendered influence: A gender role perspective on the use and effectiveness of influence tactics. *Journal of Management, 39*(5), 1156–1183.

Smith, A. N., Watkins, M. B., Ladge, J. J., & Carlton, P. (2020). Making the invisible visible: Paradoxical effects of intersectional invisibility on the career experiences of executive black women. *Academy of Management Journal, 62*(6), 1705–1734.

Solli-Sæther, H., & Gottschalk, P. (2015). Stages-of-growth in outsourcing, offshoring and backsourcing: Back to the future? *Journal of Computer Information Systems, 55*(2), 88–94.

Sooreisrafil. (2017). The steel mafia. *Sooreisrafil News*. www.sooreisrafil.com (accessed on 8 July 2024).

Sourander, A., Klomek, A. B., Ikonen, M., Lindroos, J., Luntamo, T., Koskelainen, M., & Helenius, H. (2010). Psychosocial risk factors associated with cyberbullying among adolescents: A population-based study. *Archives of General Psychiatry, 67*(7), 720–728.

Spiekermann, U. (2018). Cleaning San Francisco, cleaning the United States: The graft prosecutions of 1906–1909 and their nationwide consequences. *Business History, 60*(3), 361–380.

Srivastava, S. B., & Goldberg, A. (2017). Language as a window into culture. *California Management Review, 60*(1), 56–69.

Stadler, W. A., & Gottschalk, P. (2022). Testing convenience theory for white-collar crime: Perceptions of potential offenders and non-offenders. *Deviant Behavior, 43*(7), 804–820.

Starcke, K., Wolf, O. T., Markowitsch, H. J., & Brand, M. (2008). Anticipatory stress influences decision making under explicit risk conditions. *Behavioral Neuroscience, 122*(6), 1352.

Steffensmeier, D., & Allan, E. (1996). Gender and crime: Toward a gendered theory of female offending. *Annual Review of Sociology, 22*, 459–487.

Steffensmeier, D., & Allan, E. (2000). Looking for patterns: Gender, age, and crime. In J. F. Sheley (Ed.), *Criminology: A Contemporary Handbook* (pp. 85–127). Belmont, CA: Wadsworth.

Steffensmeier, D., Schwartz, J., & Roche, M. (2013). Gender and twenty-first-century corporate crime: Female involvement and the gender gap in Enron-era corporate frauds. *American Sociological Review, 78*(3), 448–476.

Steffensmeier, D., Schwartz, J., Zhong, H., & Ackerman, J. (2005). An assessment of recent trends in girls' violence using diverse longitudinal sources: Is the gender gap closing? *Criminology, 43*(2), 355–406.

Stephansen, E. (2020a). Et nødvendig forsvar for Shabana Rehman og Født Fri [A necessary defense for Shabana Rehman and Born Free]. *Nettavisen*. www.nettavisen.no (accessed on 8 July 2024).

Stephansen, E. (2020b). Nå er det Ernst & Young og IMDi som sitter igjen med skammen [Now it is Ernst & Young and IMDi who are left with the shame]. *Nettavisen*. www.nettavisen.no (accessed on 8 July 2024).

Stephansen, E. (2020c). Født Fri-saken har vokst til å bli en ekte skandale. Her er ni spørsmål hun må svare på [The Born Free scandal has risen into a real scandal. Here are nine questions she has to answer]. *Nettavisen.* www.nettavisen.no (accessed on 8 July 2024).

Stephansen, E. (2020d). Rykteflom i helgen: Her er tre spørsmål til statsråden [Flood of rumors this weekend: Here are three questions for the minister]. *Nettavisen.* www.nettavisen.no (accessed on 8 July 2024).

Stephansen, E. (2020e). Nå gjenstår bare prestisjen i Født Fri-saken [Now only the prestige remains in the Born Free Case]. *Nettavisen.* www.nettavisen.no (accessed on 8 July 2024).

Sterri, A., & Borge, K. (2022). How can an auditor prevent and detect white-collar crime? A convenience theory approach. *Master of Science in Business Economics Thesis*, BI Norwegian Business School, Oslo, Norway, 124 pages.

Stewart, N., & Nakamura, D. (2007). Two more D.C. tax workers removed. *Washington Post.* www.washingtonpost.com, November 10.

Stiftelsestilsynet. (2017). Stiftelsestilsynets tilsynsrapport: Stiftelsen romanifolkets / taternes kulturond [The foundation authority's inspection report: The Romani people's foundation / the cultural fund of the Tatars]. Lotteri- og stiftelsestilsynet [Lottery and foundation authority], Førde, Norway, 36 pages.

Stiftelsestilsynet. (2020). Melding om tilsyn: Født Fri [Notification of supervision]. Lotteri-og stiftelsestilsynet [Lottery and foundation authority], Førde, Norway, 3 pages.

Strand, T. (2020). Født Fri krevde 25.000 kroner for brudd på taushetsplikt: Ikke lovlig kontrakt, mener ekspert [Born Free demanded 25,000 kroner for breach of confidentiality: Not a legal contract, according to an expert]. *NRK.* www.nrk.no (accessed on 8 July 2024).

Strand, T., Bazaz, R., & Kalajdzic, P. (2020). Født Fri-ansatt: Jeg gikk tur med hundene til Shabana [Born Free employee: I went on walks with the dogs of Shabana]. *NRK.* www.nrk.no (accessed on 8 July 2024).

Strandenæs, H. F. (2020a). Født Fri-stans i utbetaling for 2. termin og iverksatt gransking [Born Free stop in payments for 2. term and initiated investigation]. Letter to Libe Rieber-Mohn at IMDi.

Strandenæs, H. F. (2020b). Tilsvarsfrist – Innhold – Kontradiksjon [Deadline for reply – Contents – Contradiction]. Letter to EY attention Øglænd, Bøe, and Antzee, 5 pages.

Strandenæs, H. F. (2020c). Stiftelsen Født Fri. Partsinnsyn og saksbehandling [The Foundation Born Free. Disclosure to Party and Handling of the Case]. Letter to Libe Rieber-Mohn at IMDi.

Strandenæs, H. F. (2020d). Brev til Lotteri- og Stiftelsestilsynet [Letter to the Lottery and Foundation Authority]. Letter to Karsten Karlsen Sunde and May Helen Vik.

Strandenæs, H. F. (2020e). Klage–Født Fri [Complaint–Born Free]. Letter to the integration and plurality directorate (Integrerings- og mangfoldsdirektoratet, IMDi), 14 pages.

Strøksnes, M. A. (2020). Når varsellampar blinker raudt [When warning lights flash red]. *Dag og Tid*, 18–23.

Sullivan, N. (2012). The somatechnics of perception and the matter of the non/human: A critical response to the new materialism. *European Journal of Women's Studies, 19*(3), 299–313.

Sundström, M., & Radon, A. (2015). Utilizing the concept of convenience as a business opportunity in emerging markets. *Organizations and Markets in Emerging Economies, 6*(2), 7–21.

Supernor, H. (2017). Community service and white-collar offenders: The characteristics of the sanction on factors determining its use among a sample of health-care offenders. *Journal of Financial Crime, 24*(1), 148–156.

Sutherland, E. H. (1939). White-collar criminality. *American Sociological Review, 5*(1), 1–12.

Sutherland, E. H. (1983). *White-Collar Crime–The Uncut Version*. Yale University Press.

Sykes, G., & Matza, D. (1957). Techniques of neutralization: A theory of delinquency. *American Sociological Review, 22*(6), 664–670.

Szalma, J. L., & Hancock, P. A. (2013). A signal improvement to signal detection analysis: Fuzzy SDT on the ROCs. *Journal of Experimental Psychology: Human Perception and Performance, 39*(6), 1741–1762.

Tabnak. (2010). The tea mafia. *Tabnak News*. www.tabnak.ir (accessed on 8 July 2024).

Tabnak. (2019). Paish program about meat import mafia. *Tabnak News*. www.tabnak.ir/fa/amp/news (accessed on 8 July 2024).

Templeton, L., Deehan, A., Taylor, C., Drummond, C., & Strang, J. (1997). Surveying general practitioners: Does a low response rate matter? *British Journal of General Practice, 47*(415), 91–94.

Thaxton, S., & Agnew, R. (2018). When criminal coping is likely: An examination of conditioning effects in general strain theory. *Journal of Quantitative Criminology, 34*, 887–920.

Theoharakis, V., Voliotis, S., & Pollack, J. M. (2021). Going down the slippery slope of legitimacy lies in early-stage ventures: The role of moral disengagement. *Journal of Business Ethics, 172*, 673–690.

Thomas, D. (2002). *Hacker Culture*. University of Minnesota Press.

Toffler, B. L. (2003). *Final Accounting: Ambition, Greed, and the Fall of Arthur Andersen*. Random House.

Tommelstad, B., & Quist, C. (2016). Politiet: Her fikk hun 25,000 kroner. VG. http://www.vg.no (accessed on 8 July 2024).

Tonoyan, V., Strohmeyer, R., & Jennings, J. E. (2020). Gender gaps in perceived start-up ease: Implications of sex-based labor market segregation for entrepreneurship across 22 European countries. *Administrative Science Quarterly, 65*(1), 181–225.

Toupin, S. (2014). Feminist hackerspaces: The synthesis of feminist and hacker cultures. *Journal of Peer Production, 5*(2014), 1–11.

Trahan, A. (2011). Filling in the gaps in culture-based theories of organizational crime. *Journal of Theoretical and Philosophical Criminology, 3*(1), 89–109.

Triana, M. C., Jayasinghe, M., Pieper, J. R., Delgado, D. M., & Li, M. (2010). Perceived workplace gender discrimination and employee consequences: A meta-analysis and complementary studies considering country context. *Journal of Management, 45*(6), 2419–2447.

U.S. Census Bureau. (2019). QuickFacts Utah. United States Census Bureau QuickFacts. https://www.census.gov/quickfacts/UT (accessed on 8 July 2024).

Ullman, S. E., & Siegel, J. M. (1993). Victim-offender relationship and sexual assault. *Violence and Victims, 8*(2), 121–134.

Ulvik, R., & Knudsen, K. (2018). Kari Lossius og Eva Karin Løvaas sier opp i Bergensklinikkene. Bergensavisen. http://www.ba.no (accessed on 8 July 2024).

Utah Attorney General's Office. (2020). White-collar Crime Offender Registry. https://www.utfraud.com/RegistryLists (accessed on 8 July 2024).

Uygur, S. A. (2020). Fraud in the charity sector in England and Wales: Accountability and stakeholder oversight (Doctoral dissertation, Royal Holloway, University of London).

Valkenhoef, G., & Tervonen, T. (2016). Entropy-optimal weight constraint elicitation with additive multi-attribute utility models. *Omega, 64*, 1–12.

Vandebosch, H., & Van Cleemput, K. (2009). Cyberbullying among youngsters: Profiles of bullies and victims. *New Media and Society, 11*(8), 1349–1371. https://doi.org/10.1177/1461444809341263.

Vic. (2020). Rasool Daniyalzadeh convicted. Vic News. www.vicnews.com.

Victor, B., & Cullen, J. B. (1988). The organizational bases of ethical work climates. *Administrative Science Quarterly, 33*, 101–125.

Virk, A. (2011). Imprisonment of women in India and the national upgrading of chastisement to mirror the United States penal system. *African Journal of Law and Criminology, 1*(1), 100–115.

Waal, F. (2010a). Står på sin forklaring. Haugesunds Avis. http://www.h-avis.no (accessed on 8 July 2024).

Waal, F. (2010b). Stuve må i fengsel. Haugesunds Avis. http://www.h-avis.no (accessed on 8 July 2024).

Wall, D. A. (2010). The internet as a conduit for criminal activity. In A. Pattavina (Ed.), *Information Technology and the Criminal Justice System* (pp. 77–98). Sage.

Wall, D. S. (2001). Cybercrime and the internet. In D. S. Wall (Ed.), *Crime and the Internet* (pp. 1–17).

Weaver, F. M., & Carroll, J. S. (1985). Crime perceptions in a natural setting by expert and novice shoplifters. *Social Psychology Quarterly, 48*(4), 349–359.

Weick, K. (1995). *Sensemaking in Organizations*. Sage.

Weisburd, D., Chayet, E. F., & Waring, E. J. (1990). White-collar crime and criminal careers: Some preliminary findings. *Crime and Delinquency, 36*(3), 342–355.

Weisburd, D., Waring, E. J., & Chayet, E. F. (2001). *White-Collar Crime and Criminal Careers*. Cambridge University Press.

Welsh, D. T., & Ordonez, L. D. (2014). The dark side of consecutive high-performance goals: Linking goal setting, depletion, and unethical behavior. *Organizational Behavior and Human Decision Processes, 123*, 79–89.

Welsh, D. T., Bush, J., Thiel, C., & Bonner, J. (2019). Reconceptualizing goal setting's dark side: The ethical consequences of learning versus outcome goals. *Organizational Behavior and Human Decision Processes, 150*, 14–27.

Welsh, D. T., Ordonez, L. D., Snyder, D. G., & Christian, M. S. (2014). The slippery slope: How small ethical transgressions pave the way for larger future transgressions. *Journal of Applied Psychology, 100*(1), 114–1127.

Wheelock, D., Semukhina, O., & Demidov, N. N. (2011). Perceived group threat and punitive attitudes in Russia and the United States. *British Journal of Criminology, 51*, 937–959.

White-collar Crime Registry, HB 378. (2015). https://le.utah.gov/~2015/bills/static/HB0378.html (accessed on 8 July 2024).

Whitty, M. T., & Buchanan, T. (2012). The online romance scam: A serious cybercrime. *Cyberpsychology, Behavior, and Social Networking, 15*(3), 181–183.

Wikstrom, P. O. H., Mann, R. P., & Hardie, B. (2018). Young people's differential vulnerability to criminogenic exposure: Bridging the gap between people- and place-oriented approaches in the study of crime causation. *European Journal of Criminology, 15*(1), 10–31.

Williams, J. W. (2008). The lessons of Enron: Media accounts, corporate crime, and financial markets. *Theoretical Criminology, 12*(4), 471–499.

Williams, M. L., Levi, M., Burnap, P., & Gundur, R. V. (2019). Under the corporate radar: Examining insider business cybercrime victimization through an application of routine activities theory. *Deviant Behavior, 40*(9), 1119–1131.

WilmerHale and PwC. (2008). Report of investigation submitted by the Council of the District of Columbia. Wilmer Cutler Pickering Hale and Dorr LLP (Counsel) and PricewaterhouseCoopers LLP (Forensic Accounting Advisors). http://www.dcwatch.com (accessed on 8 July 2024).

Wingerde, K., & Lord, N. (2020). The elusiveness of white-collar and corporate crime in a globalized economy. In M. L. Rorie (Ed.), *The Handbook of White-Collar Crime* (pp. 469–483). Wiley and Sons.

World Economic Forum. (2018). *The Global Gender Gap Report.* World Economic Forum. www.weforum.org/publications/the-global-gender-gap-report-2018/.

WSS. (2013). Women in cybersecurity. https://www.womenssecuritysociety.co.uk/wp-content/uploads/2013/07/Women-in-Cyber-Security-Final.pdf (accessed on 8 July 2024).

Yam, K. C., Christian, M. S., Wei, W., Liao, Z., & Nai, J. (2018). The mixed blessing of leader sense of humor: Examining costs and benefits. *Academy of Management Journal, 61*(1), 348–369.

Ystad, V. (2009). *Hellevik Dømt Til Fengsel.* Bergens Tidende. http://www.bt.no (accessed on 8 July 2024).

Zainabadi, M. (2008). Investigating the state of trust in Iranian society and ways to rebuild it. Research Paper No. 16, Department of Cultural and Social Studies, Research Institute Strategic Expediency Assessment Forum, Tehran, 9–17.

Zhang, Y., & Qu, H. (2016). The impact of CEO succession with gender change on firm performance and successor early departure: Evidence from China's publicly listed companies in 1997–2010. *Academy of Management Journal, 59*(5), 1845–1868.

Zhu, D. H., & Chen, G. (2015). CEO narcissism and the impact of prior board experience on corporate strategy. *Administrative Science Quarterly, 60*(1), 31–65.

Zvi, L., & Elaad, E. (2018). Correlates of narcissism, self-reported lies, and self-assessed abilities to tell and detect lies, tell truths, and believe others. *Journal of Investigative Psychology and Offender Profiling, 15*, 271–286.

Zysman-Quirós, D. (2020). White-collar crime in South and Central America: Corporate-state crime, governance, and the high impact of the Odebrecht corruption case. In M. L. Rorie (Ed.), *The Handbook of White-Collar Crime* (pp. 363–380). Hoboken, NJ: Wiley and Sons.

Index

N

S

W

Y

Z